# Breaking Feminist Waves

Series Editors
Alison Stone
Philosophy and Religion
Lancaster University
Lancaster, UK

Linda Martín Alcoff
Department of Philosophy
Hunter College
New York, NY, USA

"This series promises to invite feminist thinkers from a variety of disciplinary backgrounds to think theoretically about feminism's history and future work that needs to be done. I look forward to incorporating titles from this series into my women's and gender studies teaching."
—Alison Piepmeier, *Director, Women's and Gender Studies Program, The College of Charleston*

For the last twenty years, feminist theory has been presented as a series of ascending waves. This picture has had the effect of deemphasizing the diversity of past scholarship as well as constraining the way we understand and frame new work. The aim of this series is to attract original scholars who will offer unique interpretations of past scholarship and unearth neglected contributions to feminist theory. By breaking free from the constraints of the image of waves, this series will be able to provide a wider forum for dialogue and engage historical and interdisciplinary work to open up feminist theory to new audiences and markets.

LINDA MARTÍN ALCOFF is Professor of Philosophy at Hunter College and the City University of New York Graduate Center, USA. Her most recent books include *Visible Identities: Race, Gender and the Self*; *The Blackwell Guide to Feminist Philosophy* (co-edited with Eva Kittay); *Identity Politics Reconsidered* (co-edited with Moya, Mohanty and Hames-Garcia); *and Singing in the Fire: Tales of Women in Philosophy*.

ALISON STONE is Professor of European Philosophy at Lancaster University, UK. She is the author of *Petrified Intelligence: Nature in Hegel's Philosophy*; *Luce Irigaray and the Philosophy of Sexual Difference*; *An Introduction to Feminist Philosophy*; *and Feminism, Psychoanalysis, and Maternal Subjectivity*; and the editor of *The Edinburgh Critical History of Nineteenth-Century Philosophy*.

More information about this series at
http://www.palgrave.com/gp/series/14794

Clara Fischer • Luna Dolezal
Editors

New Feminist Perspectives on Embodiment

palgrave
macmillan

Editors
Clara Fischer
University College Dublin
Dublin, Ireland

Luna Dolezal
University of Exeter
Exeter, UK

Breaking Feminist Waves
ISBN 978-3-319-72352-5   ISBN 978-3-319-72353-2 (eBook)
https://doi.org/10.1007/978-3-319-72353-2

Library of Congress Control Number: 2017961344

© The Editor(s) (if applicable) and The Author(s) 2018
This work is subject to copyright. All rights are solely and exclusively licensed by the Publisher, whether the whole or part of the material is concerned, specifically the rights of translation, reprinting, reuse of illustrations, recitation, broadcasting, reproduction on microfilms or in any other physical way, and transmission or information storage and retrieval, electronic adaptation, computer software, or by similar or dissimilar methodology now known or hereafter developed.
The use of general descriptive names, registered names, trademarks, service marks, etc. in this publication does not imply, even in the absence of a specific statement, that such names are exempt from the relevant protective laws and regulations and therefore free for general use.
The publisher, the authors and the editors are safe to assume that the advice and information in this book are believed to be true and accurate at the date of publication. Neither the publisher nor the authors or the editors give a warranty, express or implied, with respect to the material contained herein or for any errors or omissions that may have been made. The publisher remains neutral with regard to jurisdictional claims in published maps and institutional affiliations.

Cover image: "Two Muslim Girls Wearing the Pink Hijab Scarf" by Kazuya Akimoto

Printed on acid-free paper

This Palgrave Macmillan imprint is published by Springer Nature
The registered company is Springer International Publishing AG
The registered company address is: Gewerbestrasse 11, 6330 Cham, Switzerland

Acknowledgements

The editors would like to gratefully acknowledge the Society for Women in Philosophy, Ireland (SWIPI). The idea for this book arose originally from the 2014 SWIPI conference 'Women's Bodies' which took place in Dublin, Ireland and was funded by the Irish Research Council and hosted by University College Dublin. We are grateful to Professor Maria Baghramian for her continued support and ongoing mentorship. We would also like to thank the authors, our editors at Palgrave Macmillan, and the anonymous reviewers who gave their time to provide feedback on the chapters and manuscript.

Contents

1 Contested Terrains: New Feminist Perspectives
  on Embodiment   1
  Clara Fischer and Luna Dolezal

Part I   Normative Bodies, Ethics, and Vulnerability   15

2 A Genealogy of Women's (Un)Ethical Bodies   17
  Gail Weiss

3 The Normal Body: Female Bodies in Changing Contexts
  of Normalization and Optimization   37
  Julia Jansen and Maren Wehrle

4 How Do We Respond? Embodied Vulnerability and Forms
  of Responsiveness   57
  Danielle Petherbridge

Part II New Directions in Feminist Theory 81

5 Revisiting Feminist Matters in the Post-Linguistic Turn: John Dewey, New Materialisms, and Contemporary Feminist Thought 83
Clara Fischer

6 Feminist and Transgender Tensions: An Inquiry into History, Methodological Paradigms, and Embodiment 103
Lanei M. Rodemeyer

7 Expressing the World: Merleau-Ponty and Feminist Debates on Nature/Culture 125
Kathleen Lennon

Part III Sex, Violence, and Public Policy 145

8 Are Women's Lives (Fully) Grievable? Gendered Framing and Sexual Violence 147
Dianna Taylor

9 Sex Trafficking, Reproductive Rights, and Sovereign Borders: A Transnational Struggle over Women's Bodies 167
Diana Tietjens Meyers

10 Routine Unrecognized Sexual Violence in India 183
Namrata Mitra

Part IV Pregnancy and Reproductive Technology   201

11 Performing Pregnant: An Aesthetic Investigation
    of Pregnancy   203
    EL Putnam

12 The Metaphors of Commercial Surrogacy:
    Rethinking the Materiality of Hospitality
    Through Pregnant Embodiment   221
    Luna Dolezal

Index   245

Notes on Contributors

Luna Dolezal is Lecturer in Medical Humanities and Philosophy at the University of Exeter, UK. Her research is primarily in the areas of applied phenomenology, philosophy of embodiment, philosophy of medicine and medical humanities. She is the author of *The Body and Shame: Phenomenology, Feminism and the Socially Shaped Body* (2015) and the co-editor of *Body/Self/Other: The Phenomenology of Social Encounters* (2017).

Clara Fischer is an EU Marie Skłodowska-Curie Fellow at the Centre for Gender, Feminisms, and Sexualities and Co-director of the John Dewey Research Project at University College Dublin. She is the author of *Gendered Readings of Change: A Feminist-Pragmatist Approach* (Palgrave Macmillan, 2014), co-editor of *Irish Feminisms: Past, Present and Future* (2015) and guest editor of a special issue of *Hypatia* on 'Gender and the Politics of Shame' (2018). She is completing a monograph on containment and the gendered politics of shame in an Irish context, and has research interests in the politics of emotion and embodiment, Irish feminisms, gender and austerity, and feminist-pragmatism.

Julia Jansen is the Director of the Husserl Archives and Associate Professor of Philosophy at KU Leuven. She has published widely on Kantian and Husserlian phenomenology and on aesthetics. Her research has focused, for some time, on issues of imagination in classical phenomenology and philosophy as well as in the cognitive sciences. She is the editor of the English translation of Husserl's works under the title Husserl's Collected Works, co-editor of the Phaenomenologica book series and co-editor of the journal *Phänomenologische Forschungen*. She has been teaching phenomenological feminist philosophy since 2002.

Kathleen Lennon is Emeritus Professor of Philosophy at the University of Hull, UK. Her primary research interests are in the imagination, embodiment, expression, phenomenology (particularly the work of Merleau-Ponty and Simone de Beauvoir,) gender and old age. She is working on the second edition of *Theorising Gender* and a co-authored monograph *Old Age*. Recent publications include *Imagination and the Imaginary* (2015).

Diana Tietjens Meyers is Professor Emerita of Philosophy, University of Connecticut, Storrs, USA. She has held the Laurie Chair at Rutgers University and the Ellacuría Chair of Social Ethics at Loyola University, Chicago. She works in four main areas of philosophy—philosophy of action, feminist ethics and aesthetics, and human rights. She has published five monographs. The most recent of those is *Victims' Stories and the Advancement of Human Rights* (2016). *Being Yourself: Essays on Identity, Action, and Social Life* (2004) is a collection of her articles and chapters. Her most recent edited collection is *Poverty, Agency, and Human Rights* (2014).

Namrata Mitra is Assistant Professor of English at Iona College, New York, USA. She holds a PhD degree in Philosophy and Literature from Purdue University received in 2012. Her research interests include feminist philosophy, queer theory and postcolonial literature. Her research examines representations of sexual violence in South Asian literature, comparative postcolonial theories and the place of shame in nationalist movements.

Danielle Petherbridge is Assistant Professor of Philosophy at University College Dublin, Ireland. Previously she was Irish Research Council Marie Curie International Research Fellow at Columbia University, New York. She works broadly in the area of continental European philosophy, including critical theory, phenomenology, and philosophy and literature. Her current research project, entitled *Encountering the Other*, provides an examination of theories of intersubjectivity and self/other relations across different philosophical traditions. Her book publications include: *Body/Self/Other: The Phenomenology of Social Encounters* (2017) with Luna Dolezal, *The Critical Theory of Axel Honneth* (2013), and *Axel Honneth: Critical Essays, with a Reply by Axel Honneth* (2011).

Emily Lauren Putnam is a visual artist, scholar, and writer working predominately in performance art, video, sound and interactive media. Her work draws from multiple themes and sources, including explorations of gender and sexuality, play, materialism, and the study of place, which she investigates through personal and cultural lenses. Her research focuses on continental aesthetic philosophy, performance studies, digital studies and feminist theory. She is a member of the artists' groups Mobius (Boston) and Bbeyond (Belfast). Originally from the United States, she now teaches visual culture, art history and theory at the Dublin Institute of Technology in Ireland.

Lanei M. Rodemeyer is Associate Professor of Philosophy at Duquesne University, USA. She works primarily in the areas of phenomenology, continental philosophy, the philosophy of time and feminist/gender philosophy of the body. She has published a book on Husserl's phenomenology of inner time-consciousness, *Intersubjective Temporality: It's About Time* (2006); another on phenomenology and theories of embodiment that includes diaries from Lou Sullivan, a gay male trans man, *Lou Sullivan Diaries* (1970–1980); and *Theories of Sexual Embodiment: Making Sense of Sensing* (2017).

Dianna Taylor is Professor of Philosophy at John Carroll University in Cleveland, Ohio, USA. Her research focuses on twentieth-century continental philosophy, especially the work of Michel Foucault, and contemporary feminist philosophy. She is co-editor of *Feminism and the Final Foucault* (2004) and *Feminist Politics: Identity, Difference, Agency* (2007), and is editor of *Michel Foucault: Key Concepts* (2010). Her current research brings into conversation the work of Foucault and contemporary feminist philosophers in order to theorize new ways of conceptualizing and countering the harm of sexual violence against women.

Maren Wehrle is a postdoctoral researcher and lecturer at the Department of Philosophy (Husserl Archives) at KU Leuven. Her publications include works on Husserlian and Merleau-Pontian phenomenology, philosophical anthropology, feminist philosophy and cognitive psychology. Her research focuses on issues of attention (phenomenology and cognitive psychology), embodiment, normality and normativity. Recent publications include: 'Normality and Normativity in Experience', in Doyon/Breyer: *Normativity in Perception* (2015); 'Normative Embodiment. The Role of the Body in Foucault's Genealogy. A Phenomenological Re-reading', in

The Journal of the British Society for Phenomenology (2016); and as editor (together with S. Luft) of the *Husserl Handbook*, published in 2017 by Metzler (Stuttgart).

Gail Weiss is Professor of Philosophy at George Washington University, Washington, DC, Executive Co-director of the Society for Phenomenology and Existential Philosophy, and General Secretary of the International Merleau-Ponty Circle. She is the author of *Existential Ambiguities: Beauvoir and Merleau-Ponty* (Indiana University Press, forthcoming), *Refiguring the Ordinary* (2008), and *Body Images: Embodiment as Intercorporeality* 1999), and has edited/co-edited several volumes on phenomenology and embodiment. Her research and publications bring phenomenology into conversation with contemporary work in feminist theory, critical race theory, and disability studies to address the social, political and ethical implications of non-normative bodily experiences.

CHAPTER 1

Contested Terrains: New Feminist Perspectives on Embodiment

Clara Fischer and Luna Dolezal

Feminist theory and philosophy has evinced an ongoing scholarly interest in the body and embodiment. Corporeal feminism, as it has been called by some,[1] theorizes the effects of patriarchal power structures on the female body, and hence, on women's subjectivity and social position. As we progress into the twenty-first century, despite several decades of feminist activism and scholarship, women's bodies continue to be sites of control and contention both materially and symbolically. Issues such as reproductive rights and technologies, sexual violence, objectification and normalization, motherhood, sexuality, and sex trafficking, among others, continue to be pressing concerns for women's bodies in our contemporary milieu, arguably exacerbated in a neoliberal world, where bodies are instrumentalized as sites of human capital and biopolitical forces increasingly focus on controlling the minutiae of embodied life.[2]

New Feminist Perspectives on Embodiment engages with these themes by building on the strong tradition of feminist thought focused on women's bodies, and by making novel contributions that reflect feminists'

C. Fischer (✉)
University College Dublin, Dublin, Ireland

L. Dolezal
University of Exeter, Exeter, UK

© The Author(s) 2018
C. Fischer, L. Dolezal (eds.), *New Feminist Perspectives on Embodiment*, Breaking Feminist Waves, https://doi.org/10.1007/978-3-319-72353-2_1

concerns—both theoretically and empirically (with implications for policy-making)—about gender and embodiment in the current context and beyond. The collection brings together essays from a variety of feminist scholars, who deploy diverse philosophical approaches, including phenomenology, pragmatism, and new materialisms, in order to reflect philosophically on the question of the status of women's bodies in the present day.

Given the feminist canonical engagement of the theme of embodiment, one might ask what, precisely, is new about *New Feminist Perspectives of Embodiment*? After all, there is a plethora of feminist texts on the topic, and a number of feminist theorists have charted and exposed the problematic history of the body, including the gendered body, in Western philosophy and critical thought. We view our volume as a continuation of this important, existing feminist work, with our specific contribution lying in an analysis of new technologies and policy issues in a globalized and neoliberal world, on the one hand, and the further development of feminist thought on the body, particularly addressing the theme of vulnerability, on the other.

With regard to the former, our volume includes a contribution from Tietjens Meyers, who discusses the contemporary global phenomenon of sex trafficking, which is structured by the demands of the sex industry and complicated by often contradictory national and international asylum, anti-trafficking, and human rights laws, having a direct impact on women's embodiment (through the often coercive movement and exploitation of women's bodies via trafficking and repatriation). Chapters by Dolezal and Putnam also highlight the pervasive medicalization and commercialization of pregnancy, which may, again, play out across transnational contexts and in settings where women's voices are silenced owing to technological, medicalized alienation, or to metaphors of hospitality engaged to sanitize economic framings of the use of women's bodies.

The volume also offers expositions of very recent developments in feminist theory, and how these might be employed to think fruitfully about embodiment. Lennon and Fischer draw on new materialisms as a way to theorize various dualisms, including the nature/culture dichotomy, and question whether and how the relationship between each of these realms should be negotiated in terms of our understanding of bodies and their meanings. Rodemeyer raises similar points in her explication of queer theory, noting an over-reliance on the discursive, which Fischer highlights as a common critique by new materialist and affect theorists—what she terms the "new school"—of poststructuralist and postmodern theory more generally. Fischer, Lennon, and Rodemeyer thus engage the question of how and to what extent the discursive has been and should be emphasized in its relation to the body, and trace this through feminist critique and the recent development of novel theoretical frameworks. Interestingly, they each recommend a turn towards a complimentary, canonical body of work, or at least towards lesson-learning across several theoretical paradigms. In Lennon's and in Rodemeyer's case, this is a turn towards phenomenology, with a particular focus on Merleau-Ponty by Lennon, and in Fischer's case, this is a turn towards pragmatism, specifically towards John Dewey's work. Lennon, Rodemeyer, and Fischer thus bring into conversation recent feminist thought, including new materialism and transfeminism, with canonical work to develop theoretical frameworks with which to think about the body.

Furthermore, many of the essays in the collection reflect a recent preoccupation with vulnerability in feminist scholarship, as the vulnerable body has been theorized and reconceptualized as an important starting point for understanding the ontological foundations of the human condition. In contrast to the mind/body dualism that has dominated the Western philosophical tradition—leading to a shunning of the inherent fleshiness, dependence, and vulnerability that characterizes ordinary human life—feminist theory seeks to overcome the continuing amnesia in Western philosophy about the fact that we have *all* been birthed from women's bodies, and that our existence is *necessarily* characterized by long periods of physical dependency, weakness, and bodily vulnerability, usually managed by the hands of female caregivers. The traditional denial of our fleshy existence in the Western intellectual tradition, along with its gendered foundations, has led to a concomitant "flight from vulnerability," which, as Debra Bergoffen argues, has been particularly damaging for conceptions of women's embodiment.[3] Women have been traditionally associated with the flesh, nature, and the body, and as a result, they have been denigrated, objectified, and afforded less social, political, and moral value than their male counterparts. Vulnerability as a concept in feminist theory offers possibilities for how we might ground an ethics and politics that does not deny our embodiment, but rather makes it central.[4] As embodied subjects, we are always sites of vulnerability, not just to biological forces, which might render us sick or incapacitated, and not just vulnerable in relation to others, who have the capacity to wound or to care, but crucially we are also vulnerable to sociopolitical forces, where power relations "have an immediate hold upon" the body to use Foucault's characterization.[5]

Attempting to understand our status as vulnerable subjects, in its multiple manifestations, has become a central theme of feminist thought and its significance is made manifest in this volume. For instance, Petherbridge's contribution discusses how embodied relationality and vulnerability between subjects designates both relations of power and possibilities for care through mutual embodied openness, and how these tensions might form the basis of an ethics of responsiveness. This is also a topic explored in Weiss' chapter, where she argues that considering the vulnerable body offers opportunities for ethical responses arising from positive experiences of corporeal agency. Taylor elaborates upon vulnerability in the context of sexual violence, and explores the implications of vulnerability, conceptualized as an embodied openness to others, as gendered and carrying with it the possibility of sexual harm. In Mitra's contribution, this focus on the vulnerable, gendered body is extended to an examination of embodied trauma, as she sets out how sexual violence and its effects are frequently denied in legal and public discourse, *contra* the lived experience of survivors.

As Judith Butler describes it, embodied vulnerability arises from our exposure to each other, but also to "social conditions and institutions,"[6] which means, in late capitalist societies, a vulnerability structured and exacerbated by neoliberal systems and logics. Hence, a second related and recurrent theme of this volume is neoliberalism itself, as well as its normative construction and exploitation of gendered bodies as sociopolitically vulnerable to each other in the marketplace. What happens to women's bodies that are individualized, commodified, and commercialized? What are the effects of neoliberalism on public policies concerning sex trafficking and the prevention of sexual violence, for instance, in a context where gendered bodies are objects for profit-making? How does the capitalist imperative of neoliberalism intersect with gender oppression, but also with global disparities of wealth? How have feminist theorists taken account of the neoliberal structuring of norms concerning embodiment in light of class and gender differences, and in light of trans* experiences?

These questions are addressed in various ways throughout the essays in this volume. For example, Jansen and Wehrle's contribution directly discusses how neoliberalism emphasizes individual agency and choice for women, while this is underscored by an injunction for self-optimalization that is in fact rooted in pernicious processes of normalization. Dolezal's chapter examines how the neoliberal tendency to frame many aspects of embodied life in economic terms, according to a market agenda, has concrete consequences for how the discourses surrounding commercial reproductive technologies, such as gestational surrogacy, are formulated. Through her discussion of metaphor, Dolezal demonstrates that the ideologies of neoliberalism have seeped into ordinary language, becoming so pervasive that they shape our ethical intuitions and, hence, what we feel should be socially and legally permissible. In her discussion of sexual violence, Taylor draws out neoliberalism's individuating technique of assigning personal responsibility to women for reducing or eliminating their own risk, and highlights the attendant construction of deserving and undeserving victims in a neoliberal framing focused on women's personal behaviour. Relatedly, Tietjens Meyers explores sex trafficking and the lack of protection of women's human rights in an analysis of the (forced) movement of women across transnational, economic disparities.

Through a diversity of theoretical approaches, themes, and topics, the various essays in this collection demonstrate that feminist enquiries into our status as embodied subjects are far from being resolved, nor is the conversation about embodiment coming to an end. While it is arguably well-trodden ground in feminist thought, investigating the status of the gendered body remains a pressing issue not just in academic theory, but in medicine, law, popular culture, and politics, where gendered bodies continue to be a battleground when considering issues of recent and recurrent significance, such as sexual violence and reproductive rights. *New Feminist Perspectives on Embodiment* arises from the 2014 conference "Women's Bodies," which was organized by the Society for Women in Philosophy Ireland. The rich intellectual contributions of conference participants not only provided some of the content of this volume,[7] but also demonstrated to the Editors the persistent relevance of the theme of embodiment within feminist scholarship.

New Feminist Perspectives in This Volume

New Feminist Perspectives on Embodiment is divided into four thematic sections: "Normative Bodies, Ethics, and Vulnerability," "New Directions in Feminist Theory," "Sex, Violence, and Public Policy," and "Pregnancy and Reproductive Technology," which emphasize different aspects of women's experience of embodiment and the theoretical questions and approaches which enframe them.

The essays in Part 1, "Normative Bodies, Ethics, and Vulnerability," serve, in part, to introduce some of the key philosophical paradigms which have dominated scholarship regarding women's bodies within Western thought, especially with respect to theorizations of ethics, ideas about normality and deviance, and recent feminist discussions of vulnerability as an ontological category that is intrinsically linked to human embodiment. Gail Weiss, in Chap. 2, opens the collection, exploring in detail the philosophical significance of female embodiment, especially in relation to the invisible "ideal" of the white, youthful, able male body that dominates the Western intellectual tradition. Drawing from philosophical thought that spans centuries, from Aristotle to Plato and from Beauvoir to Fanon, Weiss offers an invaluable overview of dominant philosophical ideas about embodiment that are so pervasive that they have become naturalized. Through her exegesis, Weiss demonstrates that the hegemony of consciousness/mind/reason as the source of moral agency and, hence, ethical practice continues to dominate Western philosophy. Weiss explains that it is only in relatively recent thought, particularly within feminism, that the body is portrayed as the ground of ethical obligation, rather than an obstacle to ethics and morality. Drawing on new feminist work regarding vulnerability, Weiss argues that considering the vulnerable body offers opportunities for ethical responses arising from positive experiences of corporeal agency. By highlighting some of the key themes and questions that have dominated feminist theory regarding embodiment, Weiss' chapter provides as an important conceptual framework for the chapters that follow.

In Chap. 3, Julia Jansen and Maren Wehrle explore the tensions between the "body as subject" and the "body as object," particularly in relation to female embodied experience under neoliberalism. They begin their discussion of our experience of being and having bodies as one that is fundamentally characterized by vulnerability, being "finite, exposed, and dependent on others and external forces." Our vulnerability renders us open to the world and its possibilities, but also susceptible to normalizing and disciplining forces, which can have pernicious effects, particularly, as their chapter demonstrates, on how women experience their own bodies. Through a careful phenomenological analysis of the embodied experience of the "normal"—a concept that continues to be hugely problematic when considering the social and political positioning of women's bodies—Jansen and Wehrle demonstrate that normality is not only implicated in what we might consider "optimal" bodily functioning, but is crucially a product of dominant ideologies and biopolitical forces. Drawing on the phenomenological insights of Edmund Husserl's and Michel Foucault's writing on discipline, biopolitics, and governmentality, Jansen and Wehrle's chapter provides an important conceptual frame through which we might understand how women experience their bodies as sites of agency, power, and autonomy, but at the same time, are subject to the normalizing and disciplining sociocultural and political forces of their dominant milieu. While neoliberalism emphasizes individual agency and choice, this chapter makes the important point that the neoliberal emphasis on self-optimalization is in fact rooted in pernicious processes of normalization.

Danielle Petherbridge's chapter (Chap. 4) returns us to the themes of vulnerability and ethics with respect to embodiment. Petherbridge engages with recent feminist scholarship on vulnerability in order to explore how, as intersubjective and embodied subjects, vulnerability is fundamental to social relations and how we develop as subjects. Engaging with feminist thinkers such as Judith Butler and Adriana Cavarero, Petherbridge uses the fictional work of the South African novelist J.M. Coetzee, particularly *The Lives of Animals* and *Waiting for the Barbarians*, to explore the intricacies of embodied vulnerability and its relationship to ethics and politics. As embodied vulnerability can provoke responses of both care and wounding, Petherbridge's aim is to address a pressing question when considering the utility of the concept of vulnerability within ethical discourses, namely: How are we to adequately respond to vulnerability? Using Coetzee's fictional landscapes as illustrative, Petherbridge reflects on how embodied relationality between subjects designates both relations of power and possibilities for care through mutual embodied openness and how these tensions might form the basis of an ethics of responsiveness. Weaving together reflections that span the ontological, ethical, and political dimensions of vulnerability, Petherbridge's chapter adds important insights to recent feminist scholarship on vulnerability and embodiment.

Essays in Part 2, "New Directions in Feminist Theory," focus on recent and emerging scholarship in feminist thought, with a particular emphasis on new materialisms and the formulation of transfeminism in light of the recent explosion in critical and theoretical trans scholarship. Each of these essays also engages canonical philosophical work, mainly pragmatism and phenomenology, to develop theories that reach across theoretical paradigms.

Clara Fischer's chapter (Chap. 5) engages recent feminist theorizing on the body by identifying a "new school" of post-linguistic turn feminism made up of affect theory and new materialism. In her analysis of this school's turn towards materiality and embodied affect, she specifically focuses on the confluences between John Dewey's pragmatism, and Karen

Barad's and Stacy Alaimo's new materialism in an exposition of each thinker's naturalist ontology. Among others, Fischer traces the concepts of "transaction," "transcorporeality," and "intra-action" across pragmatist and new materialist terrains, highlighting important convergences between pragmatism and new materialism, and, ultimately, arguing that pragmatism can constitute a valuable resource for contemporary feminists interested in the recent turn towards materiality.

In Chap. 6, Lanei M. Rodemeyer delineates four major paradigms in feminism and philosophy, namely the sex/gender dichotomy, queer theory, phenomenology, and transfeminism. The purpose of such a delineation lies, for Rodemeyer, in the need to draw out biases and shortcomings in specific theories, which feminism has historically undertaken with regard to supposedly neutral, but actually masculinist, philosophies. Rodemeyer begins by noting the somewhat troubled history of the relationship between feminism and transgender theory and practice—what she terms "feminist and transgender tensions"—and explains that "when we carry out analyses of gender and embodiment, the paradigms we employ can determine our outcomes – often in exclusive ways." It is precisely to avoid such pitfalls when theorizing embodiment that Rodemeyer sets out her four-fold categorization, exploring questions of essentialism and social constructionism, and the relationship between these as certain theories prioritize discursiveness or the body as a ground for analysis in and of itself. Rodemeyer presents transfeminism as a paradigm that draws on intersectionality to challenge "both simple identity politics and those positions that present the erasure of identity as an ultimate goal." In the end, Rodemeyer makes the case for a combination of approaches with which to think about embodiment in light of transgender experiences, arguing that this could ameliorate shortcomings in respective paradigms and thus provide a fruitful approach for theorists of the present.

Kathleen Lennon's chapter (Chap. 7) explores the recent movement towards new materialism in feminist theory. Lennon explores the contentious conceptual history of the nature/culture dichotomy, especially when considering feminism's fraught relationship to the natural sciences, where biological "facts" have been historically constructed to align with patriarchal ideologies regarding the social roles of men and women. Lennon brings Merleau-Ponty's phenomenology of embodied subjectivity into dialogue with recent debates in feminist theory regarding our dependence on the materiality of embodiment and the subsequent implications for gender theory. Lennon mobilizes Merleau-Ponty's theorization of embodied subjectivity in a co-constitutive relation with the world to collapse the binary of nature/culture, and hence to unsettle the question of biological sexed difference. With Merleau-Ponty's framework, Lennon demonstrates that nature can be conceived as a process with "non-determining sources which are both material and cultural," in relation to which subjects are always engaged in "creative transition."

In Part 3, "Sex, Violence, and Public Policy," chapters address important questions regarding sexual violence against women, questions which continue to be pertinent given the pervasiveness of such violence, as recently highlighted by the #MeToo social media campaign set up in response to allegations of mass sexual harassment and assault.[8] Related to this are implications for public policies, both on the issues of sexual violence and sex trafficking, which unfold in complex legal, social, and political contexts that often render harms of a gendered, sexual nature invisible as harms as such.

In her chapter (Chap. 8), Dianna Taylor uses the Steubenville case, in which a young woman was gang-raped, to prompt questions concerning the liveability and attendant grievability of women's lives in the context of ambivalent responses to women's experiences of sexual violence. Drawing on Butler's concepts of precariousness, precarity, and framing, Taylor elaborates gender as a frame that entails women's disproportionate exposure to injury, in as far as "women achieve recognition only as subordinate, devalued, and therefore not fully liveable lives," and inhabit a specific embodiment that amplifies exposure and precarity in normalizing, depoliticized conditions. This much is borne out, for Taylor, by the deterministic and fatalistic acceptance of sexual violence as a "natural" part of human existence, and the effects this has on recognizing sexual violence as violence at all. While pointing to the widespread ambivalent social response to sexual violence as evidence for the inability to recognize women's lives as fully grievable, Taylor nonetheless ends her chapter on an optimistic note, highlighting the possibility of change, given the need for the constant (re)iteration of frames, which can thus be altered.

Diana Tietjens Meyers identifies, in Chap. 9, a maligning of the human rights, including reproductive rights, of women who have been trafficked from poorer countries to work in the sex industry in more affluent countries. Meyers highlights an inherent tension between what she calls a "law enforcement gestalt" and the protection of women's human rights, which renders the United States incapable of living up to its human rights obligations as set out in the Palermo Protocol, among others. Not only does the

US emphasis on law enforcement "funnel" trafficked women "into the criminal law apparatus" (which sets the bar for residency and visa requirements much higher than the standard asylum process), but it also endangers women and their families given the risk of re-trafficking following repatriation. Added to this is the legal requirement of having to be categorized as "severely trafficked" to obtain benefits along the lines of refugees, which, as Meyers points out, is onerous on trafficked women, as it requires having to prove complete non-complicity, even non-agency, in the trafficking process. As feminists have noted, many trafficked women engage traffickers to seek better opportunities in wealthier countries, and may subsequently find that traffickers use fraud and violence to coerce them into the sex industry. Meyers notes, however, that US law requires women to show that they were subject to deception and kidnapping by traffickers at the point of origin. Ultimately, Meyers notes that the current approach to sex trafficking in affluent countries "compound[s] the dishonour done" to sex trafficking victims' "humanity, adding insult to injury."

In Chap. 10, Namrata Mitra outlines how gendered scripts of honour, shame, and nationalism in South Asia ensure that routine violence against women is rendered invisible, both legally and in the public sphere as such. Mitra draws on Susan Brison's work on trauma and the impact this has on one's sense of self, and elaborates upon Pratiksha Baxi's discussion of courtroom practices in sexual violence cases, which often erase trauma narratives entirely. By utilizing Judith Butler's concept of "framing," and her distinction between "recognition" and "recognizability," Mitra establishes that "*how* a survivor of sexual violence is recognized is not based on harms of the violence, such as trauma, persisting within the survivor's body," but is governed, rather, by "the norms of gender, sexuality, shame, honour, communal and national identity" that "forge the frames of recognizability through which someone is recognized as a survivor." Mitra then provides an insightful, brief genealogy of how such norms, including "nationalist fantasies imprinted on women's bodies," have resulted in the erasure of sexual violence in the public sphere or in its sole, patriarchal interpretation. Mitra closes her chapter by noting the important feminist resistance against routine sexual violence. She points to literature and to the activism of Meira Paibi ("Torch Bearers," a group of feminist activists who staged a daring protest in response to the gang-rape of a Manipuri woman) to highlight the possibility and urgency of "disrupt[ing] the continuous reproduction of the dominant frames of sexual violence."

The essays in Part 4, "Pregnancy and Reproductive Technology," turn to explore one of the enduring material concerns of female embodiment, that of pregnancy, childbirth, and motherhood. EL Putnam's chapter (Chap. 11) discusses the performances and artistic practices of pregnant artists, such as Marni Kotak and Sandy Huckleberry, to shed light on patriarchal constructions and norms of reproduction and maternity. By drawing on Iris Marion Young's phenomenology of pregnancy and related critiques of the deployment of alienating, antenatal technology that medicalizes birthing and reproduction, Putnam highlights the resultant marginality of women's embodied subjectivity. Yet, for Putnam, the central problematic in this context is not technology itself, as she finds, following an elaboration of Heidegger's conceptualization of technology in terms of *Gestell* (enframing), but that the specific uses of technology and their embeddedness in religious, political, and scientific discourses need to be questioned. To this end, Putnam examines religious iconography, particularly the figure of the Virgin Mary, to trace "the alienation of mothers-to-be from the embodied and phenomenological aspects of pregnancy" in the history of Western art. Ultimately, Putnam argues that a reading of pregnancy as "aesthetic experience" can redirect our attention from a teleological conception focused on the production of children towards an experiential reconfiguration of the intersubjective relationship between "the pregnant woman, the foetus, and others."

Luna Dolezal's chapter (Chap. 12) tackles the question of the ethicality of contemporary commercial surrogacy, a global practice that relies centrally on female embodiment. Dolezal demonstrates that the metaphoric landscape of contemporary commercial surrogacy practices is dominated by an economic rationality (wombs are rented, bodies are property, women are compensated). However, at the same time, concepts with a long philosophical history, such as the gift and hospitality, are invoked in order to mitigate the pecuniary aspects of surrogacy. Invoking hospitality in discourses about commercial surrogacy is, Dolezal argues, an attempt to make commercial transnational surrogacy, a practice mired in controversy and charges of exploitation and dehumanization, more palatable and alleviate questions about its potentially dubious ethicality. Dolezal examines the recent philosophical history of hospitality in the work of Levinas and Derrida, demonstrating that it is a concept with considerable gendered dimensions, where women are seen as the condition of the possibility of hospitality for autonomous male subjects, a reasoning that justifies and mirrors the power relations inherent to many transnational commercial surrogacy practices, where underprivileged women in developing countries provide the service of gestating a child for women with significantly more social and economic power. To problematize this conception of hospitality, Dolezal turns to recent feminist theory on maternity and gestation which reappropriate and reconceptualize the idea of hospitality in the context of female embodiment, particularly the recent work of Irina Aristarkhova. Aristarkhova's reconception of hospitality through "the matrix" problematizes the idea that women's pregnant flesh can merely be an indifferent vessel for the other, but instead that women's bodies are the constitutional ground for kinship, subjectivity, and human relationality. Through problematizing the metaphors and concepts which underpin and, in some sense, justify commercial surrogacy practices, Dolezal's chapter is an important contribution to contemporary debates surrounding the global medical marketplace for assisted reproductive technologies—a marketplace where many potential injustices fall on women's shoulders.

While each of the chapters in this volume offers a novel approach or perspective, the overall aim of this collection is to scrutinize and uncover some of the taken-for-granted assumptions and norms that govern how bodies are experienced, perceived, valued, and thought about in the current context. Each of the essays uniquely addresses how women's embodiment still constitutes contested terrain, thereby critically examining a variety of contemporary social and political issues that materially affect women. To be sure, the collection does not engage all of the important questions regarding gendered embodiment in contemporary times, with topics such as religious expression, disability, and aesthetic surgery, to name just a few, falling outside of the scope of the work presented here. However, with original contributions from established and emerging feminist theorists, the volume adds another important set of voices to the ongoing feminist conversation about the material, social, and cultural status of the gendered body in the present day.

Notes

1. Liz Frost. "Theorizing the Young Woman in the Body," *Body and Society* 11, no. 1 (2005): 65.
2. For example, see: Alison Phipps. *The Politics of the Body: Gender in a Neoliberal and Neoconservative Age.* (Cambridge, UK: Polity Press, 2014).

3. Debra Bergoffen, "The Flight from Vulnerability," in *Dem Erleben Auf Der Spur: Feminismus Und Die Philosophie Des Leibes*, eds. Hilge Landweer and Isabella Marcinski, 137–51, (Bielefeld: Transcript Verlag, 2016), 137.
4. See: Judith Butler, *Precarious Life: The Power of Mourning and Violence*, (London: Verso, 2004).
5. Michel Foucault, *Discipline and Punish: The Birth of the Prison*, translated by Alan Sheridan, (New York: Vintage Books, 1979), 25.
6. Judith Butler, *Frames of War: When is Life Grievable?* (London: Verso, 2016), 33.
7. In particular, see chapters from Dolezal, Fischer, Meyers, Putnam, Taylor, and Weiss.
8. Khomami, Nadia, "#MeToo: how a hashtag became a rallying cry against sexual harassment," *The Guardian*, 20th October 2017: https://www.theguardian.com/world/2017/oct/20/women-worldwide-use-hashtag-metoo-against-sexual-harassment.

Bibliography

Bergoffen, Debra. 2016. The Flight from Vulnerability. In *Dem Erleben Auf Der Spur: Feminismus Und Die Philosophie Des Leibes*, ed. Hilge Landweer and Isabella Marcinski, 137–151. Bielefeld: Transcript Verlag.

Butler, Judith. 2004. *Precarious Life: The Power of Mourning and Violence*. London: Verso.

———. 2016. *Frames of War: When Is Life Grievable?* London: Verso.

Foucault, Michel. 1979. *Discipline and Punish: The Birth of the Prison*. Trans. Alan Sheridan. New York: Vintage Books.

Frost, Liz. 2005. Theorizing the Young Woman in the Body. *Body and Society* 11 (1) 63–85.

Khomami, Nadia. 2017. #MeToo: How a Hashtag Became a Rallying Cry Against Sexual Harassment. *The Guardian*, October 20. https://www.theguardian.com/world/2017/oct/20/women-worldwide-use-hashtag-metoo-against-sexual-harassment

Phipps, Alison. 2014. *The Politics of the Body: Gender in a Neoliberal and Neoconservative Age*. Cambridge, UK: Polity Press.

PART I

Normative Bodies, Ethics, and Vulnerability

CHAPTER 2

A Genealogy of Women's (Un)Ethical Bodies

Gail Weiss

I begin with a fairly brief historical survey of the largely negative depiction of bodies more generally, and women's bodies in particular, within the philosophical tradition, starting with the ancient philosophers, continuing in the modern period, and well into the twentieth century. In the latter half of the discussion, I provide a critical analysis of contemporary feminist ethics of embodiment that I find particularly promising in addressing the positive role gendered bodies actually can and do play in ethical theory and practice. My starting point is a passage from Elizabeth Grosz's *Volatile Bodies: Toward a Corporeal Feminism*, a formative text in my own thinking about the body and an indispensable resource for anyone who seeks to address the difficult, yet truly exciting and provocative issues that arise as soon as one begins to take seriously the philosophical significance of women's bodies:

> If women are to develop autonomous modes of self-understanding and positions from which to challenge male knowledge and paradigms, the specific nature and integration (or perhaps lack of it) of the female body and female subjectivity and its similarities to and differences from men's bodies and identities need to be articulated. The specificity of bodies must be

G. Weiss (✉)
George Washington University, Washington, DC, USA

© The Author(s) 2018
C. Fischer, L. Dolezal (eds.), *New Feminist Perspectives on Embodiment*, Breaking Feminist Waves,
https://doi.org/10.1007/978-3-319-72353-2_2

> understood in its historical rather than simply its biological concreteness. Indeed, there is no body as such: there are only *bodies* – male or female, black, brown, white, large or small – and the gradations in between. Bodies can be represented or understood not as entities in themselves or simply on a linear continuum with its polar extremes occupied by male or female bodies (with the various gradations of "intersexed" individuals in between) but as a field....[1]

And, she continues:

> There are always only specific types of body, concrete in their determinations, with a particular sex, race, and physiognomy. When one body (in the West, the white, youthful, able, male body) takes on the function of model or ideal, the human body, for all other types of body, its domination may be undermined through a defiant affirmation of a multiplicity, a field of differences, of other kinds of bodies and subjectivities. A number of ideal types of body must be posited to ensure the production, projection, and striving for ideal images and body types to which each individual, in his or her distinct way, may aspire. Only when the relation between mind and body is adequately retheorized can we understand the contributions of the body to the production of knowledge systems, regimes of representation, cultural production, and socioeconomic exchange.[2]

My own goal is to contribute to this arduous labor of retheorizing the (gendered and racialized) distinction between mind and body, and ultimately, to move beyond the false dichotomy that posits them as antinomies, doomed to a struggle that neither on its own can ever win. Let us begin, then, at the beginning, by turning to the history of philosophy, a history that has, for centuries, perpetuated and reinforced an allegedly sexually and racially undifferentiated or "neutral" (yet nonetheless hierarchical) distinction between mind and body, a distinction that has privileged the experiences and reflections, dare we say, the fantasies and the illusions, of certain bodies, specifically white, male, able bodies, over all others.

Part 1: The Body as a Threat to Ethics

If we ask the question, what does the body have to do with ethics, we quickly realize that many different answers, albeit mostly negative ones, have been provided to it over the centuries. Indeed, the body's needs, desires, and affective responses have more often than not been seen as detrimental influences upon the "pure" reasoning that philosophers have historically claimed is both necessary and sufficient for making moral choices. For instance, although Plato and Aristotle, Descartes, and Kant all emphasize, in accordance with the rationalist tradition, that reason alone must guide us in choosing the best course of action in any given situation, they all also recognize that it is difficult to exercise reason if the body's own needs are not being attended to, since an unhealthy body and/or the experience of severe bodily discomfort can distract us from utilizing reason properly. To avoid being unduly influenced by our carnal appetites, they suggest that reason should govern our bodily impulses so as to prevent us from committing irrational and/or immoral actions. Since, for the rationalists, reason is a perfect, God-given faculty that only human beings possess that will unerringly lead us to make the right (rational) decisions if we use it properly, making the wrong decisions cannot be the fault of reason itself, but is rather due to our letting ourselves be guided by non-rational forces, which, not surprisingly, most frequently turn out to be our bodily needs and desires. The body, then, is historically associated with the non-rational parts of the soul or self that we share with other animals. Insofar as the body is viewed as capable of motivating our action in a manner that bypasses our faculty of reason altogether, it is not surprising that our bodily desires and demands are so frequently depicted as a threat to reason and, in consequence, morality.

This predominantly negative view of the body's influence upon our ethical reasoning within the rationalist tradition means that we cannot simply ignore the body in thinking about morality but must rather acknowledge its disruptive potential and try to minimize it as much as possible so that reason alone can guide our action and lead us to moral virtue. Accordingly, in Book IV of the *Republic*, Plato states that the faculty of reason must "rule over" the "appetitive" and "spirited" parts of the soul, yet he also asserts that each of these faculties have their own distinctive domains and must perform their own functions properly so that they are in harmony with one another. In Plato's words, "[E]ach of us ... in whom the several parts within him each perform their own task – he will be a just man and one who minds his own affair."[3]

In this compartmentalized view of the soul, each part of the soul has its own unique role to play; the just man is the one who knows what each part should be doing and how to balance them so that they are not in conflict with one another. Thus, rather than dismiss bodily needs and desires altogether, Plato suggests that they fall under the appetitive and spirited, or non-rational parts of the soul, and must be attended to in a way that does not prevent but rather promotes the exercise of reason. For, he continues, "Does it not belong to the rational part to rule, being wise and exercising forethought in behalf of the entire soul, and to the principle of high spirit to be subject to this and its ally?"[4] The harmony of the three parts of the soul, then, does not mean that they play an equal role in motivating human action; rather, this balance involves having the spirited part of the soul work in partnership with reason to restrain the dangerous influence of our bodily appetites. The goal, ultimately, is to satisfy bodily appetites in a morally acceptable manner that supports rather than violates the rational component of the soul, thereby allowing the latter to exercise its dominion over the soul as a whole. Indeed, Plato calls for the rational and spirited parts of the soul to "keep watch upon [the appetitive part], lest, by being filled and infected with the so-called pleasures associated with the body and so waxing big and strong, it may not keep to its own work but may undertake to enslave and rule over the classes which it is not fitting that it should and so overturn the entire life of all."[5]

As Donna-Dale Marcano observes in her essay, "Race/Gender and the Philosopher's Body," it is Socrates, "the exemplar of the philosopher," who displays these virtuous Platonic qualities, most notably in Plato's *Symposium*, where he

> drinks but never gets drunk, desires beautiful boys but never submits to that desire, is a soldier but one whose head is always in the sky thinking lofty thoughts. Socrates is the gadfly of Athenian society, but never attached to his family, clan, or community. Socrates transcends the body.[6]

Marcano draws out the dangerous implications of this strangely detached, disembodied paragon of human virtue in her concluding comments when she claims that

> the philosopher's body presents itself conceptually as without race and transcending race, without sex and transcending sex, without oppression and transcending oppression. The philosopher's body is human without the limiting criteria that designate the variety of bodies and thus relations to knowledge. In other words, the philosopher's body presents itself as universal, until, that is, it is challenged as particularly White or particularly male or particularly sexualized.[7]

But, of course, these challenges have themselves been fairly recent and have been posed most often by those whose race, sex, and/or sexuality calls attention to, rather than away from, their bodies; hence, we should not be surprised at how often they have been dismissed.

Though Plato's depiction of the dangers posed by the appetitive part of the soul may seem quite extreme, his concerns about the power of our bodily appetites to interfere with the exercise of reason are reinforced hundreds of years later by Descartes at the outset of his first *Meditation* when he observes: "I have freed my mind of all kinds of cares; I feel myself, fortunately, disturbed by no passions and I have found a serene retreat in peaceful solitude."[8] A few sentences later, he informs us that he is "seated by the fire, wearing a winter dressing gown," providing the reader with a sensual image of warmth and comfort, which, he implies, are the optimal conditions for utilizing his faculty of reason.[9] Letting us know that he is at ease in his armchair, calm and relaxed, in a cozy room, Descartes suggests that the philosopher must be freed from bodily cares to exercise reason in a rigorous and sustained fashion in order to determine what can be known with certainty. Here too, we see bodily desires and demands depicted as potential threats to reason, threats that must be disarmed in advance so that the philosopher can do *his* work.

Though the body is presented by these philosophers as having the potential to disrupt the use of reason, this story would be incomplete without acknowledging that both reason and the body have most frequently *not* been depicted as neutral phenomena that all human beings possess, but rather have historically been distinguished along gender lines. Thus, since Ancient times, men have been regarded as more rational than women, who in turn have been viewed as more emotional (i.e., more connected to their "bodily natures") than men. Aristotle offers a prototypical example of this association of rationality with men in the following famous passages from Book 1, Chapter 5 of the *Politics*. Beginning with the claim that "it is clear that the rule of the soul over the body, and of the mind and the rational element over the passionate, is natural and expedient; whereas the equality of the two or the rule of the inferior is always hurtful," he quickly draws the conclusion, a few sentences later, that "the male is by nature superior, and the female inferior; and the one rules, and the other is ruled: this principle, *of necessity*, extends to all mankind."[10]

Though some scholars have argued that Aristotle's views about women's "essential" inferiority to men are not as clear-cut as this passage suggests,[11] it is difficult to dispute that Aristotle is depicting men as more capable than women of exercising their rational faculties to rule over their passions. Indeed, women are presented in this passage as synonymous with the passions that need to be governed by (rational) men. As we learn in the *Nichomachean Ethics*, moreover, this ability to exercise reason to rule over the passions is the very quality that is indispensable for discerning and exhibiting the moderation that characterizes moral virtue. Aristotle implies, then, that men are naturally better suited to behave virtuously than their female counterparts.

These strong linkages between masculinity, rationality, and hence moral, political, and sexual superiority, on the one hand, and femininity, bodily emotions, and moral, political, and sexual inferiority, on the other, have been reinforced and refined over the centuries, surfacing, most notably, in Sigmund Freud's early-twentieth-century psychoanalytic explanation of female and male psychosexual development in terms of essential differences between the sex that "has" the penis and the sex that "lacks it," an account that reduces female desire to envy of the "superior" male organ that they wish to, but never can, possess. In his notorious lecture, "Femininity," Freud pronounces women to be "more narcissistic" than men, and declares that female sexuality is a "dark continent," and therefore a "problem" that resists rational explanation.[12] Moreover, Freud makes it clear that this puzzle posed by female sexuality directly influences all aspects of a woman's life, including her moral behavior and ethical judgments. Yet perhaps, as Luce Irigaray argues in *Speculum of the Other Woman*, female sexuality (and, by extension, women's moral behavior and ethical judgments) only poses an insoluble problem when one seeks to understand it, as Freud does, through a singular model derived from male sexuality. As Irigaray observes, "[A]s card-carrying member of an 'ideology' that he never questions, he insists that the sexual pleasure known as masculine is the paradigm for all sexual pleasure, to which all representations of pleasure can but defer in reference, support, and submission."[13] And since, for Freud, male and female psychosexual development provides the foundation for the development of the super-ego, which in turn is the origin of "religion, morality, and the social sense," the very capacities that Freud identifies as "the chief elements in the higher essence of man," we should not be too surprised at his claim in "The Ego and the Id" that "[t]he male sex seems to have taken the lead in all these moral acquisitions."[14] Indeed, Irigaray notes, these moral acquisitions are only available to women through a very dubious "cross-inheritance," since "the super-ego, guarantor and producer of humanity's most noble values, is, it would seem, exclusively the product of chromosomes transmitted by males alone."[15]

Part 2: The Body as the Foundation for Ethical Theory and Practice

Simone de Beauvoir's groundbreaking *The Second Sex*, first published in 1949, painstakingly documents this dominant view of women's essential inferiority compared to men, a view, she is quick to point out, that both men *and* women have bought into as truth. Her interdisciplinary, cross-cultural analysis of women's second-class status throughout history provides numerous examples of famous authors, including Freud, who present "evidence" of women's "deficient bodies" as well as their alleged deficiencies of reason and morality that, we are told, flow from their more passionate, instinctual, and/or animal-like "natures." These "essential" differences between men's and women's respective minds and bodies, she observes, have been used to justify confining women to the domestic sphere, the only domain in which they are allowed to have some moral authority. These gendered stereotypes that grant men ethical agency as the "natural rulers" and that deprive women, the ruled, of this same agency are based, she argues, not upon nature or upon reality but upon "myths" about women and men that are socially constructed, socially reinforced, and socially convenient for men (and many women) to accept. Beauvoir counters this historical association of women with bodily immanence and men with the transcendence of consciousness by arguing that "[i]n truth all human existence is transcendence and immanence at the same time."[16] As she argues in *The Ethics of Ambiguity*,[17] an existential ethics must affirm this central ambiguity of human existence rather than seeking to deny it by consigning women to immanence and offering men alone opportunities to realize their transcendence.

Beauvoir's account of human beings as both immanent and transcendent and of ethics as posing the challenge of affirming both of these characteristics simultaneously seems to offer an improvement on the rationalist model that overemphasizes reason and views the body as a threat. However, both she and fellow existentialist Jean-Paul Sartre identify transcendence exclusively with consciousness,[18] and declare this latter to be the source of human freedom and responsibility, which means that their account is more consistent with a rationalist model than it might otherwise seem. This is because Beauvoir's call to recognize women's equality to men is based upon the following two claims: (1) both men and women possess the same transcendent consciousness and (2) their bodies, while differently sexed, are equally immanent. She is not suggesting that we should recognize the body itself as a source of transcendence, but rather, in accordance with a Sartrian existential framework, she presupposes and accepts a traditional, rationalist mind/body dualism whereby the body is doomed to immanence and can only be "transcended" through the activity of consciousness.

Frantz Fanon complicates and extends the implications of Beauvoir's analysis of gender oppression in *The Second Sex* when he argues, in *Black Skin, White Masks*, that it is not all men but only the white man who has historically been seen as possessing the "superior" consciousness that denotes transcendence, while the black man (and woman) has been reduced to immanence, rendered "a slave .... to [his] appearance."[19] Fanon forcefully points out that, both symbolically and literally, colonized peoples have been degraded and dehumanized by the transcendent white gaze that consigns them irremediably to a shameful, immanent, and essentially inferior bodily existence. If they "refuse to accept this amputation" of their being, by affirming that they too possess "a soul as vast as the world, truly a soul as deep as the deepest of rivers," it is in vain, since "[t]he white gaze, the only valid one, is already dissecting me. I am *fixed*."[20] While Beauvoir traces this reduction of women to bodily immanence to a false and contradictory "myth of Woman," Fanon evokes the "myth of the Negro that," he claims, must "be destroyed at all costs."[21] For both Beauvoir and Fanon, however, the solution is the same: one must continue to assert one's transcendence, that is, one's consciousness, and hence one's humanity, in the face of those who seek to deny it, even if this effort condemns one to a life of pain and constant struggle against oppressors who will never recognize you as their genuine equal. Rather than rejecting the disembodied philosopher's body that Marcano is critiquing, then, Beauvoir and Fanon affirm its transcendent qualities and continue to present it as a universal ideal that should be realizable for all men and women, not for white, male bodies alone.

It is significant that throughout the many centuries that separate Plato and Aristotle from Beauvoir and Fanon, the view of the body as immanent and reason or the mind as transcendent has remained remarkably intact. For even as Beauvoir and Fanon, respectively, present their powerful challenges to the sexist and racist hierarchies that have enabled white men to corner the market on transcendence, thereby condemning women and people of color to the corporeal domain of immanence, they simultaneously preserve the historical status quo, which proclaims consciousness alone to be the site of human, and therefore moral, agency. Indeed, it is only in the late twentieth century and early twenty-first century that the body is increasingly portrayed, not as an obstacle to ethics, but as the very ground of ethical obligation, thereby challenging the hegemony of reason/mind as the source of moral respect and moral wisdom.

One of the most decisive rejections of the traditional view of the mind as transcendent and the body as immanent is offered by Maurice Merleau-Ponty in his 1945 *Phenomenology of Perception*. Though he does not directly address the ethical implications of his claim that the body is the subject rather than the object of perception, his account of embodied agency has provided the inspiration for many contemporary ethics of embodiment. For Merleau-Ponty, it is through the body, rather than through consciousness, that we directly engage with the world and with others. In his words, "I understand the other person through my body, just as I perceive 'things' through my body. The sense of the gesture thus 'understood' is not behind the gesture, it merges with the structure of the world that the gesture sketches out and that I take up for myself."[22] Decisively rejecting the Cartesian Cogito, the disembodied "I think" as the source of knowledge about ourselves, others, and the world, Merleau-Ponty proclaims that "[c]onsciousness is originarily not an 'I think that,' but rather an 'I can.'"[23] Though feminist and critical race scholars, including Iris Marion Young and Frantz Fanon, have criticized Merleau-Ponty for not recognizing how easily this confident "I can" may be undermined when one's body is consistently viewed as essentially inferior and/or deficient to other people's bodies, the "I can" body continues to function in Young's and Fanon's own work as an ethical ideal, even if, as they powerfully point out, it is not currently experienced as a "natural birthright" that applies to all human beings, but rather as a social privilege that enables some bodies (especially white male bodies) at the expense of others. On the positive side, as I suggest in *Body Images: Embodiment as Intercorporeality*,[24] Merleau-Ponty's account of the body-subject enables us to recognize the body not only as the source of ethical agency, but also as the source of ethical demands. These demands, I argue, are experienced as "bodily imperatives" that issue directly from our own and other's bodies and can only be met through our own and other's bodily responses; as such, they stand in marked contrast to the categorical imperatives that Kant claims are generated by reason alone.[25]

Emmanuel Levinas' chapter on "Ethics and the Face," in *Totality and Infinity*, provides an early account of the body, or, more precisely, one part of the body, as a locus of transcendence that he claims grounds the foundational ethical imperative governing interactions between oneself and others, namely "thou shalt not kill." According to Levinas, "[t]he face is present in its refusal to be contained. In this sense it cannot be comprehended, that is, encompassed."[26] This uncontainable, incomprehensible face of the Other that Levinas is describing, however, is not directly accessible through the senses, for, he continues, "It is neither seen nor touched – for in visual and tactile sensation the identity of the I envelops the alterity of the object, which becomes precisely a content."[27] Though I may actually be seeing or touching the other's face, Levinas is suggesting that these senses exhibit a "colonizing tendency" that reduces the radical otherness of the Other, the other's transcendence, to an object *for me*. For this reason, he maintains:

> The relation between the Other and me, which dawns forth in his expression, issues neither in number nor in concept. The Other remains infinitely transcendent, infinitely foreign; his face in which his epiphany is produced and which appeals to me breaks with the world that can be common to us.[28]

The face of the Levinasian Other, it seems, is a source of transcendence precisely because it is *not* reducible to "flesh and blood"; rather, it is an ineffable phenomenon whose resistance to my grasp, Levinas proclaims, "does not do violence to me, does not act negatively; it has a positive structure: ethical."[29] Though Levinas' account of the face (of the Other) as a transcendent, infinite alterity that establishes an absolute ethical obligation not to harm the other seems to move us forward in dismantling the historical association of the body with immanence and our minds with transcendence, and though it seems to function as a primordial bodily imperative, the face that he is describing is so otherworldly that it seems to transcend its own embodiment. Indeed, the Levinasian face transforms what might appear to be bodily immanence into radical transcendence, even as the actual face that I can see and touch presumably remains behind. As Judith Butler notes in her discussion of Levinas' account of the face in *Precarious Life*, "the face that at once makes me murderous and prohibits me from murder is the one that speaks in a voice that is not its own, speaks in a voice that is no human voice."[30] For it is ultimately God's disembodied voice, according to Levinas, that issues the divine command, "Thou shalt not kill," when I encounter the face of the Other.

Even though Levinas is lauded by many contemporary ethical theorists, including Butler, both for recognizing the vulnerability of the Other's face and for insisting that this vulnerability, expressed through my encounter with the flesh of the Other, is precisely what generates the ethical imperative not to harm the Other, his insistence that the face of the Other, rather than binding us together, is an absolute alterity that "breaks the world that is common to us" has been a continued point of contestation. Since the early 1990s, in fact, there has been a veritable explosion of embodied ethics most of which reject not only the limitations of the transcendence/immanence and mind/body distinctions, but also the Levinasian portrayal of the face of the Other as a site of absolute transcendence. One of the most influential of these embodied ethics has been the "dependency critique" offered by Eva Feder Kittay in *Love's Labor: Essays on Women, Equality, and Dependency*, which maintains that *bodily dependency* rather than the (alleged) autonomy of reason is the basic human condition that establishes the ground for ethical obligation.

As helpless infants, Kittay points out, our bodies demand care from other bodies; this care is itself an embodied, *ethical* activity that could never be accomplished by a mind alone. Rather than abandoning the notion of equality altogether, even though it has traditionally been understood through a Kantian and Rawlsian ethic in which each person is entitled to justice because they are individual, autonomous, rational agents, Kittay argues for what she calls "connection-based equality." This relational conception of equality does not have its source in a faculty of reason which is supposed to be universal but which can actually be impaired and may even be inoperative in some human beings, but in the universality of bodily dependency. Kittay contrasts these two very different conceptions of ethical equality as follows:

> The question for a connection-based equality is not: What rights are due me by virtue of my status as an equal, such that these rights are consistent with those of other individuals who have the status of an equal? Instead, the question is: What are my responsibilities to others with whom I stand in specific relations and what are the responsibilities of others to me, so that I can be well cared for and have my needs addressed even as I care for and respond to the needs of those who depend on me?[31]

In the years since Levinas, Carol Gilligan, and Kittay developed their respective critiques of traditional ethical theory for its privileging of an abstract, strangely disembodied faculty of reason as the ground for ethical theorizing and claims to justice, several other authors have also identified a shared condition of bodily dependency and vulnerability as the ontological foundation for ethical demands, ethical rights, and ethical responsibilities. In *Precarious Life*, for instance, Butler, argues for what she calls a "'common' corporeal vulnerability" that is ineradicable and that must be protected.[32] And more recently, in 2012, in *Contesting the Politics of Genocidal Rape: Affirming the Dignity of the Vulnerable Body*, Debra Bergoffen takes up this claim and elaborates it further. Once we have emerged from infancy, she points out, "vulnerability no longer means total dependency," and she calls upon us to "critically assess our association of vulnerability with shame and humiliation," since, she claims, "this association is misguided." Ultimately, Bergoffen maintains, "the violence of the fantasy of autonomy is more dangerous than the risks of confronting the fractured mirror and the truth of our vulnerability."[33]

With Bergoffen's suggestion that the "fantasy of autonomy" can actually promote rather than prevent ethical violence, we come full circle, for now, rather than viewing bodily needs, desires, and demands as a threat to ethical theorizing and behavior, in accordance with the rationalist tradition, many contemporary embodied ethics argue, with Bergoffen, that we have a basic ethical obligation "to affirm the dignity of our shared vulnerability."[34] For Bergoffen, the International Criminal Tribunal for the Former Yugoslavia's (ICTY) 2001 landmark conviction of three Bosnian-Serb soldiers of crimes against humanity for their rape of Bosnian-Muslim women "established the dignity of the vulnerable body," thereby exposing "the ways that the ideology of autonomy/invulnerability can neither account for our human condition nor responsibly serve as a ground of justice."[35] Insofar as this shared vulnerability constitutes a *corporeal* and not a rational source of human dignity, it meets the demands of Kittay's dependency critique, because it applies to all human bodies, and not merely to those who are deemed to have a cognitive capacity that other bodies may not possess or that they may be unable to exercise (such as during infancy, when one is unconscious or in a vegetative state, when one is severely cognitively impaired, etc.). For Bergoffen, the significance of the ICTY verdict is that it was the violation of vulnerable *women's* bodies that was for the first time declared to be a crime against humanity; moreover, the women who were violated were accorded the dignity of giving voice, in an international court of law, to their violation.

As Bergoffen notes, "[T]he court did not spell out the implications of establishing the dignity of the vulnerable body as the referent of human rights crimes. That job falls to legal theorists, philosophers, and feminists who constitute the 'we' who speak for gender justice."[36] Thus, there is still much work to be done. As she reminds us, however:

> Where we begin makes all the difference. If we start by taking the invulnerable body as the ideal of the human, a string of associations come into play that ends up denigrating vulnerability. As the human ideal, invulnerability is associated with autonomy, sovereignty, agency, power, mastery and domination. Vulnerability is seen as the anti-ideal. It is associated with passivity, dependency, subordination, powerlessness, weakness, and victimhood.[37]

Vulnerability, in short, is historically associated with women's allegedly deficient bodies, invulnerability with men's allegedly divine faculty of reason. Given this sexist (and racist) history, one might legitimately ask whether the affirmation of vulnerability as a universal human condition will be sufficient to move us beyond the binary, hierarchical logic that has historically privileged some bodies at the expense of others. For it is clear that not all bodies are equally vulnerable. Indeed, some bodies are more dependent than others, and are often less capable of recognizing, much less articulating, their violation than others. Who can or should speak for them? How should they do so? Isn't there a risk that the bodies of those who are the most vulnerable may remain unseen, unheard, and, worst of all, unresponded to if other people can simply respond by saying, "Yes, you're vulnerable, but I'm vulnerable too."?

Another, Nietzschean concern, stemming from his *On the Genealogy of Morals*,[38] is whether this feminist trans-valuation of vulnerability from weakness to strength is merely another weapon, a politics of *ressentiment* and/or "slave morality," utilized by those who are weak and relatively powerless to attack and undermine the power and privilege of those who are strong. And yet, if we are all vulnerable, that is, if vulnerability is truly a universal human experience that the profound helplessness of infancy and young childhood seems to more than confirm, then even if we acknowledge, as we surely must, that some people are indeed more vulnerable than others, it can never simply be a tool used by the weak against the strong. Even if we can dispel this particular Nietzschean concern, however, there are nonetheless clear dangers associated with the ontological privileging of vulnerability, dangers that Bergoffen, Butler, and many other contemporary theorists of embodiment feel are well worth taking. Vulnerability, in short, is not invulnerable. But, I would suggest, this may be precisely its source of strength and, ultimately, the reason why it can help us to overcome the limitations of the historical dualisms that have divided mind from body, reason from the emotions, men from women, whites from blacks, the able-bodied from the disabled, and the human from the non-human.

Acknowledging vulnerability as an ontological condition in a manner that does not make vulnerability itself invulnerable to contestation and critique means that, while it must, as Bergoffen suggests, be a starting point, we should be wary of giving it the last word, that is, of making it a conclusion. For, as history has shown us, the path from vulnerability to violation will continue to be well-trodden as long as resources are scarce, social and political recognition is withheld, and the power balance between human beings is unequal; in short, as long as we live. Indeed, as Butler observes, the Levinasian invocation of the divine prohibition, "thou shalt not kill," is so forceful precisely *because* the desire to murder, to commit the absolute violation against the other, remains a constant temptation. There is no way, then, to safeguard vulnerability once and for all from violation, just as there is no way, despite the ICTY's historic conclusion that war-time rape is a crime against humanity, to safeguard the vulnerability of women's bodies from violation. A robust ethics of embodiment, then, cannot be based on an affirmation of bodily vulnerability alone, even if we grant, with Bergoffen, that this very vulnerability is a source of human dignity.

Perhaps the most serious charge to be leveled against an ethics of embodiment grounded upon vulnerability concerns how well it can address the perennial questions of ethics, namely the questions of human freedom, responsibility, and agency. Though the vulnerable body can, I believe, generate the bodily imperatives that demand an ethical response (a response that can be heeded or disregarded), and though the response itself may create new sites of vulnerability, it can also be seen as a free, responsible, and agentic affirmation of the "I can" body. In other words, though this "I can" body is itself vulnerable physically, psychically, socially, and politically, as Fanon, Young, and Foucault have shown, it is also not reducible to its vulnerability, but rather constitutes a positive experience of corporeal agency in response to vulnerability that can and should remain an ethical ideal.

Finally, it is important to point out that since non-human beings also have vulnerable bodies, an ethics of embodiment that begins with a positive affirmation of the vulnerable body as a source of dignity and that affirms the moral efficacy of the "I can" response to the bodily imperatives generated by that vulnerability can open up new ways of understanding our moral obligations to other species. And perhaps, as Cynthia Willett argues in *Interspecies Ethics*,[39] we can even gain valuable moral lessons from these non-human others as we watch them negotiate, with pride, shame, seriousness, and humor, the perils, as well as the pleasures, of intercorporeal vulnerability.

Notes

1. Elizabeth Grosz. *Volatile Bodies: Toward a Corporeal Feminism*. (Indianapolis: Indiana University Press, 1994): 19.
2. Grosz, *Volatile Bodies*, 19.
3. Plato "Republic," in eds. Edith Hamilton and Huntington Cairns. *Collected Dialogues*, trans. Paul Shorey. (Princeton: Princeton University Press, 1980): 684 441e.
4. Plato, "Republic", 684 441e.
5. Plato, "Republic", 684 442a-b.
6. Donna-Dale Marcano, "Race/Gender and the Philosopher's Body" *Living Alterities: Phenomenology, Embodiment, and Race*. Ed. Emily S. Lee. (Albany: SUNY Press, 2014): 76.
7. Marcano, "Race/Gender and the Philosopher's Body", 77.
8. René Descartes. *Discourse on Method and Meditations*. Trans. Laurence J. Lafleur. (Indianapolis: Bobbs-Merrill Educational Publishing, 1960): 75.
9. Descartes, *Discourse on Method and Meditations*, 76.
10. Aristotle. "Politics" and "Nichomachean Ethics" in ed. Richard McKeon *The Basic Works of Aristotle*. New York: Random House, 1941: 1132 1254 5–15, my emphasis.
11. For example: Paul Schollmeier. "Aristotle and Women: Household and Political Roles" *Polis* 20, no. 1–2 (2003): 22–42.
12. Sigmund Freud. "Femininity" in James Strachey (ed.) *The Complete Psychological Works of Sigmund Freud* (The Standard Edition), vol. 22, pp. 136–157. (New York: W.W. Norton and Company, 1976).
13. Luce Irigaray. *Speculum of the Other Woman*. Trans. Gillian C. Gill. (Ithaca: Cornell University Press, 1985): 28.
14. Quoted in: Irigaray, *Speculum of the Other Woman*, 88.
15. Irigaray, *Speculum of the Other Woman*, 89.
16. Simone de Beauvoir. *The Second Sex*. Trans. Constance Borde and Sheila Malovany-Chevallier. (New York: Alfred A. Knopf, 2010), 443.
17. Simone de Beauvoir. *The Ethics of Ambiguity*. Trans. Bernard Frechtman. (Secaucus, NJ: Citadel Press, 1997).

18. See: Jean-Paul Sartre. *Being and Nothingness*. Trans. Hazel E. Barnes. (New York: Washington Square Press, 1984).
19. Frantz Frantz. *Black Skin, White Masks*. Trans. Richard Philcox. (New York: Grove Press, 2008): 95.
20. Fanon, *Black Skin, White Masks*, 119, 95.
21. Fanon, *Black Skin, White Masks*, 96.
22. Maurice Merleau-Ponty, *Phenomenology of Perception*. Trans. Donald A. Landes. (London: Routledge, 2012): 191–192.
23. Merleau-Ponty, *Phenomenology of Perception*, 139.
24. Gail Weiss. *Body Images: Embodiment as Intercorporeality*. (New York: Routledge, 1999).
25. Weiss, *Body Images*.
26. Emmanuel Levinas. *Totality and Infinity*. Trans. Alphonso Lingis. (Pittsburgh: Duquesne University Press, 1969): 194.
27. Levinas, *Totality and Infinity*, 194.
28. Levinas, *Totality and Infinity*, 194.
29. Levinas, *Totality and Infinity*, 197.
30. Judith Butler. *Precarious Life: The Powers of Mourning and Violence*. (London: Verso, 2004): 135.
31. Eva Feder Kittay. *Love's Labor: Essays on Women, Equality, and Dependency*. (New York: Routledge, 1999): 28.
32. Butler, *Precarious Life*, 42.
33. Debra Bergoffen. *Contesting the Politics of Genocidal Rape: Affirming the Dignity of the Vulnerable Body*. (New York: Routledge, 2012): 78–79.
34. Ellen Feder. *Making Sense of Intersex: Changing Ethical Perspectives in Biomedicine*. (Bloomington: Indiana University Press, 2014): 183.
35. Bergoffen, *Contesting the Politics of Genocidal Rape*, 2.
36. Bergoffen, *Contesting the Politics of Genocidal Rape*, 101.
37. Bergoffen, *Contesting the Politics of Genocidal Rape*, 101–102.
38. Friedrich Nietzsche. *On the Genealogy of Morals*. Trans. Michael A. Scarpitti. (New York: Penguin Books, 2014).
39. Cynthia Willett. *Interspecies Ethics*. (New York: Columbia University Press, 2014).

Bibliography

Aristotle. 1941. "Politics" and "Nichomachean Ethics". In *The Basic Works of Aristotle*, ed. Richard McKeon. New York: Random House.

Bergoffen, Debra. 2012. *Contesting the Politics of Genocidal Rape: Affirming the Dignity of the Vulnerable Body*. New York: Routledge.

Butler, Judith. 2004. *Precarious Life: The Powers of Mourning and Violence*. London: Verso.

Beauvoir, Simone de. 1997. *The Ethics of Ambiguity*. Trans. Bernard Frechtman. Secaucus: Citadel Press.
———. 2010. *The Second Sex*. Trans. Constance Borde and Sheila Malovany-Chevallier. New York: Alfred A. Knopf.
Descartes, René. 1960. *Discourse on Method and Meditations*. Trans. Laurence J. Lafleur. Indianapolis: Bobbs-Merrill Educational Publishing.
Fanon, Frantz. 2008. *Black Skin, White Masks*. Trans. Richard Philcox. New York: Grove Press.
Feder, Ellen. 2014. *Making Sense of Intersex: Changing Ethical Perspectives in Biomedicine*. Bloomington: Indiana University Press.
Freud, Sigmund. 1976. Femininity. In James Strachey (ed.) *The Complete Psychological Works of Sigmund Freud* (The Standard Edition), vol. 22, pp. 136–157. New York: W.W. Norton and Company.
Grosz, Elizabeth. 1994. *Volatile Bodies: Toward a Corporeal Feminism*. Indianapolis: Indiana University Press.
Irigaray, Luce. 1985. *Speculum of the Other Woman*. Trans. Gillian C. Gill. Ithaca: Cornell University Press.
Kant, Immanuel. 1956. *Groundwork of the Metaphysic of Morals*. Trans. H.J. Paton. New York: Harper and Row.
Kittay, Eva Feder. 1999. *Love's Labor: Essays on Women, Equality, and Dependency*. New York: Routledge.
Levinas, Emmanuel. 1969. *Totality and Infinity*. Trans. Alphonso Lingis. Pittsburgh: Duquesne University Press.
Marcano, Donna-Dale. 2014. Race/Gender and the Philosopher's Body. In *Living Alterities: Phenomenology, Embodiment, and Race*, ed. Emily S. Lee, 65–78. Albany: SUNY Press.
Merleau-Ponty, Maurice. 2012. *Phenomenology of Perception*. Trans. Donald A. Landes. London: Routledge.
Nietzsche, Friedrich. 2014. *On the Genealogy of Morals*. Trans. Michael A. Scarpitti. New York: Penguin Books.
Plato "Republic," in Edith Hamilton and Huntington Cairns (eds.) *Collected Dialogues*. Trans. Paul Shorey. Princeton: Princeton University Press, 1980.
Rawls, John. 1999. *A Theory of Justice*. Revised Edition. Cambridge: Harvard University Press.
Sartre, Jean-Paul. 1984. *Being and Nothingness*. Trans. Hazel E. Barnes. New York: Washington Square Press.
Schollmeier, Paul. 2003. Aristotle and Women: Household and Political Roles. *Polis* 20 (1–2): 22–42.
Weiss, Gail. 1999. *Body Images: Embodiment as Intercorporeality*. New York: Routledge Press.
Willett, Cynthia. 2014. *Interspecies Ethics*. New York: Columbia University Press.

Further Readings

Alcoff, Linda Martín. 2006. *Visible Identities: Race, Gender, and the Self.* Oxford: Oxford University Press.

Brison, Susan. 2002. *Aftermath: Violence and the Remaking of a Self.* Princeton: Princeton University Press.

Butler, Judith. 2005. *Giving An Account of Oneself.* New York: Fordham University Press.

———. 2009. *Frames of War: When is Life Grievable?* London: Verso.

Campell, Sue, Letitia Meynell, and Susan Sherman, eds. 2009. *Embodiment and Agency.* University Park: Pennsylvania State University Press.

Diprose, Rosalyn. 2002. *Corporeal Generosity: On Giving with Nietzsche, Merleau-Ponty, and Levinas.* Albany: SUNY Press.

Dreger, Alice Domurat. 1999. *Intersex in the Age of Ethics.* Hagerstown: University Publishing Group.

Doyle, Laura, ed. 2001. *Bodies of Resistance: New Phenomenologies of Politics, Agency, and Culture.* Evanston: Northwestern University Press.

Garland Thomson, Rosemarie. 1997. *Extraordinary Bodies: Figuring Physical Disability in American Culture and Literature.* New York: Columbia University Press.

Gordon, Lewis R. 1995. *Bad Faith and Antiblack Racism.* Atlantic Highlands: Humanities Press.

Heyes, Cressida. 2007. *Self-Transformations: Foucault, Ethics, and Normalized Bodies.* Oxford: Oxford University Press.

Huffer, Lynne. 2013. *Are the Lips a Grave: A Queer Feminist on the Ethics of Sex.* New York: Columbia University Press.

Kittay, Eva Feder, and Ellen Feder, eds. 2002. *The Subject of Care: Feminist Perspectives on Dependency.* Lanham: Rowman & Littlefield Publishers.

Lee, Emily S., ed. 2014. *Living Alterities: Phenomenology, Embodiment, and Race.* Albany: SUNY Press.

Mann, Bonnie. 2014. *Sovereign Masculinity: Gender Lessons from the War on Terror.* Oxford: Oxford University Press.

Miller, Sarah Clark. 2012. *The Ethics of Need: Agency, Dignity, and Obligation.* New York: Routledge.

Murphy, Ann V. 2012. *Violence and the Philosophical Imaginary.* Albany: SUNY Press.

Nussbaum, Martha. 2011. *Creating Capabilities: The Human Development Approach.* Cambridge: Harvard University Press.

Salamon, Gayle. 2010. *Assuming a Body: Transgender and Rhetorics of Materiality.* New York: Columbia University Press.

Smith, Bonnie G., and Beth Hutchison. 2004. *Gendering Disability.* New Brunswick: Rutgers University Press.

Sullivan, Nikki. 2001. *Tattooed Bodies: Subjectivity, Textuality, Ethics, and Pleasure.* Westport: Praeger.

Yancy, George, ed. 2004. *What White Looks Like: African-American Philosophers on the Whiteness Question.* New York: Routledge.

Young, Iris Marion. 2005. *On Female Body Experience: Throwing Like a Girl and Other Essays.* Oxford: Oxford University Press.

Zeiler, Kristin, and Lisa Folkmarson Käll, eds. 2014. *Feminist Phenomenology and Medicine.* Albany: SUNY Press.

CHAPTER 3

The Normal Body: Female Bodies in Changing Contexts of Normalization and Optimization

Julia Jansen and Maren Wehrle

Twofold Embodiment: The Body as Subject and the Body as Object

Being embodied means, on the one hand, to be material, visible, and subject to the physical laws that govern causality. Having a physical body means I am finite, exposed, and dependent on others and external forces, and thus vulnerable, as Butler emphasizes.[1] As a living (human) being, I also live, feel (and suffer through) my body, in virtue of which I am not only vulnerable, but also open to the world. My lived body is my center of orientation, to which all objects I perceive are relative. It is the kinaesthetic unity through which I can move freely, and change position and perspective. It also is the field within which all my tactual sensations and

J. Jansen (✉)
Husserl Archives, Institute of Philosophy, KU Leuven, Leuven, Belgium

M. Wehrle
Faculty of Philosophy, Erasmus University Rotterdam, Rotterdam, The Netherlands

© The Author(s) 2018
C. Fischer, L. Dolezal (eds.), *New Feminist Perspectives on Embodiment*, Breaking Feminist Waves, https://doi.org/10.1007/978-3-319-72353-2_3

movement sensations are localized. The lived body manifests a 'body schema', a unitary style of movement and engagement, based not only on proprioception and immediate 'knowledge' of direction, posture, and body size, but also on individual abilities, habits, acquired skills, and on a body's whole experiential past.[2]

When we analyze the way the female body is represented, and how these representations are influenced by and produced within normatively gendered institutions (e.g., the media), we address the body as a material, visible thing. When I am concerned with my 'body image', I want to know whether my body is beautiful, healthy, trained, skinny, female, male, normal, or good enough, according to the norms of our time and culture. In this sense, my body is an object I must attend to, adjust, evaluate, optimize, and compare with other bodies—a common topic for body history, feminist philosophy, and gender or queer studies. Yet, not only the body image is influenced by discourses, socio-historical structures, and norms; so is the body as subject or the body schema. In what follows, we focus mainly on the lived body and its normalization, which is always twofold: on the one hand, the lived body inevitably normalizes its experiences; on the other hand, it is subject to normalization. As Merleau-Ponty emphasized, as bodily subjects, we are situated in a world and literally *incorporate* the meanings and norms of this world in an anonymous way. Such norms are not only constitutive of the images we have of our bodies, but also have a more direct impact on our experiences, for example, on how we move, eat, sleep, and behave; on how we sense, feel, and perceive the world; and on how we relate to ourselves and others.

Human embodiment is characterized by an internal differentiation: I must *be my body* and, at the same time, *have this body*.[3] A sense of what counts as normal helps us mediate between centric and eccentric modes of embodiment and to negotiate 'internal' and 'external' perspectives on our bodies. However, such normality can never be fully achieved, and so it always remains a regulatory ideal, or an optimum we continuously strive to reestablish. This in turn moves us to constantly redefine the limits of our bodies, that is, to enhance, optimize, and technically extend them, while we simultaneously seek a supposedly lost, 'natural' identity, 'a past', as Merleau-Ponty would put it, 'which never has been present'.[4] We are not only objectified or constituted in a passive way; we are also able to actively objectify ourselves. Adjusting, controlling, and optimizing one's movements, or learning new ones often even requires, at least initially, that we focus on specific parts of our bodies.

Thus, the lived body is not only actively performing its body schema, but is at the same time under the influence of external norms and structures, and thus a target for power, practices of discipline, and normalization. At the same time, the body as object is not merely passively, externally constructed, but also enables us to distance ourselves from ourselves and to critically evaluate our experiences. This inner distance is twofold. On the one hand, it, first of all, makes neoliberal forms of (self)-normalization and optimization possible and masks them as natural, voluntary forms of self-care and mastery (in opposition to what Foucault intended when introducing these notions as possible alternatives). On the other hand, this distance within our embodiment is far from being reducible to an externally constructed constraint, and even is a precondition for reflection and freedom. In the following sections, we want to investigate this double sidedness of embodiment and how it relates to an experienced normality and to external normalization.

A Phenomenology of Normality and Optimality

What do we mean when we talk about a normal body? Is a normal body defined as the average of all existent bodies, or does it rather signify the ideal of a perfectly able and healthy body? 'Normally', we do not talk about normal bodies at all, but only of bodies that deviate from what we assume to be normal. In fact, the normal body can only take shape in contrast to bodies that are considered abnormal and thus, first of all, reveal a preexisting norm. Normal can in this sense refer to the 'usual', or to the 'optimal': while the former depends on our previous experiences of bodies, the latter defines how the body should be, for example, how it should be shaped, sized, or what it should be capable of doing. A body is in this sense 'optimal' when it most effectively fulfills its supposed tasks. However, apart from necessary organic functions and capabilities necessary for survival (such as moving and perceiving properly), these tasks have differed substantially at different times and in different cultures, and most of those differences are rather gendered than not gendered. Normality is thus not merely a descriptive category, nor does it refer to a statistical average; rather, it bears an inherent relation to an optimum, and these optima are relative to culturally and historically specific normative frameworks. For example, while in most contemporary Western societies, a 'normal' body now has to be healthy and fit, and not merely free from sickness, this was not the case before the medicalization of the eighteenth century, when sickness and pain belonged to a normal life and body.

While we have come to find it self-evident that body images are historically relative and have a normative and normalizing character,[5] the relation between the lived, experiencing body and normality is less obvious. Yet, some standards of normality are necessary for the generation of a stable and continuous experience; in this sense, normality is something we desire and require. According to Husserl, here 'normal' initially means 'concordant', in the sense that every new experience must fit into the larger temporal and thematic context of a subject's course of perception. The lived body, as a kinaesthetic system and subject of sensuous experience, is the concrete condition for concordant experience. In this sense, every normal experience relates back to a normally functioning body. What one experiences and how one experiences is in this sense dependent on one's bodily conditions. Generally, every course of experience is strictly correlated to the course of various bodily movements.[6] More concretely, this means that repeated movements or experiences turn into skills and habits that help to quickly orientate and smoothly interact with one's environment. Bodily normality represents in this regard an individual 'I can', that is, the dispositions and acquired abilities of a subject that enable her actions and movements within a given situation and environment.

Moreover, because all human subjects share common sensory and kinaesthetic skills and possibilities, this experiential access to the world is—at least formally—the same for every human being. It thus makes joint and shared experience possible, which is in turn the precondition for cooperation, communication, as well as empathy. A normal embodiment thus serves as a bridge between individual and intersubjective experience.[7] For example, embodied subjects who share a common environment develop similar skills and habits, which makes it, in turn, easier for them to anticipate the behavior of others in typical situations. Normality as concordance can therefore be understood as a stable way of 'being in the world', or as the establishment of a familiar environment.

On an individual level, the experience of one's own lived body can only be temporarily or partially experienced as abnormal, for example, in contrast with or as interruption to the normal (habitual, familiar) course of subjective experience. From a first-person perspective, the subject experiences any abnormality as a modification of normality, as something that is different from what was expected and that is recognized in reference to an overall frame of normal experience. A bodily anomaly, such as a burned finger, for example, leads to deviant sensory (in this case, tactile) data. In comparison with the 'normal' course of tactile perceptions, the subject experiences sensations stemming from the burned finger as abnormal.[8] The subjective body thus necessarily has the desire to reestablish a former normality or to create a new normality (through repeated experiences of another kind); otherwise, it no longer experiences herself or the world as concordant, evident, that is, real.

On an intersubjective level, the normal body is the measure for a common world, which serves as a basis for communication and action. In this regard, Husserl would interpret the experience of, for example, a blind subject as 'abnormal' only insofar as it 'deviates in a consistent way from the proven or true world of the experience of others'.[9] While from an individual level, the experience of a blind person is as concordant and stable as that of a seeing person, it is discordant with the average perception of a community of (seeing) subjects. Even more importantly, it is discordant with optimal perception as an epistemic norm,[10] which calls for the right subjective bodily conditions and abilities (free movement, perceptual quality, etc.), as well as for the best 'objective' circumstances (lighting conditions, perceptual distance, etc.).

However, according to Husserl, this seemingly 'objective' ideal of optimal perception usually is relative to the current interests and actions of an individual subject or a community. What is here the 'best' view of an object can vary according to special interests or practical concerns. In individual experience, optimality expresses itself mostly in the form of a *relative optimum*, relative to the subject's current actions, interests, or habitual style of experience. What would be an optimal perception of a house for, say, a pedestrian who just passes by would not be optimal enough for an architect interested in the way that house is built, or for a real estate agent who has to sell the same house. The same holds true for relative optima on an intersubjective level. Here, the relative optima are dependent on specific interest groups, be they social, political, or even recreational in nature. In everyday experience, optima are less general but highly specific or typical, which means that they are relative to individual or cultural skills, habits, and interests that have developed through specific interrelations of subjects and their environment. Normal experience is in that sense not only continuous and concordant, but, in its tendency toward an optimum, it is also highly selective.[11] The specific ways in which these selection processes take place depend on current actions and interests, as well as on the overall style of perceiving, that is, the bodily skills, habits, and the experiential history of an individual. Due to our embodiment in an intersubjective and historical world, this seemingly individual style also reflects the social norms of its time, which are literally embodied or incorporated.

If we assume (1) that normality (as concordance) depends on the previous experiences and habits of individual bodily subjects and social groups, as well as on their interests and goals (which come to define the aims of perceptions and thus their optimality), and if we assume (2) that these habits, interests, and relative optima are acquired and embedded within a historical and cultural world, then we have to conclude that what we experience as normal, even at the level of individual experience, reflects the existent norms and power relations of the respective society and time. In this sense, 'normal', and thus 'abnormal', embodiment is never neutrally referring to an individual's bodily capabilities. In fact, the 'I can', the practical bodily possibilities and skills that enable normality in experience, may turn out to be an 'I cannot', because the lived body is always also an expression of 'gender, race, class, ability, and other social and spatial privileges that some bodies enjoy more than others'.[12] In this sense, the 'I can' is an expression not only of 'embodied agency', but also of 'cultural agency'. As Iris Marion Young pointed out, a female style of bodily comportment in patriarchal societies is rather characterized by its restrictions and inhibitions.[13]

Even nowadays, there are still difficult but doable motor tasks that are taken to be self-evidently the province of boys or men and that girls or women tend to face 'with the nagging doubt that maybe "I cannot" undertake them successfully'.[14] This 'inhibition' of the moving body goes hand in hand with a constant awareness of the body as object, a constant worry about how the body appears to others. The less a woman can just *be a body* (aiming at the world and what she wants to do in it), the more she *has a body* (worrying over what the body should do and what it should look like).[15] Although women are thus often attentive to their bodies in the sense of a third-person body image, the development of a female body schema, and thus the incorporation of gendered norms, proceeds as it were 'under the radar' of explicit awareness.[16]

Normality at the level of the lived body is neither static nor simply given. That very same body must achieve it in continuous experience and actualize it in repeated movement. Normalization in this sense is thus performative.[17] However, as we have seen in the analyses of Young and Weiss, explicitly addressing one's body inhibits one's actions and one's 'normal' embodiment. Yet, if we want to resist 'normalization', understood as oppression through dominant norms, we must consciously think about how we have come to be embodied in this or that way. Precisely in order to have a 'normal' female body according to one's body image, women pay the price of not being able to move and comport themselves in an 'optimal' (unrestricted) way.[18] And even if women purposefully resist gendered expectations and conventional modes of embodiment, even if they attempt to move in a more optimal (rather than 'normal' way), this can be a cumbersome process that has to be attentively learned and thus does not feel 'natural' or 'normal' at all—not until it becomes part of an altered, rehabitualized body schema.

NORMALIZATION AND OPTIMIZATION OF FEMALE BODIES

In Foucault's analyses of discipline, a form of power that was especially characteristic of the nineteenth century, one can find an illustration of how such an implicit incorporation of norms and power relations could take place. While before the seventeenth century, power was characterized by a sovereign who literally could decide over life and death of his people, in more recent times, power is associated mostly with controlled ways of organizing life and of 'engineering' social groups. In this sense, techniques of power are directly related toward the organization and formation of bodies. Foucault speaks in this regard of two different forms of normalization that correspond to different historic implementations of power, discipline, and biopolitics. Although the latter is more characteristic of recent organizations of society, techniques of discipline are still present and even prominent in specific domains.

Discipline operates in a normalizing way in that it takes predefined norms as its starting point and tries to constitute, shape, or train bodies according to such a norm. The most famous description of normalization as discipline can be found in *Discipline and Punish*. Here, Foucault discusses different examples of power mechanisms, strategies and exercises from the eighteenth and nineteenth centuries that aim to manipulate, shape, and train the bodies of its inhabitants. This includes the control and manipulation of movements and behavior, as well as the embodied subject's time and space. As examples of discipline, he describes enforced practices in the military (marching), schools (sitting, handwriting), and factories (assembly lines). These practices follow instructions or manuals, which define every single movement and gesture: disciplining means controlling the rapidity, modality, and efficiency of their execution. For this to take place, the body must be divided into parts and functions; that is, it must be regarded as an object. The focus hereby lies on an 'uninterrupted, constant coercion' and a 'close supervision of the processes of the activity'.[19] If the movements, positions, or gestures are not executed in the 'right way', according to the respective norms (that are expressed in instructions and manuals), this will immediately result in sanctions: either directly through punishment or indirectly through the denial of recognition. In such a way, 'docile bodies' are produced, which are economically useful and effective and that stabilize prevailing norms. In this sense, the body (of a soldier, pupil, worker, etc.) is the result of repeated and intensive 'disciplined' exercise. In turn, from the perspective of the subjective body, this can be interpreted as a form of forced or prefixed habituation, that is, as a habit formation that is strictly regulated with regard to its conditions, performances, and aims.[20]

Following Foucault, Sandra Bartky interprets practices of beauty enhancements such as dieting, fitness, and cosmetics as practices of normalization. Here too, 'docile' female bodies are produced through disciplinary habit formation, namely the internalization of norms concerning how a female body should look and move—norms that impose a desire for the 'optimal' female body. Therefore, no coercion is necessary for women to adopt such disciplinary practices, but neither do they freely choose them as preferred forms of self-expression. Rather, normatively restricted habit formation effects the incorporation of (patriarchal) standards of (female) bodily acceptability. What Bartky shows with Foucault is that normalization is not something that is merely externally imposed on women by identifiable actors, but is instead something that is habitually internalized, effectively constituting a specifically 'female' subject. The continuous repetition of seemingly innocent practices of, for example, grooming, clothing, and moving, thus eventually determines not only the image a woman has of herself (her 'having a body'), but also her styles of moving, sitting, eating, and being affected by the world and others (her 'being a body'). As normative habits, these standards literally become part and parcel of her (bodily) being, which means that they are experienced not as second, but as first nature, that is, as normal in the sense of 'natural'.[21]

What this means is that the lived body is articulated in complex and also in ambiguous ways by what Gail Weiss calls 'the 3 Ns – the normal, the natural, and the normative'.[22] Each body has 'natural' constraints and capabilities, but none of them are neutrally natural. They are in practice (not necessarily in conscious thought) always already measured against standards of normality. These standards of normality, which are in the case of the lived body (not the body image) primarily directed at somebody's perceptual, kinetic, and practical possibilities, are in turn intimately linked with a sense of the optimal. However, as we have seen, what counts as 'optimal' is highly context dependent (something cannot be optimal as such, but only optimal in reference to a specific purpose or task, for which it is optimal). The fact that these purposes or tasks are highly socioculturally determined and often so prevalent that they become invisible as something one could take issue with, whatever is optimal only in light of them, ends up appearing simply as normal, or even as natural. Given that we are still much more used to exposing and critiquing processes of normalization and their normative pressures with regard to body images, the complex intertwinements of the 'the 3 Ns' on the level of the lived body often go unnoticed. What's more, their invisibility and the invisibility of their intertwinement are further facilitated by the fact that, as we argued with Husserl, lived bodies require and strive for normalization centered around optima in order to be able to take a position and orientate themselves in natural and social environments. In other words, lived bodies rely on normalization and are thus inevitably also vulnerable to modes of normalization that are constraining and oppressive. We believe that this inevitability takes on a heightened urgency in a neoliberal framework, which rejects the idea of normalization for the sake of the idea of a freely choosing subject and thus in fact increases the risks of simply undetected constraining and oppressive normalization.

(Self-)Normalization and Control of Neoliberal Female Bodies

While Bartky could still argue in the 1980s that disciplinary practices were part of a disciplinary apparatus aimed at turning women into 'docile compliant companions of men just as surely as the army aims to turn its raw recruits into soldiers',[23] this no longer seems to be an adequate description. In contemporary (especially Western) neoliberal societies, we often cannot find the typical forms of disciplinary power that Foucault considered exemplary of the nineteenth century. Instead of being disciplined to be an ideal wife or companion, women now tend to 'govern' themselves with great ambition and (pretended) pleasure. Neoliberal governmentality—a new form of power and hence a new form of subject constitution that Foucault already claimed was exemplary of our times—does not produce a docile but instead a (supposedly) free economic subject with individual tendencies, motivations, and preferences.

In the nineteenth century, the beginning era of biopolitics, scientific and political institutions aimed to locate the normal and the abnormal through measuring and defining an average. In this regard, all subjects and bodies were categorized, distributed, and evaluated against a—supposedly neutrally—measured normality. Normalization then functioned in its most literal sense, namely in categorizing and unifying the forms and behaviors of bodies. By contrast, contemporary practices of normalization are less obviously intrusive and less visible, mainly because they are now mostly executed willingly by the respective subjects themselves: in a society that is oriented toward normality—even without explicitly enforcing it through externally imposed practices of discipline—being abnormal still is unfavorable and brings disadvantages. Subjects thus 'choose' to use normalizing techniques to defend their interests and to optimize their chances in a neoliberal capitalistic society. Being 'normal', then, merely is the 'rational' to be.

This neoliberal form of normalization (which, it has to be said, does not simply replace but remains interwoven with disciplinary practices and strategies) follows a different rationality than the panoptic society of discipline. In what Deleuze has called 'societies of control',[24] there is no longer a general mechanism of normalization, which needed to exclude those who were not properly normalized. In neoliberal societies, governing is no longer a negative and exclusionary practice of surveillance and discipline, but its aim appears as 'positive' and 'productive': it supports individual interests through supporting a specific economic regime and proclaims to have the welfare of the 'population' and 'the improvement of its conditions, the increase of wealth, longevity, health'[25] as its purpose. It uses practices of organization, rationalization, enhancement, or limitation according to the principles and needs of the economy: now every subject 'freely chooses' to normalize or optimize itself, to enhance its gains (human capital) and reduce its losses in the economic market. The neoliberal female subject thus has a self-interest in optimizing her body as an object, with a calculable price and value within a job or private market. This is also expressed in a dramatic increase in self-help and optimizing literature that propagates normative practices of feminine beauty. Neoliberal practices and habits instilled in subjects are no longer connected to shame, social sanctions, or sexual rewards, but aim to construct females as a specific, and thus specifically 'targetable', group of consumers and entrepreneurs.

However, as Johanna Oksala points out, behind the mask of the glamorous ideas of personal choice and self-interest, there still hide the systematic aspects of power—domination, social hierarchies, and economic exploitation. While women apparently are now free to choose between different options, they lack the possibility to define or shape those options: women still incorporate social norms and power hierarchies through mundane techniques of normalization that then become part of their bodily subjectivity: 'Only now these techniques as well as the hierarchies they mirror and uphold are portrayed even more effectively as the consequence of individual choice.'[26]

In this context, 'optimization' is often seen as the 'rational' and 'freely chosen' alternative to normality, thereby obscuring the normalizing forces that are thus largely left unopposed. No longer being experienced as 'external' impositions, they are thus allowed to infiltrate the 'economy' of our innermost needs and desires. We now wear high heels because we want to (anything else would be a constraint of our 'freedom', after all we can wear whatever we want), and we exercise and diet *not* in order to please anybody but because we ('objectively') need to optimize our health and fitness (anything else would be against our self-interest and thus irrational).[27] Increasingly, these optimizations and 'enhancements' are not negotiated on the side of the objective body and associated body images, but on the side of the lived body. We do not want merely to 'look' fit and healthy anymore, we want to show that we 'can' run marathons, that our diet optimizes our energy levels, and that we sleep deeply and healthily at night—all monitored electronically and often documented on social media in the attempt to demonstrate that we are 'in control' of our 'balanced' lives. Given that failures to make the 'rational' choices are increasingly seen as also morally questionable,[28] our optimized bodily performance also demonstrates our moral integrity.

The new forms of neoliberal self-optimization show striking similarities with what Foucault introduced in his late Lectures as an alternative to normalizing mechanisms, the *care of the self* or an aesthetic of existence.[29] But in what sense is this self-mastery different from the neoliberal forms of normalization? The stoic concept of self-care Foucault refers to is characterized by an internal transformation of the individual through practical exercises of self-mastery and self-awareness; it presupposes freedom and a form of self-determination as well as the acquirement of a skill and a bodily optimization: one learns how to do things best in specific situations. This requires a specific form of awareness, attention to one's body, a repeated everyday training routine (meditating, dieting, gymnastics, asceticism). In Foucault, one can find three arguments as to why the care of the self does not amount to normalization. First, the aim of the respective practices is to provide the individual with autonomy and make her more independent from external circumstances; it establishes a relation to oneself that can be a source of pleasure. Second, it wants to prepare specific individuals for specific situations and therefore does not aim for a universal norm or normalization. Third, we can choose the norms we want to inhabit, the principles and teachers under which we want to subjugate ourselves. In caring for ourselves, we are thus not normalized, but we give ourselves a norm. But is this not what we do when we use fitness trackers and self-mastering tools and try to optimize our movements and appearances?

We would like to argue instead that today's forms of optimization are indeed identifiable as normalizations in the literal sense. Why? First, they aim not at an internal transformation of the individual or its independence from external circumstances. Quite the contrary, optimizing ourselves makes us deeply dependent on the tools we use, on the visibility of our objectively measurable changes, and their legitimization and recognition within the society we live in. It is thus not a transformation or active shaping of a new way of life that is central, but how this appears and is legitimized as one. Optimization is only real if it is visible, evaluated, and recognized by others: it is thus, even when it pertains to the lived body, still very intimately connected with concerns surrounding body images. Second, we tend to not acquire a specific skill that typically helps us handle a 'real-life' situation, but a skill that is specific to a certain context, for example, the context of marathon races, and that allows for our bodily performance to be compared and classified according to 'universal', that is, scientific objective standards. In this sense, we discipline ourselves to become fitter or better than the standard, a measured category or norm we believe is normal. But this norm is not less historical or contaminated by interests and power than were the prefixed norms that guided the disciplinary forms of power. Third, since we suffer disadvantages when we stay behind in the race of optimization, we are not actually free to choose the practices, principles, or teachers of optimization. This is especially relevant for people with less financial or social influence (which still is true for most women), who are forced to take any possibility to improve their chances to get financial independence and social recognition.

This perfidious logic of neoliberal optimization, which is now among the affluent increasingly replacing the logic of normalization, is afforded, encouraged, and enhanced through the developments of digital technologies. Again, it is important to see that control is twofold. It pertains not only to the body as object, but even more importantly, to the lived body. Tools of self-observation and self-documentation (from selfies to fitness watches) help us show not only what we look like, but what we can do. They also serve the digital surveillance by national governments and global corporations; and social media not only facilitate rapid multiplication and uncontrollable broadcasting, but they increasingly prevent any attempts to defend a private sphere. This also has effects on the level of embodiment, and not only on the level of the body as object and associated body images, but also on the level of the lived body. The rapidly expanding publicity of our bodies demands that we attend to our bodies more again and in new ways. It also poses new obstacles to unconstrained comportment and movement, and thus brings new inhibitions. As Paul Virilio points out, '[W]e all observe each other and compare ourselves with one another on a continual basis…every economic and political system in its turn enters the private life of all the others, forbidding any of them for free themselves for any length of time from this competitive approach.'[30] The quantitative increase in perpetual observance and (self-)control here makes a qualitative difference. Not only are there fewer and fewer opportunities to withdraw from the public eye, we are, on the contrary, constantly required to publicly demonstrate the success of our attempts at optimization and therewith our moral and rational (i.e., economic) worth.

Conclusion: What Now?

What could 'liberation' mean in a world in which we 'desire the conditions of our own subjugation' in the name of optimization masked as rational protection of self-interests?[31] This question is especially critical, since, as we have shown in this chapter, processes of not only normalization but also optimization cannot simply be eradicated. They remain constitutive of perceptual and other judgments, and of a shared world of experience and action. What Weiss has called 'thick notions' of the natural, the normal, and the normative, that is, notions that illuminate the interdependence and reciprocal reinforcement of these three dimensions, thus acquire heightened complexity because they must be understood with respect to both the body as object and the lived body, and with respect to both contingent constraining and necessary enabling aspects of normalization and optimization.

It is likely that these processes demand new conceptions of embodiment that bring physical and lived bodies together with virtual bodies that increasingly populate social media sites and Second Life spaces. Again, the tendencies are directed at the same time toward increasing visibility and increasing invisibility, namely of the contingent constraining aspects of optimization to which the neoliberal subject, who believes herself to be free, remains largely blind. Specifically, a focus on the lived body understood as the site of the dialectic between 'I can' and 'I cannot' can be of help here. That, as Pirkko Markula has pointed out, the body no longer necessarily 'corresponds to the fleshy representation of the human subject'[32] does not make it impervious to the forces we tried to outline here. A more functional approach geared toward investigating real or virtual modes of optimal performance and capability is likely to add to the complexity of available accounts of the natural, the normal, and the normative.

Moreover, since dimensions of contingent and constraining normalization and optimization are largely covered over by conceptions of choice and free will, new conceptions of embodiment will have to include phenomenological investigations of the will and of decision-making. What is important here is not only whether, from a third-person perspective, some choice for the enhancement of one's body or for the optimization of one's bodily possibilities in fact *is* free, but also how that freedom of choice is as such experienced and what aspects of this experience can account for the vehemence with which that freedom is now commonly felt and defended.

Finally, since contemporary embodiment has so much to do not only with visibility but with publicity, and given that current advances in technology and correlative practices of self-control are also linked with—equally 'rational' and allegedly 'beneficial'—demands for transparency (and the therefore unsurprising widespread consensual compliance with those demands), ongoing practices of critical reflection and resistance may also be in need of an invocation of what Édouard Glissant, in a different context, has called a 'right for opacity'.[33] Exactly what this would mean for political action and individual behavior will have to be carefully, and urgently, examined.

Notes

1. Cf. Judith Butler, *Frames of War. When Life Is Grievable* (New York: Verso 2010), 33.
2. Merleau-Ponty emphasizes that the body schema is not the result of associations established during experiences, but has to be understood as a Gestalt, that is, a meaningful whole that is irreducible to its parts. Cf. Maurice Merleau-Ponty: *Phenomenology of Perception* (New York: Routledge, 2012), 114.
3. According to Plessner, this results in a constant de-centering that gives us an 'eccentric positionality'. Cf. Helmuth Plessner, *Die Stufen des Organischen und der Mensch*. Berlin: De Gruyter, 1975.
4. Merleau-Ponty 2012, 252.
5. See, for example, Thomas W. Laqueur, *The Making of Sex. Bodies and Gender from the Greeks to Freud* (Cambridge: Cambridge University Press, 1990). Londa Schiebinger (ed.), *Feminism and the Body* (Oxford: Oxford University Press, 2000).
6. Cf. Edmund Husserl, *Analysen zur passive Synthesis*, Hua XI (Dordrecht: Springer,1966), 214–215; Edmund Husserl, *Die Lebenswelt*, Hua XXXVIII (Dordrecht: Springer, 2008), 638, 648ff., 662.
7. Because I am my body but also have it as an object, I assume this to be the case for other embodied subjects. That means that the perceived body of the other is never perceived by me purely as a physical object, but as a lived body that is owned and lived through by a subject with similar capacities and feelings. Therefore, I am able to (imaginarily) put myself in the place of the other, and to immediately assume that she has a bodily perspective that would be the same if I were in her place. An even more direct empathic relation can be seen with regard to feelings that are directly expressed through the body, such as pain, anger, or happiness (cf. Merleau-Ponty, *Phenomenology of Perception*).
8. Edmund Husserl, *Die Lebenswelt*, 640; Edmund Husserl, *Analysen zur passiven Synthesis*, 215.
9. Husserl, *Die Lebenswelt*, 657. In the same way, Husserl discusses constant cases of abnormal perceptions as borderline cases; he counts the experience of blind people, mad people, children, and animals among these cases.
10. Although one could imagine a color-blind population (cf. Husserl Ms. D 13 XIV, 31), at the moment that they meet a population of color-seeing people, Husserl believes they would acknowledge that perception with color will be better suited for a differentiated and true perception of the world. The color-blind person's perception is in this sense less optimal (Husserl, *Die Lebenswelt*, 658).
11. This aspect is often overlooked in the research literature. For example, while otherwise giving a very clear and concise presentation of normality in

Husserl, Taipale does not discuss the aspect of optimality critically in Joona Taipale, *Phenomenology and Embodiment. Husserl and the Constitution of Subjectivity* (Evanston: Northwestern University Press, 2014). The same holds true for Steinbock's groundbreaking analysis in Anthony Steinbock, *Home and Beyond: Generative Phenomenology after Husserl* (Evanston: Northwestern University Press, 1995).
12. Gail Weiss, "A Merleau-Pontian Legacy to Feminist Theory", in: *Continental Philosophy Review* 48 (2015), 84. The way we (can) move and explore our environment can also be restricted in various ways due to social and political circumstances. And *I cannot* is thus not a neutral description of individual disabilities, since it is relative to specific social and cultural situations.
13. Iris Marion Young, "Throwing Like a Girl: A Phenomenology of Feminine Body Comportment Motility and Spatiality", in: Human Studies 3/2 (1980), 153.
14. Weiss, "A Merleau-Pontian Legacy to Feminist Theory", 79.
15. This difficulty in elaborating one's body schema, or better, the dissymmetry in favor of a body image, is also characteristic of racial embodiment: Here, the white gaze of the French colonist alienates the native Antillean from her own body. See Frantz Fanon, *Black Skin, White Masks* (New York: Grove Press 2008).
16. Weiss, "A Merleau-Pontian Legacy to Feminist Theory", 81–82.
17. Not only acts of signification may be called performative (Cf. Judith Butler, *Gender Trouble* (New York: Routledge, 1990)), but so may the activities of the body. Every acquisition of skill implies the body's participation and the active discovery of its abilities and its environment. These processes are not fully regulated or fixed but entail transformations and changes, and even the discovery of new forms of movements and skills.
18. Often, what is considered to be 'normal' embodiment or bodily comportment *for women* is judged as deviant from the 'optimal', male norm of embodiment.
19. Michel Foucault, *Discipline and Punish* (London: Vintage, 1991), 137.
20. Cf. Maren Wehrle, "Normative Embodiment. The Role of the Body in Foucault's Genealogy: A Phenomenological Re-Reading," *Journal of the British Society for Phenomenology* 47 (2016), 56–71.
21. As Oksala concisely puts it: 'Habit forms the normative mechanism that produces a stable and enduring pattern of being and creates an illusion of a permanent gender core or essence.' Oksala, *Feminist Experience*, 114.
22. Weiss, "Uncosmetic Surgeries in an Age of Normativity", 105.
23. Sandra Lee Bartky: "Foucault, Femininity and the Modernization of Patriarchal Power," in *Feminism and Foucault: Reflections of Resistance*, eds. I. Diamond & L. Quinby, (Boston: Northeastern University Press 1988), 75.

24. Gilles Deleuze, "Postscript on the Societies of Control", *October* 59. (Winter, 1992), 3–7.
25. Michel Foucault, *4 Essential Works of Foucault 1954–1984* (London: Penguin Books, 1994), 217.
26. Oksala, *Feminist Experience*, 126.
27. For illuminating discussions of a 'good health imperative', see: Talia Welsh, "Fat Eats: A Phenomenology of Decadence, Food, and Health." In *Food and Everyday Life*, ed. Thomas Conroy (New York: Lexington Books, 2014); and "Unfit Women: Freedom and Constraint in the Pursuit of Health," *Janus Head* 13, no. 2 (2013): 58–77.
28. Both Weiss, "Uncosmetic Surgeries in an Age of Normativity", and Phipps, *The Politics of the Body: Gender in a Neoliberal and Neoconservative Age*, highlight the moralism that increasingly accompanies the neoliberal ideology of 'free choice'. While the choice of optimization is initially considered 'free', it is also the only 'rational' choice. Those who fail to make it, thus, easily become seen as 'irrational', which makes them immediately vulnerable to charges of moral failure. Phipps in particular stresses how thus neoliberal and neoconservative processes of normalization come to reinforce each other.
29. Michel Foucault, *The Hermeneutics of the Subject* (New York: Palgrave Macmillan, 2005).
30. Paul Virilio, *The Information Bomb* (London: Verso, 2005).
31. Cf. Judith Butler, *The Psychic Life of Power* (Stanford: Stanford University Press, 1997), 9.
32. Pirkko Markula, "Governing Obese Bodies in a Control Society", *Junctures* 11 (2008), 53–65.
33. Édouard Glissant, *Poetics of Relation*, trans. Betsy Wing, (Ann Arbor: The University of Michigan Press, 1997), 180–194.

Bibliography

Bartky, Sandra L. 1988. Foucault, Femininity and the Modernization of Patriarchal Power. In *Feminism and Foucault: Reflections of Resistance*, ed. I. Diamond and L. Quinby, 61–85. Boston: Northeastern University Press.

Butler, Judith. 1990. *Gender Trouble*. New York: Routledge.

———. 1997. *The Psychic Life of Power*. Stanford: Stanford University Press.

———. 2010. *Frames of War: When Life is Grievable*. New York: Verso.

Deleuze, Gilles. 1992. Postscript on the Societies of Control. *October* 59: 3–7.

Fanon, Frantz. 2008. *Black Skin, White Masks*. Trans. Richard Philcox. New York: Grove Press.

Foucault, Michel. 1991. *Discipline and Punish: The Birth of the Prison*. Trans. Alan Sheridan. London: Vintage.

———. 1994. In *4 Essential Works of Foucault 1954–1984*, ed. J.D. Faubion, vol. 3. London: Penguin Books.
———. 2005. *The Hermeneutics of the Subject. Lectures at the Collège De France, 1981–1982*. Trans. Graham Burchell, ed. Frédéric Gros. New York: Palgrave Macmillan.
Glissant, Édouard. 1997. *Poetics of Relation*. Trans. Betsy Wing. Ann Arbor: The University of Michigan Press.
Hardt, Michael, and Antonio Negri. 2000. *Empire*. Harvard: Harvard University Press.
Husserl, Edmund. 1966. Analysen zur passive Synthesis. In *Edmund Husserl: Gesammelte Werke*, ed. Margot Fleischer, vol. XI. Dordrecht: Springer.
———. 2008. Die Lebenswelt. In *Edmund Husserl: Gesammelte Werke*, ed. Rochus Sowa, vol. XXXVIII. Dordrecht: Springer.
Laqueur, Thomas W. 1990. *The Making of Sex: Bodies and Gender from the Greeks to Freud*. Cambridge: Cambridge University Press.
Markula, Pirkko. 2008. Governing Obese Bodies in a Control Society. *Junctures* 11: 53–65.
Merleau-Ponty, Maurice. 2012. *Phenomenology of Perception*. Trans. Donald A. Landes. New York: Routledge.
Nietzsche, Friedrich. 1968. *The Will to Power*. New York: Vintage.
Oksala, Johanna. 2016. *Feminist Experience: Foucauldian and Phenomenological Investigations*. Evanston: Northwestern University Press.
Phipps, Alison. 2014. *The Politics of the Body: Gender in a Neoliberal and Neoconservative Age*. Malden: Polity.
Plessner, Helmuth. 1975. *Die Stufen des Organischen und der Mensch*. Berlin: De Gruyter.
Schiebinger, Londa, ed. 2000. *Feminism and the Body*. Oxford: Oxford University Press.
Steinbock, Anthony. 1995. *Home and Beyond: Generative Phenomenology After Husserl*. Evanston: Northwestern University Press.
Taipale, Joona. 2014. *Phenomenology and Embodiment: Husserl and the Constitution of Subjectivity*. Evanston: Northwestern University Press.
Virilio, Paul. 2005. *The Information Bomb*. London: Verso.
Wehrle, Maren. 2016. Normative Embodiment: The Role of the Body in Foucault's Genealogy. A Phenomenological Re-reading. *Journal of the British Society for Phenomenology* 47: 56–71.
Weiss, Gail. 2015. A Merleau-Pontian Legacy to Feminist Theory. *Continental Philosophy Review* 48: 77–93.
———. 2016. Uncosmetic Surgeries in an Age of Normativity. In *Feminist Phenomenology and Medicine*, ed. Kristin Zeiler and Lisa Folkmarson Käll, 101–118. Albany: SUNY University Press.

Welsh, Talia. 2013. Unfit Women: Freedom and Constraint in the Pursuit of Health. *Janus Head* 13 (2): 58–77.

———. 2014. Fat Eats: A Phenomenology of Decadence, Food, and Health. In *Food and Everyday Life*, ed. Thomas Conroy. New York: Lexington Books.

Young, Iris Marion. 1980. Throwing Like a Girl: A Phenomenology of Feminine Body Comportment Motility and Spatiality. *Human Studies* 3/2: 137–156.

CHAPTER 4

How Do We Respond? Embodied Vulnerability and Forms of Responsiveness

Danielle Petherbridge

The notion of vulnerability has become a central category through which feminist philosophers have sought to examine the complexity of embodied interdependence. By evoking a sense of shared vulnerability, contemporary philosophers ask us to imagine ourselves into the lives of others based on a notion of corporeal openness to wounding and suffering that we experience as embodied human beings. Judith Butler, for example, suggests that there is an ethical claim contained in the experience of vulnerability that enables us to recognize our shared corporeal interdependence, an experience that evokes an empathetic relation to the other.[1] She conceives of vulnerability as revealing a fundamental form of relationality and thinks of this condition "as an ongoing normative dimension of our social and political lives."[2] Butler therefore points to a shared susceptibility to and dependence on others and attempts to construct an ethics on the basis of a "primary human vulnerability."[3] However, as she also notes, our interdependence makes us vulnerable to the unpredictability of others and the risk that a form of ethical responsiveness in the face of suffering might be withheld.

D. Petherbridge (✉)
School of Philosophy, University College Dublin, Dublin, Ireland

© The Author(s) 2018
C. Fischer, L. Dolezal (eds.), *New Feminist Perspectives on Embodiment*, Breaking Feminist Waves,
https://doi.org/10.1007/978-3-319-72353-2_4

As intersubjective beings, vulnerability is an essential part of our being and to deny it would be to attempt to exist outside the social relations within which we develop as subjects.[4] Embodied vulnerability is therefore not something that we can or want to eradicate fully; in fact, it is a constitutive element that defines us as human beings. However, the openness evoked by vulnerability is complex and multidimensional, and is characterized by both positive and negative modalities: (1) it designates a form of corporeal openness that indicates the richness of embodied experience and encounters with others and the world, at the same time as it evokes a propensity for suffering; (2) it refers to a psychological openness that affirms the individual through her relations to others and avoids monadic forms of closure; (3) it is a form of interdependence that evokes care for the subject in her needfulness, but also means she is exposed to forms of power and abuses of vulnerability.[5] The notion of vulnerability therefore designates our constitutive and needful openness to others and the dynamic open-ended nature of the human condition which is experienced in forms of both social and unsocial sociability.

How, though, do we move from a sense of openness and interdependence to positing vulnerability as the basis of an ethics of responsiveness? And what are the potential difficulties in basing an ethics on the notion of shared vulnerability when it might equally evoke wounding or caring?

In this chapter, I draw on a range of literature to examine the complexity of embodied vulnerability and the kinds of responses vulnerability evokes. Specifically, I engage with J.M. Coetzee's texts *The Lives of Animals* and *Waiting for the Barbarians*, to explore the intricacies of embodied vulnerability and bring these texts into dialogue with philosophical approaches.[6] In the first section, I explore the double-sided nature of vulnerability elucidated in the work of Judith Butler and Adriana Cavarero: first, in Butler's terms, as an ontological category that provides the ground for an ethics of non-violence based on the propensity for violence that vulnerability might evoke; second, for Cavarero, as an experience that oscillates between wounding and caring, one that points not only to our commonality but is also essential to our uniqueness as singular corporeal beings.

In the second section, I explore the complexities of vulnerability with reference to Coetzee's texts, especially the relation of embodied vulnerability exhibited in *Waiting for the Barbarians*, and Elizabeth Costello's plea for acknowledgment of her own existential vulnerability in *The Lives of*

Animals. Here, by drawing particularly on the work of Cora Diamond and Stanley Cavell, I examine the question: How are we to respond to this vulnerability? In what ways does the suffering and vulnerability experienced by Elizabeth Costello call for an empathetic response based on our openness to wounding and suffering? Moreover, I explore how the embodied relationality between the central characters in *Waiting for the Barbarians* designates a relation of power at the same time as it might represent an attempt at care and mutual embodied openness. Here, I do not mean to equate vulnerability with woundedness or injurability per se, but to point out, as Butler herself does, that if vulnerability "can become the condition of suffering, it also serves the condition of responsiveness."[7]

In the final section, I explore Cavell's and Diamond's insights further by examining the relation between embodied knowledge, vulnerability and responsiveness with recourse to a phenomenological account, and consider the way in which responsiveness to vulnerability requires acknowledgment of both commonality and difference. I also consider the complex relation between the ontological, ethical and political dimensions of vulnerability, and the way in which they might inform one another.

Embodied Vulnerability: Between Wounding and Caring

In *Precarious Life*, Butler conceives of the notion of vulnerability through what she suggests is its intrinsic association with violence. In this sense, it is the exposure to violence that, for Butler, evokes an awareness of "a primary human vulnerability" and reveals our susceptibility and dependence upon the actions of anonymous others.[8]

Butler's reflections in *Precarious Life* are written in the context of what she terms conditions of "heightened vulnerability" following September 11, when, for her, the overwhelming issue was the way in which such "unbearable vulnerability" was responded to with military violence—that is, of "fighting violence with violence." Butler's concern in the wake of the terrorist attacks, then, was how experiences of vulnerability motivated "retributive acts of aggression and violence" rather than evoking an ethical response of non-violence, which might instead appeal to our common vulnerability.[9]

Butler's appeal to vulnerability seeks to contest the liberal conception of an autonomous, individualistic subject as the norm for ethics and politics, and to replace it with one based on vulnerability and interdependence, such that our integrity and agency are understood to be "radically dependent on others," upon whom we rely for the very "persistence of our social selves."[10] Moreover, Butler's conception of vulnerability is thought in relation to the concepts of grief, loss and mourning, and the importance of these states for politics.[11] In this context, she asks not only "what makes us human?" but also "what makes for a grievable life?" In this manner, Butler makes a weak universalistic claim, arguing in a manner somewhat similar to Richard Rorty, that it is possible to appeal to a sense of common humanity—to a "we"—by means of our potential for suffering.[12] "Loss," Butler suggests, "has made a tenuous 'we' of us all."[13] For Butler, this sense of grief, loss and vulnerability provides the basis upon which one lives beyond or outside of oneself; it is the means by which we are all "undone."[14] The important point for Butler is that there is an ethical possibility contained in the experience of vulnerability, a possibility which enables us to recognize our common humanity and our collective responsibility for the lives of one another. Her central claim is that an ethics of non-violence can be grounded in an ontology of vulnerability that assumes our corporeal interdependence. In *Precarious Life*, Butler more explicitly grounds this ethical account on an ontology of vulnerability, or what she terms an "understanding of the precariousness of the Other." Here, drawing on Levinas, she suggests that this is not a matter of extrapolating from one's own experience of vulnerability to that of another, but about explaining "how it is that others make moral claims upon us, address moral demands to us, ones that we do not ask for, ones that we are not free to refuse."[15]

Butler's concern is also to critique forms of violence that tend to be reactionary, and which attempt to deny or disavow our shared vulnerability. In this sense, Butler acknowledges the ethical importance of retaining an openness, in revealing ourselves to others and delineating "the ties we have to others," the "ties or bonds that compose us" and "constitute" us as "what we are."[16] She also points to an ambiguity associated with vulnerability in the sense that it evokes not only morality, injury and violence, but also love, desire, agency and interdependence. Thus, despite beginning from the point of an association with violence, Butler also alludes to the fundamental relationality that vulnerability exposes, one that is understood not simply in terms of "I" and "thou," but as "the tie by which these terms are differentiated and related."[17] On the one hand, then, Butler, thinks of this interdependence "as an ongoing normative dimension of our social and political lives…," but on the other, she "confesses" to "not knowing how to theorize this interdependency," and this leaves her claim of ethical responsiveness to vulnerability on uncertain normative ground.[18]

Notably, as mentioned above, in *Precarious Life*, Butler seems to give more credence to an ontological basis for ethics and to imply a more seamless connection between our shared human condition of vulnerability and our ethical obligations grounded in a theory of recognition. However, in *Frames of War*, Butler shifts from the more explicit ontological account evident in *Precarious Life* to a more variegated model. In her later work, Butler seems to withdraw from the stronger claim of basing an ethics on the ontological condition of vulnerability, and instead begins from an account based on "frames" of normalization that are understood to precede acknowledgment or recognition. In this amended schema, in Butler's terms, one has to be able to apprehend the other as "a life" before they can be recognized, but this apprehension is dependent upon frames of intelligibility that structure what is knowable at all.[19]

In fact, in her later work, Butler seems to suggest that there is a somewhat fraught relation between the ontological, ethical and political dimensions of vulnerability. In *Frames of War*, she attempts to address this constellation by making a distinction between "precariousness," as an ontological category or "a generalized condition of living beings," and "precarity," as a social and political category that can address the ways in which forms of precariousness are differentially distributed or allocated.[20] Butler understands "precarity" as a political condition that is shaped by social and economic relations and through which "certain populations ... become differentially exposed to injury, violence and death."[21] Moreover, she now argues that our capacity for responsiveness "depends upon the frames by which the world is given." As a consequence, she also rejects the Levinasian sensibility that a claim might be "made upon me prior to my knowing" and is separate from the "epistemological problem of apprehending a life."[22]

In contrast to Butler, Cavarero offers an Arendtian-inspired approach to vulnerability that points to the uniqueness of singular corporeal beings. In her own meditations on vulnerability, Cavarero reflects upon the new forms of horror inflicted by the weapons of terrorism (what she terms "horrorism"), which, not being content to merely inflict death or torture, aim "to destroy the uniqueness of the body, tearing at its constitutive vulnerability." Here, Cavarero points not only to the commonality that binds us in our shared vulnerability but also to the uniqueness that is "incarnated in the singularity of vulnerable bodies."[23] In this sense, Cavarero emphasizes not only a human propensity for wounding and caring that is inscribed in the helplessness and dependence of every human being at birth, but also our singularity as unique, corporeal beings exposed to others. It is this uniqueness that "characterizes the ontological status of humans [that] is also in fact a constitutive vulnerability, especially when understood in corporeal terms."[24] For Cavarero, the "unique being is vulnerable by definition": vulnerable to interdependence with others, vulnerable to recognition from others, and vulnerable to the erasure of uniqueness. In this sense, it is important to emphasize not only a commonality we all share by virtue of being corporeal beings, but also that our uniqueness is vulnerable to and dependent upon intersubjective relations. Cavarero's insights regarding uniqueness are important for suggesting that responses to the other's vulnerability may not simply be based on commonality but instead on difference, which also means that the kinds of responses it elicits might be context-dependent as well as politically and socially specific.

Moreover, following Arendt, Cavarero highlights the notion of natality—with its double connotation of newness or uniqueness and birth—the "first scene," as she puts it, "on which the vulnerable being presents itself."[25] It is in these first moments that our interdependence with others is constituted—the "centrality of the category of birth … proclaims relationship as a human condition not just fundamental but structurally necessary."[26] As a biologically deficient and unspecialized species which is dependent on others for survival, the category of birth then becomes the nodal point for the double-sided character of the human as both a unique, singular being who requires care and the member of a species, one who shares a constitutive experience of dependence upon and exposure to others. Thus, as Cavarero intimates, primary vulnerability implies social cooperation—it "summons the active involvement" of others, whether of the "mother" or primary caregiver, or more general social and communal patterns of care and cooperation.

As an infant, each unique individual is born into patterns of constitutive relationality and it is these forms of relationality that define the category of vulnerability. As Cavarero points out, however, there is a difference between "vulnerability" and "helplessness." Although, as infants at birth, we are simultaneously defenseless and vulnerable, she wants to suggest that helplessness signifies a more situational and political category, whereas vulnerability is an ontological one. As Cavarero elucidates: "[V]ulnerability is a permanent status of the human being … whereas … helplessness depends on particular social and political circumstances."[27] These are important distinctions and I shall return to this set of issues in Part 3 below. First, though, I move to a discussion of Coetzee's texts *The Lives of Animals* and *Waiting for the Barbarians* to illustrate the ways in which vulnerability is differentially conceived and to question what kinds of responses vulnerability elicits.

How Are We to Respond? Vulnerability and Acknowledgment

At the beginning of *The Lives of Animals*, the corporeal vulnerability of the fictional character Elizabeth Costello is described by her son John Bernard as he collects her from the airport: "He is waiting at the gate when her flight comes in. Two years have passed since he last saw his mother; despite himself, he is shocked at how she has aged. Her hair, which had had steaks of gray in it, is now entirely white; her shoulders stoop; her flesh has grown flabby."[28] As a well-known novelist, "this fleshy, white haired lady" has been invited to Appleton, an American college, to speak on a subject of her choosing.[29] She has elected to speak on the lives of animals, or more properly the violence and death inflicted upon animals in their sentient vulnerability. Her reputation was established earlier in her career for her "pathbreaking feminist fiction." However, rather than drawing on this illustrious heritage, Elizabeth Costello begins her lecture at Appleton College by comparing herself to the educated ape Red Peter depicted by Franz Kafka. As an aging female writer, she explains that she feels like "an educated ape ... who stands before the members of a learned society telling the story of [her] life." For Costello, this is not meant as an ironic statement; rather, it reflects her status as an embodied animal, as "an old woman" who does "not have the time any longer to say things [she] does not mean."[30]

In addressing the apparently learned audience of academics, Costello speaks of the "horrors" of the lives and deaths of animals and contrasts the "degradation, cruelty and killing" of animals for human use to the Holocaust.[31] It is the cruelty and slaughter of animals that makes her recoil with horror; in fact, she suggests that such industrialized mass slaughter of animals "rivals anything that the Third Reich" undertook in the sense that livestock are ceaselessly brought "into the world for the purpose of killing them."[32] It becomes clear, however, that the horror which Costello tries to convey to her audience in relation to the cruelty and murder of animals belies her own woundedness. In her clumsy association of the Holocaust with cruelty to animals, Costello seems to become unhinged; the horror she associates with such cruelty traumatizes her to such a degree that she can no longer express herself adequately; she cannot seem to make her audience, her daughter-in-law or even her son understand.

As Cora Diamond suggests, what becomes apparent is that Costello herself is in fact one of the wounded animals about whom she tries to speak, but this wound is so deep that there seems to be a disconnect between her reality and the reality of those about her; they seem to exist in alternative worlds. As Diamond elucidates, Elizabeth Costello points to something painful, to some reality to which others cannot relate.[33] To adopt Diamond's insights in this context—to an account of the wound as *vulnus*—we could say that those in the audience and those family members around her try to deflect the embodied vulnerability that Costello discloses. She is wounded by the knowledge of the vulnerability we share with animals and this wound is felt at an embodied level. As Diamond elucidates it, the character of Elizabeth Costello confronts the reader with the question of what a *"genuinely embodied knowledge"* might entail.[34] The text "ask[s] us to inhabit a body," "to inhabit in imagination the body of the woman confronting, or trying to confront what we do to animals," including ourselves.[35] It also raises the issue of accepting rather than disavowing or deflecting the difficulty of reality not only of our shared vulnerability, but also of the uniqueness of the other nakedly exposed in her particular vulnerable state.

In what is arguably the penultimate passage in the text, Elizabeth Costello's son drives his mother back to the airport for her return trip home. While driving, he apologizes for his wife Norma's condescension toward his mother's philosophical musings about animal vulnerability and human cruelty, pointing to Norma's inability for empathy or sympathy toward others. As he continues muffling his half-meant apology, his mother becomes visibly distressed. "I no longer know where I am," she exclaims. "Everyday I see the evidences ... Corpses ... Fragments of corpses." She becomes increasingly distraught and tearful. But her son is perplexed. "What does she want, he thinks?"[36] He is unable to recognize that his mother's concern with the "lives of animals" is a desperate plea for acknowledgment of her own animalistic vulnerability, something she feels she shares with the corpses piled up in Nazi internment camps, and the battery farms and funeraries of industrialized animal slaughter. Yet, rather than acknowledging his mother's own suffering and vulnerability, unable to empathize with her existential pain, all he notices is the smell of old age, "of cold cream, of old flesh." Rather than extending an ethical response in relation to her vulnerability, uniqueness and alterity, instead he comforts her with words of finitude, suggesting that "it will soon be over."[37] It is this lack of responsiveness to the other's vulnerability, this inability to imagine oneself into the pain and suffering of another that highlights the difficulty of positing vulnerability as an ethical category. As Diamond suggests, it may be that those around Costello continue to resist reality. His mother is demanding something of him, but John Bernard does not know what it is she demands; her concern with the vulnerability and suffering of animals—all animals—is dismissed as the ramblings of an old woman. Elizabeth Costello is an elderly woman who is "haunted by what we do to animals"; she is wounded by this knowledge and the wound strikes deeply and isolates her from others. As Diamond reveals, then, the title of Coetzee's text is not about the animals in battery farms, of which she speaks, but about the vulnerable and wounded being at the center of the novel.[38]

Exasperated at the inability of philosophers of all kinds to be able to distinguish between "knowing" and "acknowledging" the pain and suffering of others, including human as well as non-human animals, Costello asks us to imagine what it is like to be a corpse. "For instants at a time," Costello says that she knows "what it is like to be a corpse. The knowledge repels me," she says, "[i]t fills me with terror; I shy away from it, refuse to entertain it." What is more, she suggests, "All of us have such moments, particularly as we grow older. The knowledge is not abstract—'All human beings are mortal, I am a human being, therefore I am mortal'—but embodied. For a moment we *are* that knowledge."[39] These musings threaten to collapse Costello's entire "structure of knowledge"; she feels trapped between life and death in a contradiction that causes her to panic. Yet, at the same time, it compels her to exclaim: "If we are capable of thinking our own death" in this manner, "why on earth should we not be capable of thinking our way into the life of [an other]?"[40]

There is, however, a profound difference between "knowing" and "acknowledging" the other, or the suffering or pain of the other. As Cavell articulates it, to say that "I know you are in pain" is not a statement merely of fact or certainty but instead indicates the need for an ethical response. As Cavell explains, when we use the language of "knowledge" as "acknowledgment" in this recognitive sense, what we are expressing is a sense of sympathy. But why he asks should we consider this to be an expression of sympathy? "Because your suffering makes a *claim* upon me. It is not enough that I *know* (am certain) that you suffer—I must do or reveal something (whatever can be done). In a word, I must acknowledge it, otherwise I do not know 'what (your or his) pain' means. IS."[41] Thus, in Cavell's terms, the acknowledgment of the other's vulnerability indicates a summons from the other, a solicitation to act or respond in a particular manner, to "*do* something ... on the basis of that knowledge."[42] The "failure to acknowledge" the other's pain and vulnerability is, then, the expression of "an indifference, a callousness, an exhaustion, a coldness."[43] However, as Cavell reveals, the acknowledgment of another's suffering is not guaranteed. As we have seen exemplified in the interaction between Elizabeth Costello and her son: "The claim of suffering might go unanswered" or the acknowledgment of another's vulnerability (as like my own) "may be withheld."[44]

The differences between knowing and acknowledging are powerfully explored in an alternative register in Coetzee's *Waiting for the Barbarians*. The text depicts an allegorical scene of a frontier settlement which sits perpetually teetering on the edge—waiting—in a liminal space between invasion or war, between the triumph of the Empire and the imagined threat imposed by surrounding barbarian tribes. As the narrator makes clear, authorities from the capital have demanded "that whatever might be necessary to safeguard the Empire [will] be done, regardless of cost, we have returned to an age of raids and armed vigilance. There is nothing to do but keep our swords bright, watch and wait."[45]

The affairs of the settlement have been managed by the novel's narrator, the "Magistrate," who has largely existed in a state of indifference or denial about both his own existential condition and his own complicity with the totalizing logic and cruelty of the Empire. However, when the authorities of the Empire send men from the "Third Bureau" to assess the risk of barbarian invasion and impose the logic of preemptive reprisal and revenge, the Magistrate is suddenly confronted with an ethical challenge, one forced brutally upon his conscience when he witnesses the indiscriminate torture of barbarians, including elderly men, women and children.

In the haze of hot sun, he is compelled to acknowledge the vulnerability and helplessness of a tortured barbarian woman who sits begging in the square, unable to walk due to the nature of her wounds; she seems to view him with a vacant, glassy stare. He later learns that she has been blinded by the torturers of the Empire, her eyes burnt with hot pokers, her ankles broken so that she walks "slowly and awkwardly with two sticks."[46] Out of pity and a "bleating conscience," he takes her in; he offers her "work" so that she no longer has to beg on the streets to survive.[47]

As the narrative unfolds, the Magistrate and the barbarian woman become peculiarly bound in their mutual vulnerability. The Magistrate begins a physical relationship with the woman by washing her broken feet; he handles them gently, washing slowly, "manipulating the bones and tendons ... running [his] fingers between her toes."[48] This becomes a nightly ritual of embodied vulnerability and empathy; he washes her feet and legs in "soft milky soap" and swaddles her broken ankles with clean bandages. This ritual of care soon develops into one of washing and oiling the woman's entire body, which initiates a state of giddy rapture as she lies naked before him. However, he mostly falls asleep after washing and oiling her; he does not have "a desire to enter her stocky body," but instead a desire for the intimacy of caressing and nurturing her back to health. Yet, he also has an urge to decipher the marks of torture that have been inflicted upon her body; until he understands these marks, he says he "cannot let go of her"; he searches for the truth in the wounds that have maimed her.[49]

Yet, this embodied relationality is also clearly a relation of power.[50] As "[s]he lies naked, her oiled skin glowing a vegetal gold in the firelight," he whispers searchingly: "Come, tell me why you are here." "Because there is nowhere else to go," she replies.[51] The care and acknowledgment of the barbarian woman's pain and suffering, her physical woundedness, is one entangled with the condition of her enslavement. To recall Cavarero's insights, the barbarian woman is dependent on the Magistrate in a manner that inextricably combines both her vulnerability and her helplessness. This is not merely a relation built on the acknowledgment of their common vulnerability (as an aging and weary fellow, and a tortured and wounded woman), but a politically prescribed relation between a figure of authority of the Empire and an enslaved "Other."

Nonetheless, after feeling the shame and unease, however contingent, of the torture of innocent prisoners, the Magistrate takes the woman back to her community after a perilous journey across difficult terrain. As a consequence, he is accused of colluding with the barbarians and is summarily imprisoned and tortured himself. As he lies in his makeshift cell, he is haunted by images of the woman's tortured father, who the interrogators exposed to her in all his embodied nakedness and "made him gibber with pain."[52] The Magistrate knows he is being called upon to respond, but he is uncertain exactly what response is required. At the end of the novel, he is caught in an ambivalent state: he is complicit in the workings of the Empire, yet at the same time horrified by its acts of torture and cruelty.

In torture, the Magistrate is exposed to a vulnerability he shares with the barbarian woman, a shared wounding, the cruelty of torture, the corporeal maiming and the shadow of finitude. Yet, despite her generic signification as "barbarian woman," the slave represents a singular uniqueness, to use Cavarero's terms, a particular corporeal exposure to suffering and trauma; the Magistrate wants to decipher the particular marks and wounds on her body; he traces his fingers over her broken bones; he wants to understand what has been done to her. He tries to relate to her, to communicate with her, to coax her to name and speak of the atrocities of her torture and her wounds so that he might acknowledge them. However, he is also confused about the nature of the claim she makes on him. His caress of her body and care of her wounds mask a deeper lack of understanding; he fails to grasp the depth of her condition. Although he experiences an "ethical awakening," he fails to respond in a manner that would rupture his continuing complicity with the regime of the Empire. Instead, in the closing passages, he says: "I think: 'There has been something staring me in the face, and still I do not see it.'"[53]

Embodied Knowledge, Vulnerability and Responsiveness

As Veena Das observes, one of the most important features of Coetzee's work is that it creates a form of writing that gives up authoritative narration by the author, thereby inviting the reader to form a relationship with the text that is not dominated by a masterly voice. As a consequence, the reader is open to create her own relation to the text and to respond to it in a myriad number of ways, and this in turn bestows a certain responsibility upon the reader.[54] It is perhaps this open authorial style that also enabled five official commentators of Coetzee's *The Lives of Animals* (delivered as the Tanner Lectures) to misinterpret the fictional lectures delivered by the main character Elizabeth Costello, as extolling poor philosophical arguments in defense of animal rights. The renowned moral philosopher Peter Singer is particularly perplexed by Coetzee's text: he takes Coetzee to be hiding behind a literary device to put forward his own contentious views about human cruelty to animals. As a consequence, Singer is not sure if he is meant to respond to the fictional character, Elizabeth Costello, or the author J.M. Coetzee. Singer is so thrown by Coetzee's text that he fumbles around in the dark, searching not only for an appropriate medium with which to respond, but also exasperatedly exclaiming: "All I want to know is: how am I supposed to reply to this?"[55]

Although Singer's frustrated query about how to respond on the surface appears to be aimed at his relationship to Coetzee's text, Nikolas Kompridis suggests that the reader's response to the fictional character of Elizabeth Costello should also be understood as a "normative challenge"; in other words, presented in all her naked vulnerability, Costello is calling for an ethical response. In fact, Kompridis argues that "the central theme and organizing principle of *The Lives of Animals* [is] the question of how we should respond ... [or] how we should answer and be answerable to others."[56] In this sense, it could be argued that Coetzee's text(s) raises the more general "question of human responsiveness," of what sort of responsiveness is being asked of us in the face of vulnerability. Thus, not only do fictionalized characters such as John Bernard or the Magistrate demonstrate the fraught nature of responsiveness to vulnerability, but also just as profoundly, such "failures of receptivity" extend to the failed responses of Coetzee's text by his philosophical respondents.

What does the response to a fictionalized narrative suggest about ethical responsiveness to vulnerability? It might be argued that such imaginative experiences challenge us to respond to the vulnerability of others more generally. As Kompridis suggests, the ethical challenge of Coetzee's text is about becoming receptive to the pain and suffering of others, about being receptive to pleas for acknowledgment, and to opening ourselves to challenges that might call for a new kind of response to the other.[57]

Let us return to Diamond and Cavell to explicate this notion of acknowledgment and ethical responsiveness further. As discussed above, Cavell's distinction between "knowing" and "acknowledging" provides a way in which we might understand the different forms of response we are required to make in the face of the other's vulnerability. It should be noted that Cavell's notion of acknowledgment arises in the context of a critique of skepticism and the attempt to solve the philosophical riddle of how we can know others exist. Instead of seeking a solution to this perennial philosophical problem based on some ultimate foundation or certainty, Cavell's claim is that we must simply accept the existence of others, and that such a primary level of acceptance is required before being able to "know" them.

In a manner akin to Costello's concern about the predominance of abstract thought, Cavell mounts a similar critique by pointing to the limits of knowledge and the need for a "willingness to forgo knowing."[58] Acknowledgment refers not to "knowing" the other as assumed under general rules of reason or discourse, or knowing the other by analogy, but acknowledging the other in their difference—the simple acknowledgment of the other in their otherness. As William Franke suggests, the will to know that underpins the skeptical exercise is an attempt to suppress "unknowable otherness."[59] In contrast, acknowledgment for Cavell is not one-sided; it is not a mastery of recognizing the other, but also requires the acknowledger to reveal or expose himself or herself. In his discussion of literary tragedy and our responsiveness to the characters of tragedy, Cavell writes: "What is revealed is my separateness from what is happening to them; that I am I, and here. It is only in the perception of them as separate from me that I make them present. That I make them *other*, and face them."[60] As Franke suggests, then, we cannot simply presume an "essential sameness" and "common human condition," but at the same time, need to acknowledge a fundamental separateness and dislocation in regard to the "protagonists' specific tragic fate."[61] In Cavarero's terms, this means accounting not only for the ties that bind us in a common human condition, but also for the singular uniqueness of each individual's embodied experience of and exposure to vulnerability.

As Diamond suggests, in the nakedness of her embodied vulnerability, Costello is someone who is acutely aware of the limits of language, abstract thought and philosophical argumentation. She considers that our reliance on such forms of argumentation is a way in which we make ourselves unavailable to ourselves and our own sense of what it is to be a living embodied animal. For her, abstract forms of knowledge are merely a way of distancing ourselves from our own bodily life and our capacity to respond to the bodily lives of others.[62]

Here, it is instructive to return to Diamond's insights about "embodied knowledge" and the forms of responsivity that such knowledge might entail and explore them in an alternative register. Bernhard Waldenfels has articulated a notion of responsivity that he suggests has a "strong relation to corporeality and sensibility." Drawing on Merleau-Ponty's work, he describes this receptivity to the other as "the susceptibility (*Anfälligkeit*) of a bodily being who responds to something other before this other gets a particular sense."[63] In other words, in order to respond to something, it first "has to stimulate and to affect us before it can be conceived, comprehended and interpreted as something."[64] In *Phenomenology of Perception*, Merleau-Ponty describes this kind of responsivity as requiring solicitation from something outside the subject.[65] This suggests that embodied responsivity requires an external excitation, but also that we are open to such stimulation or invitation arising from others and the world. In Waldenfels terms, responding to the other can be understood in a limited sense as taken to mean "filling in particular gaps of knowledge," but in broader terms, it also means something like "consenting to the offers" and "demands" of the other, or acknowledging their claim upon me.[66]

In the face of the other's suffering and vulnerability, we might adapt Waldenfels' view in suggesting that the claims the other makes upon me "are entwined with my own being" and are experienced at an embodied level. Following Merleau-Ponty, Waldenfels suggests that in fact the body does not merely participate in forms of responsivity toward others but is at the heart of such forms of action.[67] For Merleau-Ponty, the body constitutes our *precognitive* familiarity with ourselves and the world we inhabit: "I am aware of my body via the world," writes Merleau-Ponty, just as "I am aware of the world through the medium of my body."[68] Our intercorporeality creates a constitutive openness and vulnerability to others and means that subjects are affected by one another even on an elementary level but also potentially remain open to (social) change. For Merleau-Ponty, this always involves an embodied openness to others and the world—an openness to solicitation and dialogue. Such forms of embodied responsiveness, then, indicate that in our interactions with others, we open ourselves receptively to them rather than constituting the other in sameness, attempting to know the other at the level of abstract thought or apprehending their suffering only through the horizon of own experience.

For Waldenfels, we cannot understand subjectivity, or intersubjectivity for that matter, outside of the structures of corporeal or intercorporeal existence.[69] In his words, "the traces of the other are inscribed into corporeality itself."[70] However, this notion of corporeality or intercorporeality does not erase all difference between vulnerable bodies. The bodily nature of perception in fact grants a unique status to one's own body, as well as to the body of the other, in the sense that it points to the particularity of perceptual access and perceptual agency; the body is the nodal point that makes perception of all other objects possible. In this sense, too, it indicates that destruction of or violence against the body represents a violation of the uniqueness of others.

The phenomenological explication of embodied knowledge and responsiveness, then, provides further insights in regard to the relation between embodied knowledge and acknowledgment as articulated by Diamond and Cavell. For, on the one hand, Waldenfels' interpretation suggests that as vulnerable subjects who share an embodied condition, we are always already open to and capable of such an ethical claim being made upon us; yet, on the other hand, for such a claim to be adequately met, it must also be taken up or acknowledged by the other. The claim for ethical responsivity in the condition of vulnerability therefore requires an interplay between these different dimensions, yet it is also this complexity that builds contingency and uncertainty into the kinds of responsiveness that might follow from an openness to vulnerability.[71]

For, as we have seen above, the question of how one might respond when challenged by the vulnerability of the other is often a fraught and contingent exercise, one dependent not only on a constitutive openness to the other or a form of acknowledgment, but also on particular social and historical contexts and circumstances. As the discussion of Coetzee's texts reveals, though, just as significant as the parsing of the ontological and the ethical is the examination of vulnerability as a political category.

In this sense, *The Lives of Animals* explores an ontological or existential notion of vulnerability, one that gestures toward a universalistic ethical claim based on a shared notion of corporeal independence and openness to others, but it also depicts a disjuncture between the ontological and ethical levels. When Costello breaks down, distraught at the woundedness she shares with other animals, her son deflects this reality and pushes the notion of their shared vulnerability away, as well as his mother's own tragic relation to it.

Waiting for the Barbarians represents an equally complex picture. Although there is an underlying ontological claim about shared vulnerability in the text, the general relation between the "Empire" and the "Barbarians," as well as the particular relationship between the Magistrate and the slave woman, also demonstrates the ways in which vulnerability is clearly a political category. Moreover, the forms of vulnerability in *Waiting for the Barbarians* indicate a tension between the ontological claim and the political notion of vulnerability in specific contexts.

The text therefore gestures toward the problematic ways in which vulnerability has been mobilized as a political category used to justify forms of paternalism, risk management, militarization, or securitization and surveillance of specific groups or populations. This is clearly demonstrated in *Waiting for the Barbarians*, where the very form of life itself is structured not as an ethical relation between the Empire and the Barbarians, but as a form of existential anticipation where the Empire is always on the edge of invasion by the unknown "Other." Moreover, as we have seen, the specific relation between the Magistrate and the Barbarian woman is one based on mutual acknowledgment in the manner portrayed by Cavell, or at least a shared human condition of woundedness, care and embodied vulnerability which is laid bare each night. However, it is also predominantly a political relation, one in which the care evoked by the Magistrate toward the Barbarian woman is overlaid by power and enslavement.

In this respect, Coetzee's text reveals the importance of being alert to the ways in which certain social and political responses might impede an openness to the other's vulnerability and the capacity for acknowledgment of this shared human condition. It seems apparent that these two categories of vulnerability—the ontological and the political—imply one another and are interconnected in the sense that particular forms of evaluation overlay or filter through to inform the interpretation of ontological categories. As the discussion of Coetzee's texts reveals, sometimes the social and political form is in keeping with the ontological and universalistic claim of ethical responsiveness in the face of vulnerability, but in other circumstances, they sit in tension or such ethical claims are disavowed.

As a response to this constellation of issues, it is clear that a two-level account of vulnerability is required, while recognizing that we cannot move seamlessly from one level to the other. The first level is one based on our constitutive openness to and interdependence with others, that is, on a notion of common vulnerability that we all share as human beings that evokes embodied and affective forms of acknowledgment. This forms the ground for a universalistic claim and may constitute the background for an ethical account, but since such an account of vulnerability cannot guarantee an ethical response, it forms a background ontological or anthropological orientation that needs to be supplemented by a second dimension. The second level is a political account of vulnerability that can account for the ways in which vulnerability most often becomes politicized, for example, in responding to it through forms of paternalism, resilience, securitization and militarization, but also in terms of the uneven social and political distribution of excessive forms of vulnerability. Such unevenness of distribution and the sorts of responses outlined above are not anthropological or ontological responses to vulnerability but undeniably *political* responses that are contextually and social-historically dependent. As such, these forms of approach also require a political response such that excesses and the uneven distribution of vulnerability can be debated, contested and addressed in the public, political sphere.

However, in contrast to Butler, acknowledging that we cannot assume a seamless link between the ontological, the ethical and the political aspects of vulnerability does not mean restricting the apprehension of the other to the structuralizing forces of epistemological frames of normalization. The problem with Butler's position is that it remains unclear exactly what provides the basis for a normative account, and her latest move to a notion of "normalizing frames of intelligibility" seems to sit in tension with her claims about precariousness as a fundamental human condition, one that she suggests signals strong normative or ethical commitments. This is evident when Butler speaks of the "recognition of shared precariousness" as denoting "strong normative commitments of equality" and a "more robust universalizing of rights."[72] If our ability to perceive precariousness is structured by normative frames of intelligibility that "establish the domains of the knowable," the question becomes the following: upon what grounds can we base our judgment and reflexivity of such precarious conditions? In other words, how do we know the difference between modes of intelligibility that normalize differential distribution and normative or ethical forms of precariousness? Or put in another manner, how do we perceive suffering as suffering if what we can know or perceive is always already framed by regimes of normalization?[73] Therefore, although Butler gestures toward an ethical view of vulnerability, the lack of clarity between the terms *normativity* and *normalization* forecloses the potential of her account. As Estelle Ferrarese suggests, a politics of vulnerability points to normative expectations that do not merely assume an instituted and normalizing form, but also have instituting force that is informed by *normative* expectations.[74] Significantly, this also means that the issue of vulnerability becomes one that is opened to forms of contestation within the public sphere, where different interpretations can be voiced and debated, or struggles over the best responses to abuses of vulnerability can be waged.[75]

Although an ontological account of vulnerability cannot guarantee an ethical response, it nonetheless provides an important universalistic orientation upon which a second more normative and political account is built, and it is through a political account that normative responses are not only created, but also constantly reiterated and maintained. This means that ethical responsiveness to vulnerability is not something that we can take for granted but something that we have to work hard to establish, renew and maintain. As the Magistrate reflects in *Waiting for the Barbarians*, we have to keep our ears "tuned to the pitch of human pain." However, the knowledge of such pain is so easily contingent, and despite staring us in the face, it is easy to turn our eyes away or to close up our ears unless we remain open not only to the vulnerability of others, but also to the kinds of responses that we are called upon to make.[76]

Notes

1. This chapter builds on an earlier article entitled "What's Critical about Vulnerability? Rethinking Interdependence, Recognition and Power", *Hypatia* 31, no. 3 (Summer 2016): 589–604. Small sections of this discussion previously appeared in that paper, but here I develop an alternative analysis.
2. Judith Butler, *Precarious Life: The Powers of Mourning and Violence* (London & New York: Verso, 2004), 27; xiii.
3. Judith Butler, *Precarious Life*. Also see Butler's amended accounts in Judith Butler, *Frames of War: When Is Life Grievable?* (London and New York: Verso, 2010); Judith Butler, Zeynep Gambetti and Leticia Sabsay, *Vulnerability in Resistance* (Durham and London: Duke University Press, 2016).
4. See also Joel Anderson, "Autonomy and Vulnerability Entwined." In *Vulnerability: New Essays in Ethics and Feminist Philosophy*. eds. C. Mackenzie, W. Rogers & S. Dodds (Oxford: Oxford University Press, 2014), 143.
5. See Petherbridge, "What's Critical about Vulnerability?", 589–604; Marie Garrau. On Corine Pelluchon's, *Éléments pour une éthique de la vulnérabilité: Les hommes, les animaux, la nature*, booksandideas.net (originally in laviedesidees.fr). trans. J. Zvesper, 22 June 2012.
6. See J.M. Coetzee, *The Lives of Animals*. Edited and introduced by Amy Gutmann with responses by Marjorie Garber, Peter Singer, Wendy Doniger, Barbara Smuts (Princeton, NJ: Princeton University Press, 1999). J.M. Coetzee, *Waiting for the Barbarians* (London: Vintage Books, 2004 (1980)). Also see: Veena Das, "The Boundaries of the 'We': Cruelty, Responsibility and Forms of Life", *Critical Horizons* 17, no. 2 (2016): 168–185. Das draws on Coetzee's novel *Waiting for the Barbarians* to explore the notion of violence as a form of life. Although I take interest in this engagement, my own use of Coetzee's text is oriented around an alternative interpretation.
7. Butler, *Frames of War*, 61.
8. Butler, *Precarious Life*, 2004; Erinn Gilson, "Vulnerability, Ignorance and Oppression." *Hypatia* 26, no. 2 (Spring 2011): 332; 308.
9. Butler, *Precarious Life*, xi.
10. Butler, *Precarious Life*, 69.
11. Ann Murphy, *Violence and the Philosophical Imaginary* (New York: SUNY Press, 2012), 72.
12. Richard Rorty, *Contingency, Irony, and Solidarity* (Cambridge: Cambridge University Press, 1989).
13. Butler, *Precarious Life*, 20.

14. Butler, *Precarious Life*, 23–27.
15. Butler, *Precarious Life*, 134; 131.
16. Butler, *Precarious Life*, 22.
17. Butler, *Precarious Life*, 22.
18. Butler, *Precarious Life*, 27; xiii.
19. See: Butler, *Frames of War*, 6.
20. I would also note that there are important differences between the terms "vulnerability" and "precariousness." Whereas vulnerability designates a general openness and relationality to others, precariousness seems to evoke a permanent state of contingency and is bound to a notion of finitude and mortality. As Catherine Mills notes, there is also a constant slippage between these terms in Butler's work and the difference is not fully worked through. See Catherine Mills, "Normative Violence, Vulnerability, and Responsibility." *Differences* 18, no. 2, (2007): 133–56.
21. Butler, *Frames of War*, 25.
22. Butler, *Frames of War*, 180; 3.
23. Adriana Cavarero, *Horrorism: Naming Contemporary Violence*. Trans. W. McCuaig (New York: Columbia University Press, 2009), 8.
24. Cavarero, *Horrorism*, 20.
25. Cavarero, *Horrorism*, 20–21.
26. Cavarero, *Horrorism*, 30.
27. Cavarero, *Horrorism*, 31. Cavarero's distinction between the ontological and the political dimensions (vulnerability and helplessness, respectively) are well-taken, although in *Horrorism*, she does not provide a full account of the way in which these dimensions might be interrelated, or the detail of how they might inform an ethical theory of responsiveness. Her account of the corporeal uniqueness of singular beings is, however, central to the development of the kind of approach being gestured at here.
28. Coetzee, *The Lives of Animals*, 15.
29. Coetzee, *The Lives of Animals*, 16.
30. Coetzee, *The Lives of Animals*, 18.
31. Coetzee, *The Lives of Animals*, 21.
32. Coetzee, *The Lives of Animals*, 21.
33. Cora Diamond, "The Difficulty of Reality and the Difficulty of Philosophy", *Partial Answers: Journal of Literature and the History of Ideas* 1, no. 2 (June 2003), 1–26.
34. Cora Diamond, "The Difficulty of Reality", 12–13 (my italics).
35. Cora Diamond, "The Difficulty of Reality", 12–13.
36. Coetzee, *The Lives of Animals*, 69.
37. Coetzee, *The Lives of Animals*, 69.
38. Cora Diamond, "The Difficulty of Reality."
39. Coetzee, *The Lives of Animals*, 32.

40. Coetzee, *The Lives of Animals*, 32–3.
41. Stanley Cavell, *Must We Mean What We Say?* (Cambridge & London: Cambridge University Press, 1976), 263; Nikolas Kompridis, "Recognition and Receptivity: Forms of Narrative Response in the Lives of the Animals We Are", *New Literary History* 44, no. 1 (Winter 2013): 1–24; 13.
42. Cavell, *Must We Mean What We Say?*, 257.
43. Cavell, *Must We Mean What We Say?*, 264.
44. Cavell, *Must We Mean What We Say?*, 266.
45. J.M. Coetzee, *Waiting for the Barbarians* (London: Vintage Books, 2004 (1980)), 41.
46. Coetzee, *Waiting for the Barbarians*, 27.
47. Coetzee, *Waiting for the Barbarians*, 29.
48. Coetzee, *Waiting for the Barbarians*, 30.
49. Coetzee, *Waiting for the Barbarians*, 32–3.
50. See my article "What's Critical about Vulnerability?" for arguments against the fusion of power and violence in the context of vulnerability.
51. Coetzee, *Waiting for the Barbarians*, 43.
52. Coetzee, *Waiting for the Barbarians*, 88.
53. Coetzee, *Waiting for the Barbarians*, 170.
54. Veena Das, "The Boundaries of the 'We'", 168–9.
55. Peter Singer in J.M. Coetzee, *The Lives of Animals*, 86.
56. Kompridis, "Recognition and Receptivity", 5; 16.
57. Kompridis, "Recognition and Receptivity", 20–21.
58. Stanley Cavell, *Disowning Knowledge in Seven Plays of Shakespeare* (Cambridge: Cambridge University Press, 2003), 95; see also William Franke, "Acknowledging Unknowing: Stanley Cavell and the Philosophical Criticism of Literature." *Philosophy and Literature* 39, no. 1 (April 2015): 248–258.
59. Franke, "Acknowledging Unknowing", 252.
60. Cavell, *Disowning Knowledge*, 109; see Franke, "Acknowledging Unknowing", 256.
61. Franke, "Acknowledging Unknowing", 257.
62. Diamond "The Difficulty of Reality", 7–9.
63. Bernhard Waldenfels, "Responsivity of the Body: Traces of the Other in Merleau-Ponty's Theory of Body and Flesh" in *Interrogating Ethics: Embodying the Good in Merleau-Ponty*, eds. James Hatley, Janice McLane and Christian Diehm (Pittsburgh: Duquesne University Press, 2006), 91–106; 95.
64. Waldenfels, "Responsivity of the Body", 96.
65. See, for example, Maurice Merleau-Ponty, *Phenomenology of Perception*, trans. Colin Smith (London and New York: Routledge, 2002) 422–423; see Waldenfels, "Responsivity of the Body", 96.

66. Waldenfels, "Responsivity of the Body", 99.
67. Waldenfels, "Responsivity of the Body", 102.
68. Merleau-Ponty, *Phenomenology of Perception*, 94–5.
69. See Diane Perpich, "Moral Blind Spots and Ethical Appeals: A Response to Bernhard Waldenfels", in *Interrogating Ethics: Embodying the Good in Merleau-Ponty*, eds. James Hatley, Janice McLane and Christian Diehm (Pittsburgh: Duquesne University Press, 2006), 107–131; 111.
70. Waldenfels, "Responsivity of the Body", 106.
71. See Perpich, "Moral Blind Spots and Ethical Appeals", 121. Whereas Perpich offers this as a critique of Waldenfels for oscillating between two contradictory positions: either we are always open to the other's ethical claim or it requires recognition to have valiancy, I suggest this is a productive way to think about the ontological openness to others that vulnerability entails. However, this also explains why our openness to others is not always enough to ensure an ethical response, in the sense that it also requires an active ethical response on the part of the subject. Such ethical responsiveness is most convincingly understood in terms of Cavell's notion of acknowledgment or Axel Honneth's notion of recognition.
72. Butler, *Frames of War*, 28–9.
73. Although in *Frames of War*, Butler explains that in order to persist, normative regimes must be "reiterated," my suggestion is that this does not fully answer the question of the basis upon which we can judge what constitutes better or worse forms of life, or better and worse forms of vulnerability.
74. Estelle Ferrarese, *Vulnerability* (Boston: Brill, 2018) forthcoming.
75. I do not have the scope to develop the detail of this alternative account within the confines of this chapter. In other work, I suggest that a modified theory of recognition as developed by Axel Honneth is the most productive way to address some of these issues. See my discussion in "When Is One Recognizable?" forthcoming.
76. Coetzee, *Waiting for the Barbarians*, 5; 22; 170.

Bibliography

Anderson, Joel. 2014. Autonomy and Vulnerability Entwined. In *Vulnerability: New Essays in Ethics and Feminist Philosophy*, ed. C. Mackenzie, W. Rogers, and S. Dodds. Oxford: Oxford University Press.

Butler, Judith. 2004. *Precarious Life: The Powers of Mourning and Violence*. London/New York: Verso.

———. 2010. *Frames of War: When Is Life Grievable?* London/New York: Verso.

Butler, Judith, Zeynep Gambetti, and Leticia Sabsay. 2016. *Vulnerability in Resistance*. Durham/London: Duke University Press.

Cavarero, Adriana. 2009. *Horrorism: Naming Contemporary Violence.* Trans. W. McCuaig. New York: Columbia University Press.

Cavell, Stanley. 1976. *Must We Mean What We Say?* Cambridge/London: Cambridge University Press.

Coetzee, J.M. 1999. *The Lives of Animals.* Edited and Introduced by Amy Gutmann with responses by Marjorie Garber, Peter Singer, Wendy Doniger, Barbara Smuts. Princeton: Princeton University Press.

———. 2004. *Waiting for the Barbarians.* London: Vintage Books. (1980).

Das, Venna. 2016. The Boundaries of the 'We': Cruelty, Responsibility and Forms of Life. *Critical Horizons* 17 (2): 168–185.

Diamond, Cora. 2003. The Difficulty of Reality and the Difficulty of Philosophy. *Partial Answers: Journal of Literature and the History of Ideas* 1 (2): 1–26.

Ferrarese, Estelle. 2018. *Vulnerability.* Boston: Brill.

Franke, William. 2015. Acknowledging Unknowing: Stanley Cavell and the Philosophical Criticism of Literature. *Philosophy and Literature* 39 (1): 248–258.

Garrau, Marie. 2012. On Corine Pelluchon's. *Éléments pour une éthique de la vulnérabilité: Les hommes, les animaux, la nature*, booksandideas.net. (originally in laviedesidees.fr). Trans. J. Zvesper, 22 June 2012.

Gilson, Erinn. 2011. Vulnerability, Ignorance and Oppression. *Hypatia* 26 (2): 308–332.

Kompridis, Nikolas. 2013. Recognition and Receptivity: Forms of Narrative Response in the Lives of the Animals We Are. *New Literary History* 44 (1): 1–24.

Mills, Catherine. 2007. Normative Violence, Vulnerability, and Responsibility. *Differences* 18 (2): 133–156.

Murphy, Ann. 2012. *Violence and the Philosophical Imaginary.* New York: SUNY Press.

Perpich, Diane. 2006. Moral Blind Spots and Ethical Appeals: A Response to Bernhard Waldenfels. In *Interrogating Ethics: Embodying the Good in Merleau-Ponty*, ed. James Hatley, Janice McLane, and Christian Diehm. Pittsburgh: Duquesne University Press.

Petherbridge, Danielle. 2016. What's Critical About Vulnerability? Rethinking Interdependence, Recognition and Power. *Hypatia* 31 (3): 589–604.

Rorty, Richard. 1989. *Contingency, Irony, and Solidarity.* Cambridge: Cambridge University Press.

Waldenfels, Bernhard. 2006. Responsivity of the Body: Traces of the Other in Merleau-Ponty's Theory of Body and Flesh. In *Interrogating Ethics: Embodying the Good in Merleau-Ponty*, ed. James Hatley, Janice McLane, and Christian Diehm. Pittsburgh: Duquesne University Press.

PART II

New Directions in Feminist Theory

CHAPTER 5

Revisiting Feminist Matters in the Post-Linguistic Turn: John Dewey, New Materialisms, and Contemporary Feminist Thought

Clara Fischer

Feminist theorising on the body and on emotion has recently undergone a revival of sorts, as a cohort of "new" materialists and affect theorists have advocated a move away from philosophical preoccupations with culture, cognition, and language, towards a focus on corporeality, ontological immanence, and affect. Much of this work proposes the need for contemporary theory to disavow the "linguistic turn" and to return to the material world of bodies and embodied affects. What this approach assumes, more or less explicitly, is a loss of feminist concern with such topics at some stage in the past, and an imperative to recover same in order to avoid feminist thought being compromised or unproductive in the present. Some critiques have been mounted against the new affect and materialist theorists, notably with regard to their emphasis on "newness" and "recovery" in light of feminist work clearly highlighting a continuous engagement with materiality and affect.[1] Moreover, I have also argued that the new school

C. Fischer (✉)
University College Dublin, Dublin, Ireland

© The Author(s) 2018
C. Fischer, L. Dolezal (eds.), *New Feminist Perspectives on Embodiment*, Breaking Feminist Waves,
https://doi.org/10.1007/978-3-319-72353-2_5

does not always, as professed by it, provide anti-dualistic and holistic ways of thinking about the body, mind, culture, language, and emotion.[2]

Indeed, much work by the new affect and materialist theorists treats these categories—mind and body—atomistically, as it requires distinctions between cognition and affective experiences, between thought and feeling, between minds and bodies, and, ultimately, between culture and nature, in order to revalue such oppositionals in its claims to a distinctly "new" theoretical approach. For the new school distinguishes itself from the old by reinstating nature, the body, and affect as important, although neglected, theoretical concerns, and by moving beyond perceived reductions and confines of poststructuralist thought. In its quest to do so, though, much of the new school's revaluation of nature, bodies, and affects (on the one hand), and culture, mind, cognition, and language (on the other), simply elevates one group of supposed oppositionals in favour of the other.[3] Thus, an ontology of materiality and affect—presumed to be instant, primal, spontaneous—supplants concerns with what are now taken to be constrictions posed by culture, language, cognition, and the mind.

Given the shortcomings of this approach—its maintenance of dualisms, notably the mind/body dualism, and its strict atomism—I will, in this chapter, proffer the anti-dualistic thought of the pragmatist philosopher John Dewey. Pragmatism has, in fact, been re-appropriated by one of the main proponents of the "turn to affect," Brian Massumi, but his use of William James serves the project of said elevation of materiality and affect over and above thought, language, and culture.[4] James's work on emotion, which can easily be read as a reduction of emotion to bodily states and as an elision of cognition altogether,[5] seems to chime nicely with Massumi's work, which seeks to limit the importance and relevance of cognition and culture in favour of the neo-vitalist immanent, spontaneous, bodily, affect.[6]

By utilising Dewey's thought to examine what place pragmatism might assume in debates on contemporary, post-linguistic turn feminism, I draw on pragmatism's strengths: its anti-dualism, naturalist ontology, and fallibilist epistemology. Moreover, Dewey's exposition of organic beings that are constantly created by and in turn create their environments avoids inverting dualistic oppositionals or collapsing these into each other. My presentation of pragmatism will rely heavily on Dewey's conception of habituated, transacting beings. For many new materialists, contemporary theorising adversely presents bodies as abstractions and removes the "fleshiness" of corporeal existence from the feminist, critical lens.[7] Pragmatists, though, especially those drawing on Dewey, have long recognised the concrete, bodily existence of beings, who are thoroughly enmeshed and continuously co-constituted in their worlds through habits.

As I have previously noted, pragmatism underwent its own revival at just about the time the affective and new materialist turns were announced by critical theorists in a variety of disciplines.[8] Unfortunately though, beyond Massumi, there does not appear to have been any substantial engagement by affect and new materialist thinkers with (neo)pragmatist thought,[9] and, as will be seen, the "new" school actually echoes concepts and ideas that are central to pragmatism. To illustrate this, I will explicate Dewey's work on habit and nature alongside theories by two new materialist thinkers, Stacy Alaimo and Karen Barad. Alaimo and Barad develop the concepts of "trans-corporeality" and "intra-action," respectively, which pragmatist readers will quickly recognise as reminiscent of Dewey's "transaction." The purpose of delineating these ideas in conjunction with each other is not to claim some kind of territorial, prior stake to common ground, but to highlight the fact that feminists have recourse to a philosophical tradition spanning the better part of 200 years that is similarly equipped with the resources and tools needed for dealing with shortcomings identified by the affect and new materialist critiques. For the criticisms raised by the new school in terms of feminist theoretical emphasis are, on my reading, often legitimate.

Feminists rightly critique certain contemporary critical work for being too narrowly focused on language and abstraction instead of on concrete materiality. Indeed, this has been a common critique of Judith Butler's work, in particular, including by prominent feminist-pragmatists.[10] However, some new materialist and affect theorists' stronger claim to feminist theory's wholesale forgetting of the body, nature, and affect or emotion cannot be sustained, especially since it ignores the feminist and pragmatist work that has been ongoing, even right through the pronouncement of the material and affective turns on embodiment and emotion.[11] My gripe with the "new" school then is this: much like Hemmings and Ahmed, I think its presentation as an entirely novel paradigm risks erasure,[12] including of existing feminist and pragmatist work; its lack of engagement with pragmatism neglects a philosophical tradition that holds the answers to many of the shortcomings it legitimately identifies in (some!) contemporary, critical theorising[13]; and its revaluing of nature, materiality, and affect or emotion often results in an atomism and a reversal of the very dualisms it claims to undermine, as bodily immanence and affect take priority over cognition and culture.[14]

Given these concerns, my task for this chapter is threefold: I will redress the elision of pragmatism in the conversation around affect theory, new materialisms, and contemporary feminist theorising; I will trace some of the confluences between Dewey's work on nature and materiality, and the new materialist work of Alaimo and Barad; and finally, I will show that pragmatism can form a useful resource for those interested in redressing new materialist concerns about concrete embodiment and materiality in post-linguistic turn feminist theory.

Pragmatist Silences and Echoes in the Post-Linguistic Turn New School of Feminism

Affect theorists and new materialists have heralded a period of renewed engagement with materiality and embodied emotion that is often presented in contrast to contemporary theory, specifically, poststructuralism and social constructivism. This "return" to nature, to bodily spontaneity and vitalism, is supposed to revert feminists and political theorists to concerns that they have, latterly, neglected owing to their preoccupation with language and culture.[15] According to Alaimo and Hekman, feminist theory stands "at an impasse" owing to its retreat to "culture, discourse, and language."[16] In their exposition of Silvan Tomkins' work, Sedgwick and Frank attribute this to contemporary theory's "hypervigilant antiessentialism and antinaturalism."[17] Both new materialisms and affect theory thus critique the limitations placed on critical thought by virtue of the linguistic turn and its paranoid fear of essentialism,[18] and propose transgressing this through the recovery of material immediacy, bodily spontaneity, or affective vitalism. As such, they develop theories that centrally reposition materiality and/or affect as part of that materiality.[19]

Some of the pronouncements by affect and new materialist theorists in terms of newness are, as noted, problematic. Moreover, there is a tendency to treat mind, body, thought and feeling atomistically as one oppositional is elevated in a bid to reprioritise what the new school believes has been neglected in recent critical thought. For example, in Massumi's work, bodily feeling is severed from and prioritised over cognition, as feeling is presented as prior to—and by implication more important than—thought.[20] This extends to debates on nature and culture, as nature is elevated to countermand its perceived marginality in feminist theory to such an extent that it leads to the possibility of culture's erasure—as Vicki Kirby asks, could it be that "culture was really nature all along?"[21] While I appreciate the desire to redress what has, according to the new school, been too long maligned in feminist theory, I think such efforts must proceed along truly anti-dualistic lines that do not reduce certain categories to others or maintain problematic dichotomies. To be fair, much affect and new materialist work sets out to do so, and Kirby's assertion that "the meat of the body *is* thinking material"[22] certainly looks promising for those of us excited by the renewed cross-disciplinary interest in anti-dualistic theorisations of materiality, affect, and emotion.

What seems incongruous, though, in light of the renewed search for anti-dualistic theory that embraces nature, materiality, and concreteness is the general oversight of pragmatism. Pragmatist philosophy has long constituted a framework for theorists sceptical of the linguistic paradigm and its implications in terms of the theoretical remoteness of bodies and lived bodily practices. Pragmatism, as a *lived* philosophy, emphasises action, corporeal embeddedness, and political meliorism in a naturalistic ethics and ontology. Its core paradigm is experience, rather than language. As such, it circumvents many of the shortcomings of the linguistic turn highlighted by the new school. That is not to say that theorists should disavow the lessons leant from thinkers' turn to language during the course of the twentieth century. Certainly, the insight that language can act as an instrument of power is one that is deeply relevant to critical theorists' work,[23] as is the move from foundationalism.[24] It should be said that the neo-pragmatist turn also included a retreat from experience in favour of language by certain thinkers, such as Richard Rorty and Robert Brandom, as they used the linguistic paradigm to reconfigure pragmatism in its image. Like Koopman, though, I think that a pragmatist focus on non-foundational experience can be maintained by contemporary critical theorists while still acknowledging insights gained from the linguistic turn.[25]

Notably, the new materialist theorists with whom I will be engaging in this chapter also resist rewinding the clock to a pre-linguistic turn era. They represent nuanced exemplars of the "new school," acknowledging and even utilising theoretical tools developed by postmodern theorists—Barad, for instance, draws on Butler's concept of performativity.[26] They note the impossibility of an uncritical, amnesic return to modernism, and point to the need "to build on rather than abandon the lessons learned in the linguistic turn."[27] My contention, in this chapter, is that feminists interested in a move towards materiality, affect, emotion, and nature would do well to turn to pragmatism and more recent neo-pragmatist work while, similarly, avoiding a naïve, forgetful backtracking to modernism. Feminists, indeed critical theorists more generally, will be richly rewarded for doing so, as pragmatism is at least partly capable of redressing the concerns of new materialist and affect theorists, and neo-pragmatists have long read pragmatism through a contemporary, feminist critical perspective that forms an alternative or supplement to the poststructuralist and deconstructionist linguistic paradigm.[28]

In what follows, I will focus particularly on John Dewey's embodied, habituated, transacting "organism" as just such a resource for feminists. This pragmatist conception of (the human) being inhabiting and shaping environments is much more immediately materialist, "fleshy," and experiential when compared to similar expositions of the linguistic-turn variety.[29] It forms part of a truly anti-dualistic approach to what is the central problematic of the new materialist and affect theoretical agenda: to reimagine the relationship between nature and culture, or the material and the discursive, in such a way as to redress the neglect of the former categories. As noted, on my reading of work by the new school, this rebalancing between oppositionals often fails, as the revaluation of the formerly neglected categories goes too far, thereby inverting dualisms rather than redressing them. However, a Deweyan, naturalistic conception of the transacting self inhabiting the world can constitute, for feminists, a model of anti-dualistic theorising that conceives of nature and culture (and the related dichotomies of thought and feeling, body and mind) in less antagonistic and mutually accommodating terms.

Moreover, certain new materialist concepts, developed to reconceive of the relationship between nature and culture come, as noted, astonishingly close to the classic pragmatism the new school largely overlooks. This is particularly evident in the exposition of Barad's and Alaimo's ontological models, which prize organicism, relationality, and materiality. Pragmatism espouses a similar ontological naturalism, as Dewey, in particular, was heavily influenced by Charles Darwin.[30] Dewey was born the same year *On the Origin of Species* appeared—a book he noted for having introduced "a new intellectual temper," with "the very words origin and species" presenting "an intellectual revolt."[31] For Dewey, Darwinism entailed a complete rethinking of an essentialist, foundationalist metaphysics of fixity and stasis in favour of a more malleable, transformative, and transforming naturalistic ontology.[32] It is from this that Dewey develops moral, epistemological, and political theories that centrally assume organic beings to be *in* the world, indeed, to be simultaneously productive of and produced by their worlds. As will become clear below, this deep-seated concern with Darwinism and naturalism holds specific implications for how pragmatists theorise the nature-culture relationship, and the possibility of reconciling entrenched philosophical dualisms such as mind/body, and thought/feeling.

Given Dewey's strong preoccupation with Darwinism, it seems, again, puzzling that new materialist and affect theorists have not drawn on his thought to develop the kind of naturalistic, agentic, anti-dualistic resources they seek. Elizabeth Grosz, for instance, draws on Darwin to explicate "biological and cultural emergence," and to redress "feminists' resistance to his work."[33] Indeed, several theorists of the new school turn to scientists in a bid to revalue what is presented as the universally elided in feminist theory—the body, material immediacy, and vitalist affect—hence, Barad's utilisation of work by the physicist Niels Bohr.[34] While there is of course nothing the matter with drawing on such scientific work directly, one wonders why philosophical appropriations of such work—including by pragmatists and, notably, feminist-pragmatists such as Jane Addams[35]—do not figure in the texts by the new school. Grosz, Barad, and Alaimo make fleeting references to pragmatism, but do not pursue their ideas in conversation with pragmatist work.[36] As will become clear, this is particularly odd given the strong echoes of pragmatist ideas prevalent in some of the new school's theorising. In what follows, I will trace some of these echoes by sketching Barad's, Alaimo's, and Dewey's naturalist ontologies, and by identifying the recursiveness of a conception of the organic, embodied being in continuous *transaction*.

Tracing *Transaction* Across Pragmatist and New Materialist Ontologies

Barad's "Intra-action" in a Diffractive, Butlerian-Bohrian Ontology

In her article, "Posthumanist Performativity: Toward an Understanding of How Matter Comes to Matter," later reworked in *Meeting the Universe Halfway*, Karen Barad develops a theory of "agential realism" to reconfigure "the familiar notions of discursive practices, materialization, agency, and causality, among others."[37] This is done against the backdrop of that central problematic identified by the new school: the ascendancy of language and culture and the concomitant disregard for materiality in feminist thought. In Barad's view, "language has been granted too much power ... Language matters. Discourse matters. Culture matters. There is an important sense in which the only thing that does not seem to matter anymore is matter."[38] Barad's theory, then, seeks to reposition matter by bringing together feminist and queer theoretical work with Niels Bohr's scientific writings. The idea is to develop a riff on Butler's notion of performativity—"an agential realist elaboration of performativity" that "allows matter its due as an active participant in the world's becoming, in its ongoing intra-activity."[39] Like other new materialists, Barad thus rejects matter as passive substance onto which culture and language etch meaning. Matter here is agentic, surpassing the discursive-material relation, as it "intra-acts" in and with its world(s).

Barad adapts Butler's thought to develop a posthumanist, materialist account of performativity. She thereby recognises and builds on the "discursive factors that are important to the process of materialization,"[40] while adding to this the neglected dimension of "the material constraints and exclusions, the material dimensions of agency."[41] Thus, she supplements what she views as Butler's incomplete account—which explains "how *discourse* comes to matter," but not "how *matter* comes to matter"—and counters the dualism she thinks Butler maintains in her "reinstalling [of] materiality in a passive role."[42] Bohr is drawn on to make this a "diffractive,"[43] transdisciplinary reading of performativity that develops an "agential realism" and builds on his opposition to Newtonian physics. Accordingly, Bohr rejects an "inherent distinction between the object and the agencies of observation,"[44] replacing a Newtonian framework based on the division between knower and object of knowledge, representationalism, and metaphysical individualism,[45] with a "philosophy-physics"[46] positing epistemological "wholeness" (or "inseparability") and "phenomena."[47] These phenomena are, on Barad's reading of Bohr, "physical-conceptual (material-discursive) intra-actions," with "the neologism 'intra-action' ... signify[ing] *the mutual constitution of object and agencies of observation within phenomena* (in contrast to 'interaction,' which assumes the prior existence of distinct entities)."[48] The upshot of this model of new materialist, performative metaphysics, then, is a rethinking of the relationship between knower (measurement) and object of knowledge,[49] and between the discursive and the material. An ontology of mutually emergent entities restores agency to matter, and undercuts representationalism in an epistemology that eliminates distance between knower and what can be known.

Alaimo's "Trans-corporeality" in the "Ethical Space of Nature"

Stacy Alaimo presents us with a similar exposition of a naturalistic metaphysics that reprioritises matter in a sea of otherwise linguistic and social constructivist feminist theory. She laments feminism's "flight from nature,"[50] and, like Barad, holds that a too narrow focus "on how various bodies have been discursively produced ... casts the body as passive, plastic matter."[51] In contrast to this, she develops the notion of "trans-corporeality" to highlight the inseparability of human beings—"the corporeal substance of the human"—from "the environment."[52] Trans-corporeality thus grounds humans in the "more-than-human world," while reconfiguring "the environment" as "a world of fleshy beings, with their own needs, claims, and actions."[53] Drawing on new materialist work by Barad, among others, her posthumanist concept of trans-corporeality indicates travel "across different sites" and attributes agency to materiality beyond the human/environment dichotomy.[54] It does this by "open[ing] up an epistemological 'space' that acknowledges the often unpredictable and unwanted actions of human bodies, non-human creatures, ecological systems, chemical agents, and other actors."[55] We have here, then, a naturalistic conception of "fleshy" beings in their worlds that champions the inseparability of human beings and environments, and that revalues the more-than-human as agentic.

Interestingly, Alaimo links this conception of trans-corporeality to specific examples delineating the intertwining of nature and human beings, for, as she explains, "'nature' is always as close as one's own skin."[56] Nature is thus foregrounded in a way that counters its depiction as inertness, "empty space," or "resource,"[57] as "environmental health, environmental justice, the traffic in toxins, and genetic engineering, to name a few"[58] illustrate precisely the *trans-*, or cross-travelling element, of trans-corporeality as it envelopes both humans and environments. Indeed, in her examination of toxic bodies, Alaimo illustrates trans-corporeality in terms of the pervasive and universal impact toxins have on a variety of bodies, regardless of their immediate proximity to toxic sources. Citing the contamination of Inuit breast milk, Alaimo argues that even in cases of physical remoteness from pollution, the world's beings are subject to a "chemical stew" in our "blood and tissues," which shows us that our fates, our physical well-being, is enmeshed with and depends upon that of "the rest of the planet."[59] Moreover, she notes, we do not yet know the effects of the swathes of chemicals we discharge, nor the effects they have on each other and on our "inter- and intra-act[ing] bodies and 'environments.'"[60] Her example of toxic bodies thus highlights trans-corporeality as a means of thinking about materiality "not as a utopian or romantic substance existing prior to social inscription, but as something that always bears the trace of history, social position, region, and the uneven distribution of risk"[61] as we "imagine ourselves in constant interchange with the environment."[62]

Dewey's "Transacting" Organism in a Naturalist Ontology

In Dewey's post-Darwinian, naturalist ontology, the organism—whether human being or animal—is positioned within nature as a matter of constant adaptation with its environment.[63] He notes that "life goes on in an environment; not merely in it but because of it, through interaction with it. No creature lives merely under its skin; its subcutaneous organs are means of connection with what lies beyond its bodily frame, and to which, in order to live, it must adjust itself."[64] Dewey develops the concept of "transaction" and refers sometimes also to "interaction," which denotes the co-constitutive relationship between the "organism" and its environment—that is, the organism simultaneously produces and is produced by its environment. Thus, "the career and destiny of a living being are bound up with its interchanges with its environment, not externally but in the most intimate way."[65] Human beings are rooted in the world in full recognition of the fact that environments shape us while we shape our environments.

Dewey undercuts the strict distinction between human beings and nature, although he also resists collapsing one category into the other. He maintains that "living as an empirical affair is not something which goes on below the skin-surface of an organism: It is always an inclusive affair involving connection, interaction of what is within the organic body and what lies outside."[66] By still referring to an "inside" and "outside" in the wider context of a constantly, mutually adapting organism-environment dyad, he avoids reducing organism to environment and environment to organism. Rather, these form mutually dependent, if separately recognisable categories in a holistic ontological model of natural adaptation. As Shannon Sullivan helpfully describes it, Dewey's "transaction" can be understood through the metaphor of "the stew."[67] Rather than reducing ingredients to a non-differentiated soup as a melting pot would do, or maintaining the separateness of ingredients as a salad might, the stew allows vegetables to keep—to a certain extent—their individual shape and flavour, while also allowing for the mutual flavouring of ingredients by each other. As such, "the stew demonstrates ... how the notion of transaction takes us beyond the dualism of atomism [of organism and environment] and its flip side of ontological collapse."[68]

Transaction is always ongoing, and since we develop through constant adaptation *with* and *in* the world, there is no pre-adaptive organism that can be extracted and examined from outside of nature. This has distinct epistemological and moral implications for Dewey. He rejects the philosophical dichotomy between mind and body, arguing instead for "a body-mind, whose structures have developed according to the structures of the world in which it exists."[69] On top of this, he adopts a distinctly pragmatist epistemology—fallibilism—which questions objectivity resulting from the bird's eye view, and troubles the classic distinction between knower and object of knowledge.[70] Notably, at the centre of Dewey's presentation of the organism that constitutes and is in turn constituted by its environment lies the concept of habit. Our particular fund of habits is unique to us and explains our particular way of being in the world, as it structures our transactions. As Sullivan explains, "[O]rganisms' bodying generally occurs in patterned, rather than random ways. Bodying is constituted by habits, which are an organism's acquired styles of activity."[71] It is through (sometimes repetitive) action, indeed, *trans*action, that being comes to be constituted.[72]

The Promise of Pragmatism for Contemporary Feminism

With that said, it should be evident that distinct areas of overlap emerge from the (admittedly brief) sketch of Barad's, Alaimo's, and Dewey's ontological thought and their respective concepts of "transaction," "intra-action," and "trans-corporeality." Alaimo's "trans-corporeal" framing of "fleshy" being in a world where none of us are immune from toxic perils, and where human beings and the "more-than-human world" depend on and are informed by each other, is strikingly similar to Dewey's notion of the embedded organism that is formed by and simultaneously forms its environments through transaction. By rejecting a disjunction between human beings and their environments, Alaimo attributes an agency and capacity for change to nature that, long ago, also formed the ground of Dewey's penchant for Darwinism. It is precisely nature's capacity to shape—and in turn be shaped (by the organism)—that excited Dewey, as it provoked the possibility of transformation and the agency this usually requires. Moreover, it allowed a move away from a static, closed metaphysics of fixed essences towards a much more open, continuously adapting, and therefore potentially transforming ontology. On both Dewey's and Alaimo's accounts, this means that nature is agential, transforming, and transformative. This is a far cry from the passive and unresponsive nature that gets inscribed by culture and language, by *human* agency, in theories of triumphant human mastery over environment, and redresses the elision of materiality and nature that the new school identifies in poststructuralist and deconstructionist feminist thought.

The question of nature's agency also figures prominently in Barad's exposition of "intra-action," which similarly dispels ideas based on the strict separability of entities. For Barad, "matter is an agentive factor in its iterative materialization … agency is a matter of *intra*-acting…agency is doing/being in its intra-activity."[73] The resemblance to the Deweyan, habituated organism that continuously creates itself and its world is obvious here. Habits, that is, our doings and beings, lend a particular style, as Sullivan notes, to bodying through transaction with our environments. Pragmatism's focus on practice, on action, indeed, *trans*action, when placed in the context of a naturalist ontology, draws attention to the ways in which we are constantly co-constituted, materialised, through habituated doing/being. Notably, this is a *mutual* relationship between organism and environment that presupposes nature as agentic and capable of change. Dewey's naturalism thereby meets the new materialist vision of an active, changing matter and nature, for, as Barad notes, "matter is not immutable or passive."[74]

The consequences for theorising knowledge that arise from a naturalist ontology are also similarly shared by Dewey and Barad. The question is: if human beings are thoroughly embedded in the natural world, then how can we stand outside of what it is we are enquiring into? Moreover, if humans are inseparable from nature, and exist in constant adaptation to it, then how is a bird's-eye-view conception of knowledge possible? In both Barad's and Dewey's cases, the distinction between knowledge and object of knowledge, and the assumption that we can indeed stand outside of what we are enquiring into, is rejected. Barad draws on Bohr's work to elaborate on this, while Dewey develops a fallibilist theory of enquiry that allows for the object of enquiry to be impacted and changed by our very enquiry.[75]

In sum, it should be clear that there are interesting overlaps between the preoccupations of some members of the new feminist school of post-linguistic turn theorising, particularly with regard to the development of a naturalist ontology. I have tried to highlight some of the converging themes within this, and to point to pragmatist resources that can be usefully drawn on by feminists interested in the contemporary turn towards materialism and affect. It is regrettable that much of the work by the new school has not (yet) engaged pragmatism in its reimagining of the relationship between nature and culture, mind and body, and feeling and cognition. Despite the fact that contemporary philosophical concepts, such as "post-humanism" or Butler's "performativity," obviously postdate the classic pragmatists, the foregoing shows that pragmatism forms a vibrant tradition for feminists interested in redressing the critiques raised by the new school. As such, I recommend engaging with the legitimate criticisms of the new materialist and affect theorists by drawing on pragmatism, to allow for a post-linguistic turn feminism that refrains from erasing the important existing and ongoing feminist-pragmatist work to which the new school clearly has a philosophical affinity.

Notes

1. S. Ahmed, "Imaginary Prohibitions: Some Preliminary Remarks on the Founding Gestures of the 'New Materialism'," *European Journal of Women's Studies* 15, no. 1 (February 1, 2008): 23–39. Clare Hemmings, "Invoking Affect: Cultural Theory and the Ontological Turn," *Cultural Studies* 19, no. 5 (2005): 548–67.
2. Clara Fischer, "Feminist Philosophy, Pragmatism, and the 'Turn to Affect': A Genealogical Critique," *Hypatia: A Journal of Feminist Philosophy* 31, no. 4 (2016): 810–26.
3. Ibid.
4. Ibid.
5. William James, "The Emotions," in *The Principles of Psychology, Vol. II* (Cambridge, Mass.: Harvard University Press, 1981). William James, "The Physical Basis of Emotion," *Psychological Review* 101, no. 2 (1994).
6. Interestingly, the feminist-pragmatist philosopher Shannon Sullivan draws on James to redress what she perceives as dualisms held by cognitivist theorists of emotion. However, I think it is precisely the fact that James can be read as being exclusively concerned with emotion as non-cognitive, bodily phenomenon—"emotion is necessarily, inevitably, and entirely a bodily phenomenon"—that renders James problematic as a theorist capable of

undoing mind-body and emotion-cognition dualisms. See Shannon Sullivan, *The Physiology of Sexist and Racist Oppression* (Oxford: Oxford University Press, 2015), 35.

7. Stacy Alaimo, "Trans-Corporeal Feminisms and the Ethical Space of Nature," in *Material Feminisms*, ed. Stacy Alaimo and Susan Hekman (Bloomington, IN: Indiana University Press, 2008), 237–64, p. 238.

8. Fischer, "Feminist Philosophy, Pragmatism, and the 'Turn to Affect': A Genealogical Critique."

9. Brian Massumi, *Parables for the Virtual: Movement, Affect, Sensation* (London: Duke University Press, 2002). As noted, though, Massumi re-appropriates James for a reductive and atomistic conception of affect and emotion to develop an ontology of affect; see Fischer, "Feminist Philosophy, Pragmatism, and the 'Turn to Affect': A Genealogical Critique."

10. See Shannon Sullivan, *Living Across and Through Skins: Transactional Bodies, Pragmatism, and Feminism* (Bloomington and Indianapolis: Indiana University Press, 2001).

11. Fischer, "Feminist Philosophy, Pragmatism, and the 'Turn to Affect': A Genealogical Critique."

12. Hemmings, "Invoking Affect: Cultural Theory and the Ontological Turn" and Ahmed, "Imaginary Prohibitions: Some Preliminary Remarks on the Founding Gestures of the 'New Materialism'."

13. The negation of pragmatism in this work stems also from the tendency by some prominent affect and new materialist theorists to equate all contemporary critical theory with poststructuralism or deconstruction; see Fischer, "Feminist Philosophy, Pragmatism, and the 'Turn to Affect': A Genealogical Critique."

14. See also Ruth Leys, "The Turn to Affect: A Critique," *Critical Inquiry* 37 (2011): 452–58.

15. Coole and Frost thus speak of the "lively immanence of matter associated with new materialisms"—see Diana Coole and Samantha Frost, "Introducing the New Materialisms," in *New Materialisms: Ontology, Agency, and Politics* (London: Duke University Press, 2010), 1–43, p. 9.

16. Stacy Alaimo and Susan Hekman, "Introduction: Emerging Models of Materiality in Feminist Theory," in *Material Feminisms*, ed. Stacy Alaimo and Susam Hekman (Bloomington, IN: Indiana University Press, 2008), 1–19, 1.

17. Eve Kosofsky Sedgwick and Adam Frank, "Shame in the Cybernetic Fold: Reading Silvan Tomkins," in *Touching Feeling: Affect, Pedagogy, Performativity*, ed. Eve Kosofsky Sedgwick (London: Duke University Press, 2003), 93–121, 111.

18. The issue of essentialism is a complex and contested one within the new school, with several theorists remaining sceptical of ascribing essences and

innate characteristics to existents, and others, notably Elizabeth Grosz, championing a gender essentialism that reifies the gender binary—see Elizabeth Grosz, *In the Nick of Time: Politics, Evolution, and the Untimely* (Durham & London: Duke University Press, 2004). For a critique of this, see Gill Jagger, "The New Materialism and Sexual Difference," *Signs: Journal of Women in Culture and Society* 40, no. 2 (2015): 321–42.
19. Hence my subsuming of both affect theory and new materialisms under the heading of the "new school."
20. Massumi, *Parables for the Virtual: Movement, Affect, Sensation*, 29.
21. Vicki Kirby, "Natural Convers(at)ions: Or, What If Culture Was Really Nature All Along?," in *Material Feminisms*, ed. Stacy Alaimo and Susan Hekman (Bloomington & Indianapolis: Indiana University Press, 2008), 214–35, 214.
22. Ibid, 221.
23. I have previously theorised Jane Addams' tale of the "devil baby" as a precursor to the stylistic, communicative differences identified by Iris Marion Young in terms of questions of power and democratic deliberation—see Clara Fischer, "Pragmatists, Deliberativists, and Democracy: The Quest for Inclusion," *Journal of Speculative Philosophy* 26, no. 3 (2012): 497–515.
24. For a more in-depth discussion on the debate between those pragmatists favouring language and those defending the primacy of experience, including the role anti-foundationalism played therein, see Colin Koopman, "Language Is a Form of Experience: Reconciling Classical Pragmatism and Neopragmatism," *Transactions of the Charles S. Peirce Society* 43, no. 4 (2007): 694–727.
25. Ibid.
26. Karen Barad, *Meeting the Universe Halfway: Quantum Physics and the Entanglement of Matter and Meaning* (London: Duke University Press, 2007).
27. Alaimo and Hekman, "Introduction: Emerging Models of Materiality in Feminist Theory," p. 6.
28. In 1991, Charlene Haddock Seigfried, the progenitor of contemporary feminist-pragmatism, asked: "Where are all the pragmatist feminists?" Over two decades later, there are numerous theorists working in feminist-pragmatism; several books problematising classic pragmatists from a feminist perspective have been published; and classic feminist-pragmatists, especially Jane Addams, have been "restored" to the philosophical and pragmatist canon—see Charlene Haddock Seigfried, "Where Are All the Pragmatist Feminists?," *Hypatia: A Journal of Feminist Philosophy* 6, no. 2 (1991): 1–20. Charlene Haddock Seigfried, *Pragmatism and Feminism: Reweaving the Social Fabric* (Chicago: University of Chicago Press, 1996). Erin McKenna, *The Task of Utopia: A Pragmatist and Feminist Perspective*

(London: Rowman & Littlefield, 2001). Sullivan, *Living Across and Through Skins*. Maurice Hamington and Celia Bardwell-Jones, eds., *Contemporary Feminist Pragmatism* (New York: Routledge, 2012). Erin C. Tarver and Shannon Sullivan, eds., *Feminist Interpretations of William James* (University Park, PA: The Pennsylvania State University Press, 2015). Charlene Haddock Seigfried, ed., *Feminist Interpretations of John Dewey* (University Park PA: The Pennsylvania State University Press, 2002). Maurice Hamington, ed., *Feminist Interpretations of Jane Addams* (University Park, PA: The Pennsylvania State University Press, 2010).

29. In Chap. 4 of *Gendered Readings of Change*, I proposed a feminist-pragmatist conception of the self precisely as an alternative model to too deterministic and too fluid, that is, poststructuralist, conceptions.

30. Although my focus in this chapter is on Dewey's naturalist ontology, it is also important to note contemporary pragmatist resources on animals and the environment, including Erin McKenna, *Pets, People, and Pragmatism* (New York: Fordham University Press, 2013); Erin McKenna and Andrew Light, eds., *Animal Pragmatism: Rethinking Human-Nonhuman Relationships* (Bloomington, IN: Indiana University Press, 2004); Andrew Light and Eric Katz, eds., *Environmental Pragmatism* (New York: Routledge, 1996); and Erin McKenna, "We Are Hers," *The Pluralist* 6, no. 3 (2011): 34–43.

31. John Dewey, *The Influence of Darwin on Philosophy and Other Essays in Contemporary Thought*, ed. Larry A. Hickman (Carbondale: Southern Illinois University Press, 2007), 5.

32. I have set out at length the role change and stasis play in Dewey's philosophy, and whether his model of change is one feminists can appropriate—see Clara Fischer, *Gendered Readings of Change: A Feminist-Pragmatist Approach* (New York: Palgrave Macmillan, 2014).

33. Grosz, *In the Nick of Time: Politics, Evolution, and the Untimely*.

34. Barad, *Meeting the Universe Halfway: Quantum Physics and the Entanglement of Matter and Meaning*.

35. Seigfried, *Pragmatism and Feminism*, 226, see also Chap. 9.

36. See Grosz, *In the Nick of Time: Politics, Evolution, and the Untimely*, 7. Barad, *Meeting the Universe Halfway: Quantum Physics and the Entanglement of Matter and Meaning*, 147. Stacy Alaimo, *Bodily Natures: Science, Environment, and the Material Self* (Bloomington & Indianapolis: Indiana University Press, 2010), fn. 3, 159.

37. Karen Barad, "Posthumanist Performativity: Toward an Understanding of How Matter Comes to Matter," in *Material Feminisms*, ed. Stacy Alaimo and Susan Hekman (Bloomington, IN: Indiana University Press, 2008), 129.

38. Barad, *Meeting the Universe Halfway: Quantum Physics and the Entanglement of Matter and Meaning*, 132.
39. Ibid, 136.
40. Ibid, 194.
41. Ibid, 192.
42. Ibid.
43. Ibid, 25.
44. Ibid, 196.
45. Ibid, 195.
46. Ibid, 122.
47. Ibid, 196.
48. Ibid, 197.
49. Barad notes that, for Bohr, "theoretical concepts are defined by the circumstances required for their measurement," and that therefore, "there is no unambiguous way to differentiate between the object and the agencies of observation," 196.
50. Alaimo, *Bodily Natures: Science, Environment, and the Material Self*, 4.
51. Alaimo, *Bodily Natures: Science, Environment, and the Material Self*, 3. Many of Alaimo's ideas discussed here can also be found in Alaimo, "Trans-Corporeal Feminisms and the Ethical Space of Nature."
52. Alaimo, *Bodily Natures: Science, Environment, and the Material Self*, 2.
53. Ibid.
54. Ibid.
55. Ibid.
56. Ibid.
57. Ibid, 2.
58. Alaimo, "Trans-Corporeal Feminisms and the Ethical Space of Nature", 239.
59. Alaimo, *Bodily Natures: Science, Environment, and the Material Self*, 18.Ibid.
60. Ibid, 21.
61. Alaimo, "Trans-Corporeal Feminisms and the Ethical Space of Nature", 261.
62. Alaimo, *Bodily Natures: Science, Environment, and the Material Self*, 22.
63. Unfortunately, a more comprehensive exposition of Dewey's naturalism and his concept of "transaction" lies beyond the scope of this chapter. For more detailed accounts, see Sullivan, *Living Across and Through Skins*. And Fischer, *Gendered Readings of Change: A Feminist-Pragmatist Approach*.
64. John Dewey, *Art as Experience*, ed. Jo-Ann Bodyston, Later Work (Southern Illinois University Press, 2008), 19.
65. Ibid.

66. John Dewey, *Experience and Nature*, ed. J A Boydston, *John Dewey: The Later Works, 1925–1953*, vol. 1: 1925 (Carbondale & Edwardsville: Southern Illinois University Press, 2008), 215.
67. Sullivan, *Living Across and Through Skins*, 15–16.
68. Ibid, 16.
69. Dewey, *Experience and Nature*, 211.
70. For a fuller account of fallibilism and Dewey's "theory of inquiry" (he disliked the term "epistemology"), see Larry A. Hickman, "Dewey's Theory of Inquiry," in *Reading Dewey: Interpretations for a Postmodern Generation*, ed. Larry A. Hickman (Bloomington & Indianapolis: Indiana University Press, 1998), 166–86.
71. Sullivan, *Living Across and Through Skins*, 30.
72. Again, a much more comprehensive exposition of habit sadly has to be forgone here—for further details, see Chaps. 3 and 4 in Fischer, *Gendered Readings of Change: A Feminist-Pragmatist Approach*.
73. Ibid, 235.
74. Ibid, 151.
75. Hickman, "Dewey's Theory of Inquiry."

Bibliography

Ahmed, S. 2008. Imaginary Prohibitions: Some Preliminary Remarks on the Founding Gestures of the 'New Materialism'. *European Journal of Women's Studies* 15 (1): 23–39.

Alaimo, Stacy. 2008. Trans-Corporeal Feminisms and the Ethical Space of Nature. In *Material Feminisms*, ed. Stacy Alaimo and Susan Hekman, 237–264. Bloomington: Indiana University Press.

———. 2010. *Bodily Natures: Science, Environment, and the Material Self*. Bloomington/Indianapolis: Indiana University Press.

Alaimo, Stacy, and Susan Hekman. 2008. Introduction: Emerging Models of Materiality in Feminist Theory. In *Material Feminisms*, ed. Stacy Alaimo and Susam Hekman, 1–19. Bloomington: Indiana University Press.

Barad, Karen. 2007. *Meeting the Universe Halfway: Quantum Physics and the Entanglement of Matter and Meaning*. London: Duke University Press.

———. 2008. Posthumanist Performativity: Toward an Understanding of How Matter Comes to Matter. In *Material Feminisms*, ed. Stacy Alaimo and Susan Hekman. Bloomington: Indiana University Press.

Coole, Diana, and Samantha Frost. 2010. Introducing the New Materialisms. In *New Materialisms: Ontology, Agency, and Politics*, 1–43. London: Duke University Press.

Dewey, John. 2007. In *The Influence of Darwin on Philosophy and Other Essays in Contemporary Thought*, ed. Larry A. Hickman. Carbondale: Southern Illinois University Press.

———. 2008a. *Art as Experience*, ed Jo-Ann Bodyston. Later Work. Carbondale/Edwardsville: Southern Illinois University Press.

———. 2008b. *Experience and Nature*, ed. J A Boydston. *John Dewey: The Later Works, 1925–1953*. Vol. 1: 1925. Carbondale/Edwardsville: Southern Illinois University Press.

Fischer, Clara. 2012. Pragmatists, Deliberativists, and Democracy: The Quest for Inclusion. *Journal of Speculative Philosophy* 26 (3): 497–515.

———. 2014. *Gendered Readings of Change: A Feminist-Pragmatist Approach*. New York: Palgrave Macmillan.

———. 2016. Feminist Philosophy, Pragmatism, and the 'Turn to Affect': A Genealogical Critique. *Hypatia: A Journal of Feminist Philosophy* 31 (4): 810–826.

Grosz, Elizabeth. 2004. *In the Nick of Time: Politics, Evolution, and the Untimely*. Durham/London: Duke University Press.

Hamington, Maurice, ed. 2010. *Feminist Interpretations of Jane Addams*. University Park: The Pennsylvania State University Press.

Hamington, Maurice, and Celia Bardwell-Jones, eds. 2012. *Contemporary Feminist Pragmatism*. New York: Routledge.

Hemmings, Clare. 2005. Invoking Affect: Cultural Theory and the Ontological Turn. *Cultural Studies* 19 (5): 548–567.

Hickman, Larry A. 1998. Dewey's Theory of Inquiry. In *Reading Dewey: Interpretations for a Postmodern Generation*, ed. Larry A. Hickman, 166–186. Bloomington/Indianapolis: Indiana University Press.

Jagger, Gill. 2015. The New Materialism and Sexual Difference. *Signs: Journal of Women in Culture and Society* 40 (2): 321–342.

James, William. 1981. The Emotions. In *The Principles of Psychology*, vol. II. Cambridge, MA: Harvard University Press.

———. 1994. The Physical Basis of Emotion. *Psychological Review* 101 (2): 205–210.

Kirby, Vicki. 2008. Natural Convers(at)ions: Or, What If Culture Was Really Nature All Along? In *Material Feminisms*, ed. Stacy Alaimo and Susan Hekman, 214–235. Bloomington/Indianapolis: Indiana University Press.

Koopman, Colin. 2007. Language Is a Form of Experience: Reconciling Classical Pragmatism and Neopragmatism. *Transactions of the Charles S. Peirce Society* 43 (4): 694–727.

Leys, Ruth. 2011. The Turn to Affect: A Critique. *Critical Inquiry* 37: 452–458.

Light, Andrew, and Eric Katz, eds. 1996. *Environmental Pragmatism*. New York: Routledge.

Massumi, Brian. 2002. *Parables for the Virtual: Movement, Affect, Sensation*. London: Duke University Press.

McKenna, Erin. 2001. *The Task of Utopia: A Pragmatist and Feminist Perspective*. London: Rowman & Littlefield.

———. 2011. We Are Hers. *The Pluralist* 6 (3): 34–43.
———. 2013. *Pets, People, and Pragmatism*. New York: Fordham University Press.
McKenna, Erin, and Andrew Light, eds. 2004. *Animal Pragmatism: Rethinking Human-Nonhuman Relationships*. Bloomington: Indiana University Press.
Sedgwick, Eve Kosofsky, and Adam Frank. 2003. Shame in the Cybernetic Fold: Reading Silvan Tomkins. In *Touching Feeling: Affect, Pedagogy, Performativity*, ed. Eve Kosofsky Sedgwick, 93–121. London: Duke University Press.
Seigfried, Charlene Haddock. 1991. Where Are All the Pragmatist Feminists? *Hypatia: A Journal of Feminist Philosophy* 6 (2): 1–20.
———. 1996. *Pragmatism and Feminism: Reweaving the Social Fabric*. Chicago: University of Chicago Press.
———, ed. 2002. *Feminist Interpretations of John Dewey*. University Park: The Pennsylvania State University Press.
Sullivan, Shannon. 2001. *Living Across and Through Skins: Transactional Bodies, Pragmatism, and Feminism*. Bloomington/Indianapolis: Indiana University Press.
———. 2015. *The Physiology of Sexist and Racist Oppression*. Oxford: Oxford University Press.
Tarver, Erin C., and Shannon Sullivan, eds. 2015. *Feminist Interpretations of William James*. University Park: The Pennsylvania State University Press.

CHAPTER 6

Feminist and Transgender Tensions: An Inquiry into History, Methodological Paradigms, and Embodiment

Lanei M. Rodemeyer

As feminist philosophers, we work to be sensitive to all types of embodiment, whether identified through gender, ability, age, race, or any other marker. But we still commit errors. At least I do. As a cisgender,[1] white woman without disability, I can be blind to my advantages. It is an ongoing project to remain aware of my positions of privilege. However, relatively recent events, such as the 2014 publication of Sheila Jeffrey's *Gender Hurts* (a book that is explicitly anti-trans while positioning itself as feminist), heated debates between calls to censor anti-trans authors/speakers and proponents of free speech (especially in the UK),[2] and the multiple, complex issues arising from *Hypatia*'s publication of an article comparing "transgenderism" to "transracialism"[3] indicate for me the following insight: that my own struggle to decentralize my privileged positions is also staged within a greater context of relations between feminist and transgender projects (as well as other approaches such as critical theories of race).

L. M. Rodemeyer (✉)
Duquesne University, Pittsburgh, PA, USA

© The Author(s) 2018
C. Fischer, L. Dolezal (eds.), *New Feminist Perspectives on Embodiment*, Breaking Feminist Waves,
https://doi.org/10.1007/978-3-319-72353-2_6

It therefore seems valuable to recall some of the history of tensions between feminist work and transgender that lie in the background of current issues.[4] For this reason, within the context of my overall argument, I will be turning to specific moments that highlight some of these tensions. These moments will serve as material for my analyses, but they will also act as reminders that, while we might have the best intentions, cisgender, white feminists speak from a position of privilege. This might be "old news," but I believe it is important to remain cognizant of the fact that feminist theory and transgender studies have not had a smooth, congenial history. While we might strive for alliance or "affinity," taking note of historical and theoretical tensions—as well as the privileged positions some of us hold—remains crucial for our current projects.[5]

But this chapter is not meant to be a mere refresher course on the history of feminist and transgender relations (one which would, admittedly, serve primarily a cisgender audience). Rather, I wish to address the fact that, when we carry out analyses of gender and embodiment, the paradigms we employ can determine our outcomes—often in exclusive ways. Now, many feminists have demonstrated that philosophical paradigms, supposedly "neutral," contain masculine bias as well as other normative presumptions. But—turning the tables on feminist theorists—Vivane Namaste has criticized queer and contemporary feminist theorists in a similar way: She argues that, by abstracting the question of "gender" from economic and social factors, feminist theorists have neglected essential aspects of transgender experience while, at the same time, they hold "transgender" up as a prime example for their theories. Building upon Namaste's insight, I wish to examine four paradigms[6] that have been employed to analyze gender and embodiment[7] in philosophy and feminist theory: (a) sex/gender, (b) queer, (c) phenomenology, and (d) transfeminism. While doing so, I will indicate how the limitations of certain methods affect their analyses of both gender and embodiment, especially in light of transgender experience. I will also consider how tactically engaging two or more approaches[8] at once could offset the shortcomings of each taken alone.

Sex/Gender

The paradigm of sex/gender employs the dichotomy of a material or biological sex and a socially constructed gender. As we all know, it is no longer the predominant approach for feminists, although it used to be. While this dichotomy may be notable because of its historical influence, it is even more important to examine because theorists working within this paradigm are compelled to place embodiment—including individual, sensory experiences and gender identity—on the side of either materiality or social construction. This has led to troubling attitudes about embodiment and even more problematic claims about transgender.

In 1979, Janice Raymond accused trans women of two things: (1) succumbing to patriarchal culture in their desire to become women, and (2) raping cisgender women by infiltrating their minds and safe spaces.[9] In order to make the latter claim, Raymond must presume that biological sex is an essential, material quality, and thus, that trans women are necessarily male. Only then can Raymond claim that trans women are capable of raping cisgender women. But to make the former claim, Raymond must also presume the social construction of gender, and further, that this social construction is the source of women's oppression. Any insistence that gender is experienced as "real"—which Raymond understands trans people to do—therefore challenges the understanding of gender as socially constructed. In Raymond's mind, then, trans people undermine the feminist project of fighting against women's oppression by claiming that gender is somehow a material reality. Raymond's condemnation of trans people is thus a two-pronged attack that relies upon both sides of the sex/gender dichotomy, and trans people appear either deceptive (knowing that gender is socially constructed but denying this fact) or deceived (believing that socially constructed gender is real).[10]

Raymond's position also reveals the limitations of this dichotomy with regard to embodiment. Embodiment includes the sensed feeling of one's gender, but this sensed feeling can only be understood as either material sex or social construction within the paradigm of sex/gender. Any sense of gender identity that does not align with material sex will challenge its link to materiality, however, and any sense of gender that exceeds how gender is institutionally or linguistically constructed will call the construction of gender into question. When some trans people insist that the sense of their gender does not align with their material sex, their sensed embodiment can be perceived to cut through the borders of materiality and social construction. The dichotomy of sex/gender does not allow for sensed feelings of gender and embodiment that might lie outside the division of matter and social construction, and any claims to the contrary appear to attack not only this paradigm but also the feminist projects that rest upon it. Trans persons whose experiences do not align with a sex/gender divide[11] are therefore vilified as furthering the oppression of women, and descriptions of their sensed embodiment are reworked to support the paradigm of sex/

gender, effacing any authority those trans people might have to describe their own experiences. For this reason, the paradigm of sex/gender is incapable of properly addressing the diversity of transgender embodiment—and the diversity of embodiment in general. Worse, it provides theoretical justification for those who oppose transgender rights, even today.

Raymond's position continues to be reflected in work by trans-exclusionary radical feminists[12] such as Sheila Jeffreys. In *Gender Hurts*—published by Routledge in 2014[13]—Jeffreys praises Raymond's work as "groundbreaking," while lamenting the "almost complete absence of feminist critical work" on the topic of "transgenderism."[14] Similar to Raymond, Jeffreys argues that "transgenderism" is a threat to feminist projects because it reifies patriarchal gender stereotypes.[15] Gender stereotypes can only be reified, though, if they are understood as socially constructed, and as opposed to a material sex, and thus Jeffreys, too, relies upon the sex/gender dichotomy for her position.[16] Julie Bindel, another trans-exclusionary radical feminist, follows a similar line of thinking: Trans women are impostors because of their material male sex, and trans men are women who have betrayed the cause of feminism. Bindel famously concludes a 2004 article by saying, "I don't have a problem with men disposing of their genitals, but it does not make them women, in the same way that shoving a bit of vacuum hose down your 501s does not make you a man."[17] For trans-exclusionary radical feminists such as Jeffreys and Bindel, the paradigm of sex/gender is fundamental to their condemnation of transgender, and any possibility for an embodied sense of gender beyond this dichotomy is excluded.

Sandy Stone was explicitly mentioned by Raymond as an example of a trans woman who exerted male privilege in cisgender women's spaces,[18] and in her response, Stone points to the limitations of the sex/gender paradigm. Stone describes the diversity of gender experience while also indicating the gender narratives that limit or exclude trans voices. Given the absence of trans voices in theories about transgender, Stone suggests the development of a "counterdiscourse": "Rather, we can seize upon the textual violence inscribed in the transsexual body and turn it into a reconstructive force."[19] Stone refers to Judith Butler's descriptions of butch/femme relations that reveal many more layers than simply an assimilation of heterosexual culture. For Stone, transgender embodiment displays multiple layers that go beyond any sex or gender binary. She points out, "We need a deeper analytical language for transsexual theory, one which allows for the sorts of ambiguities and polyvocalities which have already so productively informed and enriched feminist theory."[20] In this way, Stone's "Posttranssexual Manifesto" is more than just a response to Raymond. Rather, it provides an argument for gender paradigms that reflect the ambiguity and diversity of gendered embodiment.

Stone employs the language of queer theory in her article. She explicitly cites Judith Butler, and her call for "counterdiscourses" is a move clearly influenced by queer gender theory. Within queer approaches, materiality is itself discursive, performative, and/or socially constructed. While these factors are not exactly the same, I will address them generally under the term "queer," based upon three major shared presumptions: (a) their rejection of our access to a material body, (b) their emphasis on the discourses surrounding both sex and gender, and (c) their understanding that sex and gender only appear material through the discourses that present them as such. But while this new movement addresses certain weaknesses of the sex/gender paradigm, it subsumes embodiment entirely into the discursive realm.

Queer Approaches to Sex and Gender[21]

As seen in Stone's response to Raymond, queer theory allows scholars to analyze gendered embodiment through multiple discourses. "Queer" reflects the fluidity of gender, the many influences in play in how gender is experienced, and the ways in which gender embraces the contradictions, paradoxes, infiltrations, and blendings of gendered meanings. For this reason, queer theory is an extremely important approach within trans studies, and many trans theorists identify as queer and/or adopt queer positions when carrying out their projects. However, in spite of its advantages, the queer paradigm also has two major limitations.

First, queer approaches usually argue that materiality is itself only discursive. Materiality is a notion that leads us to believe that actual matter underlies it. The position that materiality is purely discursive, in itself, may not necessarily be a problem, and the arguments offered are quite convincing. However, sensed embodiment, because of its traditional link with materiality, is usually lumped in with it. Any individual or embodied senses of gender are thus only understood within the context of discourses about materiality rather than on their own ground. And this is where the problem arises: By denying embodiment its own ground, queer approaches tend to deny or minimize the authority from which I can speak about my sensory, embodied experiences. These experiences are understood as merely one discourse among many, or more commonly, they are merely reflections of dominant discourses about my embodiment. This lack of authority is especially detrimental for trans people, whose authority has already been dismissed by medical and psychological approaches to gender: When some trans people point to the "reality" or "materiality" of their embodied experiences, they appear naïve or misguided from a queer perspective, and their claims are treated as such. But in many cases of trans scholarship, the reference to "materiality" or "reality" could be a reference to sensed embodiment on its own ground. As Jay Prosser points out,

> There is much about transsexuality that must remain irreconcilable to queer: the specificity of transsexual experience; the importance of the flesh to self; the difference between sex and gender identity; the desire to pass as "really-gendered" in the world without trouble; perhaps above all […] a particular experience of the body that can't simply transcend (or transubstantiate) the literal.[22]

But while an argument in favor of material existence for itself may result in inconsistencies (and Prosser admits this in a later work[23]), the sensory foundation for embodiment is left unaddressed. Thus, queer approaches both exclude the possibility of sensory, embodied experiences arising from their own ground and undermine the authority of those trans persons who speak about a material, "real," or sensory basis to their gender and embodiment.

Second, a queer understanding of gender tends toward a conceptual understanding that excludes economic, class, or racial situations. As Viviane Namaste argues, the fact that many trans women are prostitutes is excluded from queer analyses. But this work is required for many trans women to live as women. "It is in and through work that the gender of transsexual women is constituted. […] Labor is a missing category of contemporary Anglo-American feminist theory."[24] Namaste also points out that prostitution is a labor that falls upon many trans women of color who are lower class. Economic and racial factors, simply put, are integral to how many trans people live their gender. By leaving these components out of their analyses, queer theorists exclude essential aspects of gender. So, when queer analyses employ a distilled version of "the" transgender person as an example of gender theory, or when they cite trans autobiographies as examples, they not only fail to consider crucial components that are integral to transgender, but also run the risk of failing to represent gender properly. In addition, Namaste demonstrates that abstract analyses of gender carried out by cisgender theorists benefit those theorists with recognition and possible promotion, but they do not benefit the trans persons who act as examples for their theories. "Although Anglo-American feminist theory has focused on transvestites and transsexual women for nearly twenty years now, it is clear that the knowledge gained has been of little benefit to transsexual women ourselves."[25] Thus, there are several consequences to queer approaches to gender: First, transgender individuals are employed as case studies without being in a position to share in the analyses and contribute their own input, and their authority is denied. Second, the sensory feelings that can be fundamental to our embodied sense of gender are either rejected or subsumed as mere discourse, eliminating the possibility of embodiment on its own ground. Third, the concrete, lived situations that are essential to gender are avoided, missing crucial aspects of transgender lives and leading to skewed analyses of gender. And finally, while academic analyses of gender may further the careers of the cisgender theorists who carry them out, they do nothing to serve the trans people who are engaged as examples of the theory. Thus, in addition to drawing relatively narrow (and thereby possibly inaccurate) conclusions, queer theoretical approaches to gender can indirectly cause harm—even without the intention to do so.[26]

Two classic examples of queer gender theorists who employ transgender as paradigms to prove their theories—criticized repeatedly in trans scholarship—are Marjorie Garber and Bernice Hausman. Garber argues that transgender experience demonstrates the social construction of gender (and implicitly, sex): "The phenomenon of transsexualism is both a confirmation of the constructedness of gender and a secondary recourse to essentialism—or, to put it a slightly different way, transsexualism demonstrates that essentialism *is* cultural construction."[27] According to Garber, transsexuals resort to gender essentialism while they are themselves living proof of gender construction. Within the queer paradigm, the move to argue that matter is socially constructed necessitates that any and all claims about the body must be understood as socially constructed. Given this, descriptions by trans people about their gender, and especially those who claim that they "are" a specific gender, must be understood through the lens of social construction.[28]

References to sensory embodiment are ignored or understood only through discourse, and concrete lived aspects of gender, such as race and class, are left out of consideration.

Bernice Hausman turns to medical and psychological discourses in order to argue that "transsexualism necessarily depends upon a relation to developing medical discourses and practices."[29] In order to support her position, Hausman intentionally reads trans authors against themselves: "[T]he story told in this chapter is an attempt to subvert the official story put forth by transsexual autobiographers."[30] While Hausman also reads official medical statements about transgender through a "subversive retelling," she neglects to attend to the fact that transgender voices are already filtered through the medical and psychological descriptions of their "cases." By carrying out a subversive reading of trans autobiographies in turn, she contributes to a history of adapting descriptions offered by trans writers to serve particular theories.[31] Even worse, she implies that transsexuals are themselves incapable of carrying out critical readings of gender because of their "gender confusion." As Prosser points out,

> Whereas the gender-confused use transsexual autobiography to verify their gender confusion, critical readers (presumably having no gender confusion to verify) apparently get to see through the internal problematics of these texts: as if transsexuals were not critical thinkers and readers; indeed, as if one couldn't be a transsexual and a critic at the same time.[32]

Trans subjects thus experience yet another erasure that rides upon the heels of their erasure within medical and psychological discourse.[33]

More recently, Gayle Salamon argues for the social construction of gender through analyses of descriptions given by trans men. Like Garber and Hausman, Salamon has no wish to vilify trans men, and in fact, she is sympathetic to many of the struggles they face. However, she reads the descriptions of sensory embodiment offered by trans men primarily in her effort to prove her theory that material embodiment—including all embodied sensory experience—is socially constructed. Thus, whether she is reading with or against the trans men whom she cites (given that some trans men understand their embodiment through social construction and others do not), she insists that their claims regarding their embodied sense of gender can only be evidence for the social construction of gender. "Intersex people and transpeople demonstrate that sex is assigned rather than discovered, [...] and thus offer a challenge to the notion that gender may travel, but sex is firm ground."[34] Salamon's argument is interesting, however, in that she takes great pains to demonstrate that sensory embodiment, including any "inner" sense of gender identity, must be socially constructed. Embodiment, according to Salamon, *cannot* stand on its own ground, because it is necessarily discursive. "Were bodily feeling able to deliver a certainty about either the body or the identity of the self apart from the body, it would be able to do so only *because it is structured like language.*"[35] While this is not the place to engage her arguments in detail,[36] it is important to note that, by relegating all sensory embodiment to social construction, Salamon undermines the authority of trans people to speak of any embodied experiences that appear in excess of social constructs: "It would seem problematic to suggest that such a subject possesses an absolute agency to determine his or her gender identity if the conviction about that identity hinges on a feeling that is impossible to resist and compels submission rather than conferring any sort of mastery."[37] Salamon, like many queer theorists, appears to be haunted by the dichotomy of sex/gender, so, once matter is found problematic, the only other option must be social construction.

Thus, we find two important aspects of gender—individual, sensory embodiment and the concrete, material conditions that are integral to gender—denied in many queer analyses of gender, and especially those that employ transgender as an example. Nevertheless, because it recognizes the pervasiveness of discourse in our experiences, and because it allows for the diversity of gender experience, queer theory remains an important paradigm for analyses of gender and transgender—and it is a paradigm that is often employed in trans studies. But further methods are needed that can reflect the aspects that are refused by queer approaches, and thus we turn now to phenomenology.

The Phenomenological Method

One of the primary advantages of phenomenology is that it demonstrates how different types of objects appear. Physical things appear under different conditions than numbers. This is due to the fact that physical things follow different necessary laws than numbers do. According to Edmund Husserl, these are two distinct "regions" of objects. The paradigm of sex/gender works with two regions of objects—the material and the socially constructed—and the attempt to negotiate embodiment between two separate regions is one reason why this paradigm faces so much difficulty. The queer paradigm shifts everything to a single region, broadly understood, that of discourse or social construction. This makes the position of queer theory much more effective in its work to address the narratives that determine gender in various ways. But the limitation of queer theory arises from its strength: While circumscribing its scope of objects within only one region (that of discourse), it may achieve internal coherence, but it is also challenged by anything that might exceed the discursive realm. By definition, queer theory must deny or subsume anything that appears to exceed discourse. From a phenomenological perspective, however, the material and the discursive are not the only two possible regions. According to Husserl, the sensory body has its own essential laws. Sensory experiences do not necessarily have causal relations between each other the way material objects (such as billiard balls) do, even if the material aspect of the body is subject to causal laws. Pain can lead to despair, or it can lead to desire; there is more than just mechanical determination between a pain and what follows from it. Sensory experiences also do not simply follow linguistic structure, even if consciousness is always directed toward meaning. Sensations have their own motivation regardless of grammatical structures, so feelings can arise that surprise us, feelings for which we have no names. Sensory embodiment is its own ground of experience, one that—as has become apparent in the prior sections—can be important in light of gender theory and transgender existence.

But phenomenology also has its limitations. While the phenomenological method is not one that simply generalizes from a particular experience, it does examine an individual experience in order to determine the essential structures that enable it to appear. So, if I am doing phenomenology properly, I will not take my personal experiences and impose them upon other people; I will only understand that the essential conditions (such as temporal flow) that enable my own experience should be the same conditions for any other, similar experience. But this focus upon individual experience and essential structures can draw my attention away from the importance of narratives and social discourses to my embodied experiences. It can also lead me to focus on myself if I am not careful. For this reason, I have argued elsewhere that Husserl's phenomenology would benefit by being coupled with queer theory (and vice versa) in order to address issues of embodiment and gender more completely.[38]

But I am not the first to have made this suggestion: In 1998, Henry Rubin already questioned whether some queer methods do not further erase transgender voices. By dismantling subjectivity in general, Rubin argues, queer approaches tend to appropriate or gloss over transgender subject positions. Thus, Rubin recommends coupling "discourse analysis" with a phenomenological approach:

> Discursive genealogy can historicize phenomenological accounts, while phenomenology can insert an embodied agent-in-progress into genealogical accounts. I have come to believe that phenomenology and genealogy are complementary methods that augment one another's strengths.[39]

Rubin argues that a phenomenological approach, which acknowledges the importance of first-person experience to theoretical analyses of embodied and gender experience, can provide an effective counterbalance to "discursive genealogy" or queer theory. At the same time, an approach that attends to discursive and historical relations can offset any privileging of the self that ignores social, cultural, linguistic, and institutional relations—the latter being a possible danger of the phenomenological approach.[40] For this reason, combining queer theory with phenomenology becomes appropriate, if not even necessary, for transgender theory. By coupling two methods with one another, Rubin suggests, we can counteract the negative side effects that each one tends toward individually.

Gayle Salamon also points to phenomenology as an important method for transgender studies. She argues that, in phenomenology, "gender and sex can be understood as delivered to the subject through a felt sense rather than determined by the external contours of the body, thus circumventing a view of sex or gender that understands either to be a matter of bodily morphology as given."[41] In this way, Salamon acknowledges the importance of a felt sense of embodiment that is reducible to neither matter nor mind. In fact, elsewhere, Salamon turns to Merleau-Ponty's notion of "flesh" as an apt description of embodiment. Flesh is neither matter nor mind, but partakes in both, and yet it is somehow also more than the sum of the two. For Salamon, this description applies to trans embodiment as well: "Merleau-Ponty's description of flesh sounds in several crucial aspects like a description of transgenderism or transsexuality: a region of being in which the subject is not quite unitary and not quite the combination of two different things."[42] But because Salamon defines matter itself as socially constructed, her understanding of "flesh" as "between" matter and mind ultimately places flesh and our felt sense of embodiment on the side of "mind" and social construction.[43] In this way, Salamon employs the "flesh" of trans embodiment as evidence for her argument that embodiment and gender are socially constructed (discussed above). Nevertheless, Salamon describes Merleau-Ponty as especially useful for trans studies, and points to other phenomenologists such as Heidegger, de Beauvoir, Levinas, Fanon, and "even Husserl" as useful for trans studies.[44]

In some of my own work, I integrate phenomenology with trans studies, but my approach has not been unproblematic, either. In 2014, I argued that Husserl's notion of *Leib* establishes a ground of sensed embodiment distinct from either the material or socially constructed aspects of the body. Unfortunately, I made this argument in the hopes that this terminology would be useful for "the" intersex person and "the" transsexual. In this sense, I was committing the same errors that I criticize above, employing transgender (and intersex) as paradigms for gender theorizing, and lumping a variety of experiences under these umbrella terms. I regret having made those errors—errors that reflect my own blind spots as a cisgender woman. Nevertheless, I find that Husserl's notion of *Leib* and Merleau-Ponty's "flesh" both refer to an experiential realm that cannot be reduced to either matter or discourse. While embodiment is clearly informed by both its materiality (muscles, bones, hormones, cells, synapses, chromosomes, etc.) and discourse (history, social traditions, institutions, beliefs, language, etc.), it also arises from its own basis through pain, pleasure, tension, excitement, and other sensations that may or may not resonate with its material and discursive components. When I sense my body to be in conflict with the discourse about it, or when my embodied experiences do not appear within discourse—but they do appear to me—then the *Leib* becomes recognizable as its own structure. Thus, embodiment can be seen as a distinct ground of experience, one that is important for gender theory as well as for trans studies.

While phenomenology can be extremely useful for trans studies, as well as for feminist theorizing of gender and embodiment, it is not the only method appropriate for gender studies—nor should it be. As Rubin made clear, phenomenology works best when combined with queer theory so that each corrects the other's imbalances. But trans theorists often engage more than one approach in ways that both combine and transform our understanding of gender.

Trans/Feminisms

The notion of "transfeminism" is not new, and it incorporates a variety of ways in which trans scholarship and feminism can be associated with one another.[45] Of note is the employment of "intersectionality" in much transfeminist work, where the constitution of embodiment and the oppression a person may experience are understood through the multiple ways she appears to herself and to others. As such, transfeminism problematizes both simple identity politics and those positions that present the erasure of identity as an ultimate goal. Identities are lived—and troubled—through how we take them up, but they are also experienced through oppressive forces that regulate, limit, and punish any transgression from the norm or ideal. Thus, transfeminism often challenges feminist positions that work with simple identities without recognition of the multiple and shifting identities and oppressions that intersect in the individuals who live them. But it also contributes to feminist work by clarifying the layers of oppression that intersect through gender, race, culture, ethnicity, ability, etc. Given this, I would like to look, first, at an argument by Viviane Namaste, who employs intersectionality in the style of transfeminism, even though she does not identify herself as transfeminist in this article. Then, I will turn to two articles from a special issue of *TSQ: Transgender Studies Quarterly* entitled "Trans/Feminisms." In doing so, I would like to focus on the following: How trans scholarship engages critically with feminist positions through intersectionality; how trans feminist scholarship often combines approaches in order to provide more nuanced analyses of gender and embodiment; and how embodiment appears through these combined approaches.

Viviane Namaste's position is quite critical of contemporary feminist approaches to gender, as indicated earlier. But she also offers a provisional set of principles that could yield more productive analyses as well as serve the populations being studied. She suggests that feminist theorists employ a more empirical approach, one that attends to the details surrounding a situation, in order to offset the narrow focus often taken in abstract analyses of gender. In addition to this, she points to relevance, equity of community participation, and ownership as key to studies of indigenous communities that do not appropriate or colonize those communities or their knowledges. Such principles, she argues, ought to be employed by feminist theorists as well:

An insistence on empirical approaches to theory, and the integration of principles of relevance, equity in participation, and ownership would radically transform the production of academic feminist knowledge in the Anglo-American world. [...] If people are marginalized in and through the production of knowledge, then a truly transformative intellectual practice would collaborate with such individuals and communities to ensure that their political and intellectual priorities are addressed.[46]

In this way, Namaste suggests combining both empirical and community-based anthropological approaches with feminist analyses of gender. Only by integrating these different approaches into one another can we alleviate some of the problems arising from abstract gender paradigms. In addition, her critique of Anglo-American feminism is precisely that it lacks acknowledgment of the intersections of gender, race, economics, knowledge, health issues, and so on that are essential to transgender embodiment. Feminism must correct this error by recognizing the many shifting identities in play in the embodiment of gender, and it can do so through combining approaches from other disciplines with its own gender analyses.

In 2016 (partially in response to Jeffreys' *Gender Hurts*), *TSQ: Transgender Studies Quarterly* published a special issue entitled "Trans/Feminisms." The guest editors "mark the trans/feminist relation with a slash, which signals both the connections and disjunctions between these two categories. The expansive collection of articles [...] revisit, reframe, interrogate, unpack, upend, and confound expectations for both terms."[47] Reese simpkins' "Trans*feminist Intersections," for example, discusses intersectional and material becoming, as well as their political expressions. Although simpkins' approach is very much in line with queer presumptions, where materiality is understood through discursive identity, he argues for a "material dynamism" that reflects our shifting identities and how they integrate with our changing contexts of marginalization and privilege: "A trans*feminist politics of becoming is based on this dynamic materiality in which identities, identifications, and subjectivities are produced anew every time they are (re) articulated."[48] Simpkins' "dynamic materiality" reflects the shifting of our identities that arise from material embodiment and how that embodiment is marked within differing events and power regimes. While simpkins' discussion remains quite abstract, and thus could fall under critiques such as Namaste's, his argument demonstrates a more nuanced understanding of "materiality." "Dynamic materiality" is more than simple, concrete matter, and thus, it might be open to reflecting sensed embodiment as well as lived situations.

Micha Cárdenas' "Pregnancy: Reproductive Futures in Trans of Color Feminism" challenges not only white and women-of-color feminism, but also queer theory. Each of these positions misses the specific experience of trans women of color—an intersection of multiple oppressions that has its own specificity:

> While I once thought taking hormones was a good experiment
> an ethico-aesthetic experimental life act in the spirit of Delueze and Guattari,
> now I realize what a masculinist, colonialist dream that was.[49]

Feminist and queer theoretical approaches, argues Cárdenas, have neglected the importance of reproduction to trans women of color. Cárdenas speaks not only about the political or discursive aspects of her experience, although these are important; rather, she also describes her embodiment when she is taking estrogen and then when she stops, and both embodiments are presented within the context of her desire to reproduce:

> Now, after so many years of taking them,
> I realize that in these pills there is a home for me, these pills, and all the changes they've brought to my body and life,
> have brought me to a place of commitment to building a home and a family.[50]

Cárdenas' pregnancy is the recognition of life in the millions of sperms she is able to "bank," but in order to do so, she must return to a male body, one filled with testosterone, growing black hairs in her cleavage, enduring mood swings, food cravings, and changes in the shape and texture of her body. The sensory ground of her embodiment is essential to her gender, even as her embodiment and gender shift through and between traditional gender lines. Sensory embodiment—and gender—are clearly not stable elements. In other words, referring to sensory embodiment is a reference to a ground of experience, but as such, that ground can be shifting and changing.

Trans scholarship that focuses on trans experience and the philosophical issues that arise from it, and transfeminist scholarship that employs an intersectional approach to critiques of identity as well as new analyses of gender, therefore, continue to bring embodied experience to theories of gender in new ways—beyond a simple presumption of material sex, beyond reference to ideal notions of a gender binary, and also beyond the social construction of gender. Without denying the importance of any of these aspects of gender, trans and transfeminist scholars also point to concrete embodiment as an intersection of many levels of experience. In doing so, they often combine a variety of methods in order to offset the problematic presumptions that can be the driving force behind any one theory. And, in fact, trans scholarship also examines its own presumptions. As Paisley Currah notes, "Indeed, we may have reached the point at which the transgender-cisgender binary [...], the grid of intelligibility that has recently come to dominate much trans studies and advocacy, now may obscure more than it reveals."[51] Given the malleability of embodied experiences and our lived situations, then, even the division between trans- and cisgender must ultimately be challenged. Nevertheless, we cannot lose our ground, whether that ground is one of personal experience or empirical facts, of situational limitations or sensory embodiment.

Acknowledgment I would like to thank the editors of this volume for inviting me to contribute this chapter, as well as for their helpful and detailed feedback through several revisions. Many thanks also to the anonymous reviewers who helped me gain an insight into my own goals for this chapter. Finally, thanks to my father, who played with my son for hours while I worked on a final draft.

Notes

1. "Cisgender" is a term that refers to gendered embodiments where one's gender assigned at birth correlates with how one lives and experiences one's gender. Here, it also serves as an indicator of the position of privilege held by those who experience their gendered embodiment in a way that is normatively accepted.
2. See Susan Stryker and Talia M. Bettcher, "Introduction: Trans/feminisms," *TSQ: Transgender Studies Quarterly*, Vol. 3, No. 1–2 (2016), 6.
3. Rebecca Tuvel, "In Defense of Transracialism," *Hypatia*, Vol. 32, Issue 2 (Spring 2017), 263–278. I hesitate to mention Tuvel's article here, as the issues surrounding its publication were much bigger than any problems within the article itself. Nevertheless, Tuvel's article reflects some of the errors I have made in the past, which I discuss later in this chapter.
4. Although race will be indicated as an important aspect of trans embodiment, I will be unable to address racial embodiment explicitly given the limitations of this chapter.

5. Along the same lines of these reflections, Sarah Ahmed writes of "affinity" as a way to analyze transphobia while also acknowledging her position of cis privilege. Sara Ahmed, "An Affinity of Hammers," *TSQ: Transgender Studies Quarterly*, Vol. 3, No. 1–2 (2016), 22–34.
6. This list of paradigms is certainly not exclusive. Psychoanalysis, for example, is another extremely important paradigm that has been employed to describe transgender, and it has also been taken up by feminists and trans scholars, both critically and affirmatively. Given the limitations of this article, I am unable to address it here.
7. Embodiment can be understood in many ways, but it especially focuses upon the sensory feeling of being in one's body. Here, sensory feeling goes beyond the traditional "five senses," including also bodily form and movement (proprioception), inner feelings (such as tension, excitement, or exhaustion), and surface feelings on the skin as an interface between the world and myself. In addition, I am including concrete lived situations, such as the economic, health, and racial factors addressed by Viviane Namaste (2000, 2009), as important layers of embodiment and gender.
8. Although they are not equivalent, I will be using the terms "paradigm," "method," and "approach" somewhat interchangeably in this chapter.
9. Janice G. Raymond, *The Transsexual Empire: The Making of the She-Male*. (Boston: Beacon Press, 1979), 99 and 104.
10. Raymond's argument also includes a more subtle claim that trans women cannot claim (or re-claim) the name of women because they have not experienced a life of sexual oppression as women. This argument is based less upon material embodiment than upon the importance of a personal history of sexist oppression. By this analysis, Raymond allows for intersex persons who were raised as girls to claim the name of women, but excludes trans women who grew up as boys. Raymond, *Transsexual Empire*, 114–116. See also Talia Mae Bettcher's analysis in "Intersexuality, Transgender, and Transsexuality," *The Oxford Handbook of Feminist Theory*. (Oxford University Press, 2016), 411–12. However, while this move troubles Raymond's reliance upon a material basis for her claims—indeed, she later re-emphasizes the essential material grounds of her argument—it ultimately reifies history in a sense similar to her understanding of the material or biological grounds to sex.
11. This is not to say that no trans people experience their embodiment as evidence of a sex/gender divide. Indeed, some trans people understand gender identity as similar to—if not related to—a biological grounding, while how gender is expressed remains culturally constructed. However, many descriptions offered by trans people also challenge the dichotomy of sex/gender, and this is my focus here. I might also note that, if gender identity is materially grounded, then the conflict between birth anatomy and gender

identity reveals a materiality that is, at the very least, paradoxical. Given this, the notion of materiality as a simple and obvious density becomes problematized, challenging the sex/gender divide in yet another way.
12. Cristan Williams provides a compelling description of some events in the history of radical feminism, demonstrating that not all radical feminists are trans-exclusionary, and in fact, that early radical feminists actually defended trans women from attacks. Cristan Williams, "Radical Inclusion: Recounting the Trans Inclusive History of Radical Feminism," *TSQ: Transgender Studies Quarterly*, Vol. 3, No. 1–2 (2016): 254–8.
13. It would be worthwhile to reflect upon how Jeffreys' manuscript passed through the review process at such a notable press as Routledge. Given the limitations of this chapter, I cannot do so here.
14. Sheila Jeffreys, *Gender Hurts: A Feminist Analysis of the Politics of Transgenderism* (London and New York: Routledge, 2014), 11.
15. She even goes so far as to compare "transgenderism" and "the transgendering of children" with eugenics. Jeffreys, *Gender Hurts*, 123–141.
16. It is important to note that Jeffreys' book was very critically reviewed by Tim Johnston on *Hypatia Reviews Online*.
17. Published online in *The Guardian*, January 31, 2004.
18. Raymond, *Transsexual Empire*, 101–3.
19. Sandy Stone, "The *Empire* Strikes Back: A Posttranssexual Manifesto," in *The Transgender Studies Reader*, ed. Susan Stryker and Stephen Whittle. (New York and London: Routledge, 2006), 230.
20. Stone, "*Empire* Strikes Back," 231.
21. I must note that queer theory is an approach that problematizes the very notion of paradigms or methods understood in any strict sense.
22. Jay Prosser, *Second Skins: The Body Narratives of Transsexuality* (New York: Columbia University Press, 1998), 59.
23. Jay Prosser, *Light in the Dark Room: Photography and Loss* (Minneapolis: University of Minneapolis Press, 2004), 163–181.
24. Viviane Namaste, "Undoing Theory: The 'Transgender Question' and the Epistemic Violence of Anglo-American Feminist Theory," *Hypatia* 24/3 "Transgender Studies and Feminism: Theory, Politics, and Gendered Realities" (2009), 20.
25. Namaste, "Undoing Theory," 27.
26. See Prosser (1998, especially pp. 21–60), Namaste (2000, especially pp. 9–23), and Namaste (2009) for further development of these critiques. I address Namaste's (2009) position more extensively below.
27. Marjorie Garber, *Vested Interests: Cross-Dressing & Cultural Anxiety* (New York and London: Routledge, 1992), 109.
28. Judith Butler has also been criticized for her discussion of transgender people, especially regarding the death of trans prostitute Venus

Extravaganza. See Prosser (1998, 45–50) and Namaste (2000, 13–14). Although Butler presents a relatively more informed view of transgender experience in later texts, her position of the performativity of gender remains problematic for at least some scholars. See Namaste (2009) and Rodemeyer (2018, 64–7).
29. Bernice L. Hausman, *Changing Sex: Transsexualism, Technology, and the Idea of Gender* (Durham and London: Duke University Press, 1995), 4.
30. Hausman, *Changing Sex*, 141.
31. It is interesting to note that Hausman is extensively cited by Jeffreys as support for her position that "transgenderism" is socially constructed.
32. Prosser, *Second Skins*, 132.
33. Hausman explicitly chooses to ignore texts by "marginalized" trans people (such as sex workers), on the basis that they are marginal within the community of trans people and thus do not represent the "official" position of "public transsexuals." In addition to appearing rather circular, Hausman's argument essentially eclipses experiences and individuals that are fundamental aspects of trans experience. (Hausman, *Changing Sex*, 141–2.) Viviane Namaste's response (2009) to such tendencies in feminist theory is discussed below.
34. Gayle Salamon, *Assuming A Body: Transgender and Rhetorics of Materiality* (New York: Columbia University Press, 2010), 190.
35. Salamon, *Assuming a Body*, 83. Emphasis in original.
36. I address Salamon's arguments in much more detail elsewhere (Rodemeyer 2018, 71–6).
37. Salamon, *Assuming a Body*, 83.
38. See Rodemeyer (2017, 2018).
39. Henry S. Rubin, "Phenomenology as Method in Trans Studies," *GLQ: A Journal of Lesbian and Gay Studies* 4:2 (1998), 279.
40. In fact, Rubin's recommendation of a phenomenological approach as a corrective to discourse analysis follows upon his critical assessment of Hausman's *Changing Sex*. Rubin, "Phenomenology as Method," 266.
41. Gayle Salamon, "Phenomenology," *TSQ: Transgender Studies Quarterly*, Vol. 1, No. 1–2 (2014): 154.
42. Salamon, *Assuming a Body*, 65. Salamon reasons in her second chapter that the notion of "flesh" would be quite useful in analyses of gender and trans embodiment, but she never mentions it again in the remainder of her book.
43. Salamon, *Assuming a Body*, 88–93. It is interesting to note that Salamon points to Husserl's phenomenology as pointing beyond matter or the body as "real."
44. Salamon, "Phenomenology," 154–155.
45. A brief review of works that fall under the heading of "transfeminism" is deftly treated in Susan Stryker and Talia M. Bettcher, "Introduction:

Trans/Feminisms," *TSQ: Transgender Studies Quarterly*, Vol. 3, No. 1–2 (2016): 9–12.
46. Namaste, "Undoing Theory," 27.
47. Paisley Currah, "General Editor's Introduction," *TSQ: Transgender Studies Quarterly*, Vol. 3, No. 1–2 (2016): 3.
48. Reese simpkins, "Trans*feminist Intersections," *TSQ: Transgender Studies Quarterly*, Vol. 3, No. 1–2: 233.
49. Micha Cárdenas, "Pregnancy: Reproductive Futures in Trans of Color Feminism," *TSQ: Transgender Studies Quarterly*, Vol. 3, No. 1–2: 51.
50. Micha Cárdenas, "Pregnancy," 51.
51. Currah, "Introduction," 3.

Bibliography

Ahmed, Sara. 2016. An Affinity of Hammers. *TSQ: Transgender Studies Quarterly* 3 (1–2): 22–34.

Bettcher, Talia Mae. 2016. Intersexuality, Transgender, and Transsexuality. In *The Oxford Handbook of Feminist Theory*, 407–427. New York, NY: Oxford University Press.

Bindel, Julie. 2004. Gender Benders, Beware. *The Guardian*, January 30. https://www.theguardian.com/world/2004/jan/31/gender.weekend7. Accessed 6 Mar 2017.

Cárdenas, Micha. 2016. Pregnancy: Reproductive Futures in Trans of Color Feminism. *TSQ: Transgender Studies Quarterly* 3 (1–2): 48–57.

Currah, Paisley. 2016. General Editor's Introduction. *TSQ: Transgender Studies Quarterly* 3 (1–2): 1–4.

Garber, Marjorie. 1992. *Vested Interests: Cross-Dressing & Cultural Anxiety*. New York/London: Routledge.

Hausman, Bernice L. 1995. *Changing Sex: Transsexualism, Technology, and the Idea of Gender*. Durham/London: Duke University Press.

Jeffreys, Sheila. 2014. *Gender Hurts: A Feminist Analysis of the Politics of Transgenderism*. London/New York: Routledge.

Johnston, Tim R. 2014. Review of Gender Hurts: A Feminist Analysis of the Politics of Transgenderism, by Sheila Jeffreys. *Hypatia Reviews Online*. http://hypatiareviews.org/reviews/content/275. Accessed 6 Mar 2017.

Namaste, Viviane. 2000. *Invisible Lives: The Erasure of Transsexual and Transgendered People*. Chicago/London: The University of Chicago Press.

———. 2009. Undoing Theory: The 'Transgender Question' and the Epistemic Violence of Anglo-American Feminist Theory. *Hypatia* 24 (3): 11–32.

"Transgender Studies and Feminism: Theory, Politics, and Gendered Realities."

Prosser, Jay. 1998. *Second Skins: The Body Narratives of Transsexuality*. New York: Columbia University Press.

———. 2004. *Light in the Dark Room: Photography and Loss*. Minneapolis: University of Minneapolis Press.
Raymond, Janice G. 1979. *The Transsexual Empire: The Making of the She-Male*. Boston: Beacon Press.
Rodemeyer, Lanei. 2014. Feminism, Phenomenology, and Hormones. In *Feminist Phenomenology and Medicine*, ed. Kristin Zeiler and Lisa Käll. Albany: SUNY Press.
———. 2017. Husserl and Queer Theory. *Continental Philosophy Review* 50 (3): 311–334.
———. 2018. *Lou Sullivan Diaries (1970–1980) and Theories of Sexual Embodiment: Making Sense of Sensing*. Cham: Springer.
Rubin, Henry S. 1998. Phenomenology as Method in Trans Studies. *GLQ: A Journal of Lesbian and Gay Studies* 4 (2): 263–281.
Salamon, Gayle. 2010. *Assuming A Body: Transgender and Rhetorics of Materiality*. New York: Columbia University Press.
———. 2014. Phenomenology. *TSQ: Transgender Studies Quarterly* 1 (1–2): 153–155.
Simpkins, Reese. 2016. Trans*feminist Intersections. *TSQ: Transgender Studies Quarterly* 3 (1–2): 228–234.
Stone, Sandy. 2006. The *Empire* Strikes Back: A Posttranssexual Manifesto. In *The Transgender Studies Reader*, ed. Susan Stryker and Stephen Whittle, 221–235. New York/London: Routledge. Originally Published in *Body Guards: The Cultural Politics of Gender Ambiguity*, ed. Julia Epstien and Kristina Straub. New York: Routledge, 1991.
Stryker, Susan. 2006. My Words to Victor Frankenstein Above the Village of Chamounix: Performing Transgender Rage. In *The Transgender Studies Reader*, ed. Susan Stryker and Stephen Whittle, 244–56. New York and London: Routledge. Originally Published in *GLQ: A Journal of Lesbian and Gay Studies* 1(3). Gordon & Breach Science Publishers: 1994.
Stryker, Susan, and Talia M. Bettcher. 2016. Introduction: Trans/Feminisms. *TSQ: Transgender Studies Quarterly* 3 (1–2): 5–14.
Tuvel, Rebecca. 2017. In Defense of Transracialism. *Hypatia* 32 (2): 263–278.
Williams, Cristan. 2016. Radical Inclusion: Recounting the Trans Inclusive History of Radical Feminism. *TSQ: Transgender Studies Quarterly* 3 (1–2): 254–258.

CHAPTER 7

Expressing the World: Merleau-Ponty and Feminist Debates on Nature/Culture

Kathleen Lennon

The relationship between feminism and science has not always been a happy one, not only because women have been so under-represented in that domain, but also because the natural sciences, particularly biology, evolutionary psychology, neurophysiology, and ethology, have been put to work ideologically, to legitimate certain kinds of roles for women and men. These sciences have been, and still are, something of a battleground regarding what constitutes male and female natures. Critiques of such science as ideological made explicit the cultural situatedness of science and its mediation by the social structures and imaginaries in which scientists are placed. Scientific theories, it has been argued, have a contingency which needs recognising.[1] In response, what has been termed *the new materialism* identifies a project of bringing 'the materiality of the human body and the natural world into the forefront of feminist theory and practice,'[2] in the face of, what has been claimed were, overly constructivist accounts emerging from such feminist critiques.[3] I want to place these debates in the context of the more general question of 'what it means to understand human beings as part of nature, and how we can think nature starting from our situation within it,'[4] linking the feminist discussions to

K. Lennon (✉)
University of Hull, Hull, UK

© The Author(s) 2018
C. Fischer, L. Dolezal (eds.), *New Feminist Perspectives on Embodiment*, Breaking Feminist Waves,
https://doi.org/10.1007/978-3-319-72353-2_7

the writings of Merleau-Ponty. I will suggest that the picture which Merleau-Ponty offers, of our bodies expressing the world, undercuts the nature/culture dichotomy and provides a metaphysics which resonates with those feminist writers who themselves resist it.

Culture Constructs Nature

First, it is worth reminding ourselves of the arguments which led feminists to be suspicious of the account of nature as sexed, offered by much biological and related science. Sex difference research has been a thriving area for at least the last 200 years. There are two fundamental assumptions underlying this work. First is the assumption that the binary division of bodies into male and female is part of the biological order of the world. Within this assumption, facts about our biology provide an explanatory grounding for our sexed categories, in a way that makes a division into male and female a recognition of objective facts of nature, which, in some sense, demand attention. Objective here means having a unifying factor which is independent of our practices of classification. I will return to this claim. The second key assumption of much scientific work on sex differences is that the assumed objective division into male and female bodies is accompanied by other differences, associated psychological and behavioural dispositions which have consequent effects on social positionality. The differences picked out are supposed to both causally explain and sometimes justify the differing social positions which men and women typically occupy. For example, it is claimed: 'People with the female brain make the most wonderful counselors, primary school teachers, nurses, carers therapists ... People with the male brain make the most wonderful scientists, engineers ... musicians, architects ... toolmakers.'[5] The defence of sex differences of this kind is given causal anchorage in the hormones and chromosomes which contribute to distinct bodily characteristics and/or evolutionary theory and/or in claimed physical differences in male and female brains. It is sex differences of this psychological and behavioural kind, of course, which feminist writers have been most concerned to contest. And, as Deborah Cameron notes,[6] from the 1990s, a 'steady trickle of books ... about the sex differences of men and women' has developed into 'a raging torrent'; from scientific papers which appear to suggest cognitive or behavioural differences, to popular science books and self-help books designed to aid communication across the presumed gap between men (who are from Mars) and women (who are from Venus), to coin an ubiquitous current usage.

If biological explanations are to be offered for psychological and behavioural differences between men and women, then these differences must themselves be established. Clearly there are, if we look around us, wherever we are, a large number of psychological and behavioural differences between those classified as men and those classified as women. But if these are to be biologically based, then they must not be differences which vary historically or cross culturally. And once we add that restriction, then the characteristics for which we might seek biological explanations become much less and highly contested. The candidates tend to concern differences in aggression, sexual, and nurturing behaviour, and differences in linguistic, spatial, and systematising ability.[7] But a problem with these approaches is the way the categories show such a large area of overlap. Strength endurance, intelligence (however measured), spatial and linguistic abilities, and aggression (however measured) are all such that, even where there seems to be some weighting towards male or female (some men so far have faster marathon times), there are many members of the other category who outperform those in the group to which the trait is supposed to be attached. (Women marathon runners are clearly faster than most men are.) Deborah Cameron and others have discussed the claim that women have higher communication skills and men greater systematising ones, which are fundamental to Baron-Cohen's work.[8] It is quite unclear here how both sets of skills are to be defined. What counts as systematisation or communication? Context inflects what we are prepared to count as each. Moreover, whatever definitions we adopt, we find that the supposed differences are numerically very small: '[I]n almost every case the overall difference made by gender is either small or close to zero.'[9] What is much more significant than differences between women and men are differences within the category women and within the category men— together with large areas of overlap across the sexed categories. In the face of this, feminists have explained the constant stream of work attempting to establish such differences as being a result of a cultural obsession with sex differences.

Perhaps the most telling objections to many of these attempts to anchor behavioural sex differences in biology comes from biologists themselves, many of them feminist. They contest *the model of biological mechanisms* found within much work in evolutionary psychology and the discussions concerning male and female brains. As Fine points out: 'For decades brain development has been thought of as an orderly adding in of new wiring that enables you to perform ever more sophisticated cognitive functions...But our brains, as we are now coming to understand are changed by our behaviour, our thinking, our social world.'[10] Biologist Ruth Bleier encourages us 'to view biology as potential, as capacity ... Biology itself ... develops in interaction with and response to ... our environment.'[11] The *plasticity of the brain* means not only that it is reorganised in response to stimuli, but also that the same function can be taken over by different parts of it. Anne Fausto-Sterling points out 'organisms-human and otherwise-are active processes ... material anatomic connections in the brain respond to external influences ... environment and body co produce behavior and ... it is inappropriate to try to make one component prior to the other.'[12] The picture which such biologists are offering us is not one in which the brain is irrelevant to how we behave, but one in which it is itself open to modification and development. It is not a picture in which pre-given male and female patterns of response are hardwired into brains in a way that was selectively adaptive in our pre-history.

The insight that science is inflected with culture has been applied not only to the research into psychological and behavioural sex differences, but also to the claim that the sexed binary itself is an objective and necessary biological fact. But on this issue there has been much less agreement between the feminist writers interrogating the biological accounts. For many writers, the sexed kinds 'male' and 'female' are biological kinds, reflecting a naturally occurring grouping of properties, which have important causal effects, particularly within the biology of reproduction. Alison Stone, for example, accepts that the biology of sex difference is messy. The several distinct biological markers of maleness and femaleness—visible morphology, hormones, and chromosomes—are not always found together, a point we will return to below. But nonetheless, she claims, there is a natural division anchored in the key characteristic, namely 'the ability to make a distinctive contribution to reproduction i.e. for females, to gestate, give birth to and breast feed babies.'[13]

However, suggestions that such a binary framework is not necessary, but contingent, have also come from several sources. Attention to the genealogy of particular scientific theories, for example, the theories of sex hormones,[14] has shown that their emergence rested not only on gendered cultural assumptions, but also on contingencies such as the availability of urine from gynaecological clinics or mares' urine from stables, enabling the production and investigation of the so-called female sex hormone. Nelly Oudshoorn pointed out that as work progressed, the original assumption that each sex was governed by its own hormones gave way to the recognition that 'male' and 'female' hormones are present in both sexes. Here, was a possibility for dualistic notions of male and female to be abandoned, and a variety of sexed positions to be introduced. Given the cultural context, however, traditional classifications prevailed, yielding a theoretical framework within which the hormones were viewed as working in distinct ways to produce two discreet categories.

Such critical work was reinforced by biologists, who make clear that the several distinct biological markers of maleness and femaleness—visible morphology, hormones, and chromosomes—are not always found together. Biologist Anne Fausto-Sterling[15] has drawn attention to the fact that bodies which possess the usual male (XY) or female (XX) chromosomal make-up can have a variety of external genitalia and secondary sex characteristics. Anne Fausto-Sterling's work identifies at least five possible classificatory types suggested by different patterns of biological clustering.[16] Were we interested in classifying in relation to fitness for reproduction, this wider range of categories would seem to serve this purpose more accurately. Some clusters facilitate reproduction and some do not. There will be bodies fit for reproduction which contribute to the process in one way. There will be bodies fit for reproduction which contribute to it in another way. Then there will be bodies that are not fit for reproduction and do not fit into either of these categories. What does seem clear is that a classification in terms of possession of properties causally relevant to reproduction does not map neatly onto our everyday binary classification into male and female. This is not to reject the contribution to be made by biological science, but to suggest that the evidence it produces has been systematised in ways that reflect pre-established social binaries.

This point has been most famously argued by Judith Butler,[17] who claims that our cultural attachments to masculinity and femininity, as a division of social and behavioural characteristics tied to heterosexuality, have conditioned our mode of interpreting the biological data. 'There is no recourse to a body that has not already been interpreted by cultural meanings,' she claims, 'hence sex could not qualify as a pre-discursive anatomical facticity.'[18] We view biological factors as requiring a binary division into two sexes because of a performatively constructed binary gender to which heterosexuality is central. It is 'the epistemic regime of presumptive heterosexuality,'[19] she says, which structures the understanding of biology. What we count as nature, all these accounts conclude, is constructed in terms of our cultural presuppositions.

What If Culture Was Really Nature All Along?[20]

The arguments discussed above, both those concerning psychological and behavioural sex differences, and those concerning the sexed binary itself, all work in one direction, the perspective that culture mediates what we count as nature. As Gill Jagger points out: 'These studies help to make evident the boundary articulations and exclusions involved in the constitution of sexed identity and ... reveal the role of cultural constructions of sexual difference.'[21] It is into that context that arguments, now identified under the term *new materialism*,[22] emerged to argue, in a contrary direction, that 'culture' is not something that can float free of, be unconstrained by nature. These materialist writers claim that, in stressing the role of culture in constituting our accounts of reality, as the above arguments have done, the material itself has lost agency. To correct such a deficit, what is stressed instead is that, although culture 'structures how we apprehend the ontological, it doesn't constitute it.'[23] Instead, culture itself is viewed as anchored in, interwoven with nature. Nature is viewed as something which itself *is an agent* in the formation of culture. There is a world that shapes and constrains our knowledge, even though, such new materialist writing accepts, we cannot get at that world in an unmediated way. Such a focus is linked to a renewed interest in biological accounts of the body. There is a general thought here that it is one thing to show that biology does not solely determine behavioural and psychological dispositions, but it is going too far to make biology *irrelevant* to sexed embodiment.[24] Surely, it might be thought, there are facts about my body which bear *some relation to* my identity as male or female or intersex or transex? Aren't there some biological features which suggest/ground the cultural distinctions we adopt? For these theorists, this involves rethinking the nature/culture dichotomy to recognise that it is not just that nature and/or matter are products of culture but that culture is also in some sense a product of nature. Indeed, nature is that without which culture wouldn't exist at all.

In some versions of this view, there is a return to prioritising the nature side of the nature/culture dichotomy. Elizabeth Grosz suggests that there is a certain absurdity 'in objecting to the notion of nature, or biology itself, if this is (even in part) what we are and will always be. If we *are* our biologies, then we need a complex and subtle account of that biology if it is to be able to more adequately explain the rich variability of social, cultural and political life ... How does biology-the structure and organisation of living systems—facilitate and make possible cultural existence and social change?'[25] Grosz makes these remarks in the context of a paper exploring the work of Darwin, encouraging us not to be afraid of Darwinian ideas, for these ideas give us 'a dynamic and open ended understanding of the intermingling of history and biology.'[26] Grosz here seems to be stressing the points made by feminist biologists which we have highlighted above, namely the openness of biological processes, their interaction with environmental factors, and the plasticity of our brains in response to them. Nonetheless, she draws some problematic conclusions, which do not seem required by the new materialist motivations. In embracing natural selection, she appears to give it *a foundational explanatory role* so that 'language, culture, intelligence, reason, imagination memory—terms commonly claimed as defining characteristics of the human and the cultural—are all equally effects of the same rigorous criteria of natural selection.'[27] Consequently, natural selection also plays a role with regard to the social relations between men and women. 'Darwin affirms,' she says, 'a fundamental continuity between the natural and social, and the complicity ... of the social with the selective procedures governing the order and organisation of the natural.'[28] Here, we seem not just to have opened a conversation between nature and culture, but to have assumed nature has the originating explanatory role. Moreover, this account privileges a particular account of that nature, evolutionary theory, as providing us with the master narrative.[29] It is one thing to argue that we cannot ignore the contribution which nature itself makes to the terms in which we make sense of it. But to allow for the possibility of constraints is not necessarily to assign a particular biological account a privileged position in articulating the nature of those constraints.

For Grosz, Darwinian evolutionary theory requires 'genetic material from two sexes,'[30] and this she equates with it requiring a binary sexual difference; 'he makes,' she says, 'sexual difference one of the ontological characteristics of life itself.'[31] But here, her work seems to run counter to the feminist biologists we discussed in the previous section. The very openness of biological processes which she herself has stressed, and which is insisted on by biologists such as Anne Fausto-Sterling, seems in conflict with such a position. In contrast to Grosz, Riki Lane, in discussing transsexuality, argues that 'mobilizing a reading of biology as open-ended and creative supports a perspective that sees sex and gender diversity as a continuum, rather than a dichotomy—put simply, "nature" throws up all this diversity and society needs to accept it.'[32] And Fausto-Sterling points out: 'Were we in Europe and America to move to a multiple sex and gender ... system ... we would not be cultural pioneers. Several Native American cultures ... define a third gender which may include people we would label as homosexual, transsexual, intersexual, but also people we would label as male and female ... Groups such as the Hijras of India contain people we in the West would label intersexes, transsexual, effeminate men and eunuchs ... Anthropologists debate how to interpret ... [these] systems. What is important, however, is that the existence of other systems suggests that ours is not inevitable.'[33]

What we need, then, in negotiating these debates is a framework which respects the agency of what we term nature, without handing priority to any given account of that nature. And this is found in other writers included under the new materialist umbrella.[34] Donna Haraway's work,[35] for example, is hailed by many as materialist, but it pulls in a different direction from Grosz's work on Darwin. Working always 'within the belly of the beast,'[36] as she says (the beast here being our scientific and technological cultures), she unravels the 'non-determining sources which are both material and cultural, and in relation to which individual subjects and social groups are moments, always engaged in creative transition.'[37]

Haraway's writings are centrally important in establishing not only the way culture mediates our understanding of nature, but also the impossibility of maintaining any dualism of 'nature' and 'culture.' The *nature/cultures* with which she concerns herself resist disentanglement into biological grounding and derived formations. Rather, the two are irrevocably intertwined. Her excavation of how what counts as nature for us emerges is multifaceted. It involves, in addition to scientific experimentation, movements of multinational capital (e.g., the story of Dupont),[38] the deconstruction of dominant metaphors within the scientific text, and the weaving of the biotechnological accounts into a dialectical relationship with the surrounding cultural artefacts. This is to recognise that our account of what we take to be nature emerges from a complex interaction of scientific investigations, cultural metaphors, and the networks of technology, which condition theory. It is not to deny that there is something independent of our conceptualisations which sets constraints on what can be said about it. What we cannot do is disentangle the bit which is *given* from our ways of thinking about it:

> [T]he practices of the sciences force one to accept two simultaneous, apparently incompatible truths. One is the historical contingency of what counts as nature for us; the thoroughgoing artifactuality of a scientific object of

knowledge that makes it inescapably and radically contingent ... and simultaneously scientific discourses make claims ... physically ... they have a sort of reality to them which is inescapable. No scientific account escapes being story laden, but it is equally true that stories are not all equal here. Radical Relativism just won't do.[39]

What I want to suggest is that Merleau-Ponty's account of our *expressing the world* makes sense of these apparently incompatible truths.

Expressing the World

The debates summarised above, between feminists drawing attention to the social and cultural constructedness of biological theory, and feminists who give an explanatory priority to, for example, evolutionary accounts of nature, can be compared to the debates between empiricism and intellectualism as addressed by Merleau-Ponty. Within his discussion, empiricism is the view that, in perception, sensory data are given to us unmediated; while intellectualism is the view that perception is structured and organised by thought, prior to our awareness. Both the materialism and the constructivism of the debates outlined above are more sophisticated than either of those positions. But between the poles of recognising the pull of the world versus recognising the constituting role of subjects, they are positioned nearer opposing ends. In *Phenomenology of Perception*, Merleau-Ponty rejects both poles: 'Empiricism cannot see that we need to know what we are looking for, otherwise we would not be looking for it, and intellectualism fails to see that we need to be ignorant of what we are looking for, or equally again we should not be searching.'[40] In the account which he offers, of our practices of *expressing the world*, he saw himself as supplanting the opposing poles which inform both positions.

For Merleau-Ponty, our expressive gestures, including language, *bring the world to articulation*. Expression is 'the simultaneous articulation of ... body and ...world.' Gestures 'presuppose a perceived world shared by everyone in which the sense of the gesture unfolds and is displayed.'[41] In *Phenomenology of Perception*, the possibility of our expressing the world hinges on our embodiment within it and a bodily relation between us and the world. We can express nature only because we are part of it. These bodily relations provide an interrogation of the world. We are able to express it as a result of our embodied anchorage in it. This, however, is not an act of a *constituting* subject, constructing the features of the world, but of an *expressive* one. What is offered is a world which comes into focus alongside us, by means of creative expressive acts, whose legitimacy rests on their being able to be recognised and taken up by others. But our expressions, linguistic or otherwise, are not operating simply as signs, to draw attention to a world whose characteristics could be grasped independently of the gestures. That is not possible. The world, he says, is accomplished through us, our expressions being 'so many ways of singing the world.'[42]

For Merleau-Ponty, the *initiation* of expressive content is a central focus of concern. An 'initiating gesture—gives a human sense to the object for the first time.'[43] It is such initiation that offers us insights into the nature of expression itself, and into the way in which a capacity for expression distinguishes our mode of being in the world. 'All perception, all action which presupposes it … every human use of the body is already primordial expression, the primary operation which first constitutes signs as signs … inaugurates an order and founds an institution or tradition.'[44] An initiating gesture, then, brings into view an aspect of the world, makes it accessible to ourselves and others. This gesture is a creative one; its expressive possibility resting on it finding a public, on it succeeding as an act of communication.

In *Phenomenology*,[45] he discusses a demonstration by a geometer of the characteristics of a triangle. This demonstration, he suggests, is not reached via a logical definition of 'triangle,' but by engagement with a triangle, an extension of its lines (even if only in imagination), which makes manifest its possibilities, 'a configuration … towards which my movements are directed.'[46] This is possible 'because my perception of the triangle [is] not so to speak congealed and dead; the drawing of the triangle on the paper [is] … shot through by lines of force, untraced yet possible directions … born everywhere in it … bursting with indefinite possibilities, of which [what is] … actually drawn is merely one particular case'[47] The proof of the geometer is therefore a creation, in the face of an initial triangle encountered as open with possibilities. He reiterates this point in a discussion in *The Prose of the World*: '[W]hen I introduce a new line into a drawing that changes its signification.'[48] These creative acts do not arise in a void, but against the background of previous significations which leave open possibilities (of which more below).[49] The geometer in providing us with insights about the figure is making evident something new about it, which others, on following the demonstration, can also find there. For Merleau-Ponty, these acts 'give us a world to express and think about that envelops and exceeds [our] perspectives, a world that announces itself in lightening signs as a spoken world or an arabesque.'[50] Our expressive acts yield a world announcing itself. Consequently, 'our expressive significations of the world ... have a truth: "truth which does not resemble things ... and without any predestined instruments of expression ... which is nonetheless truth."'[51] It is truth if, in a move which here brings Merleau-Ponty close to Heidegger,[52] the world announces itself in the expressive act. Aspects of it become available to us.

In *Phenomenology of Perception*, the stress is on our active embodiment giving form or shape mutually to itself and the world. In the later work on institution, *Institution and Passivity*,[53] this picture is developed into that of a process, both instituted and instituting, passive and active, which yields the meaning, the significance, which makes up the world for us. The distinction between *constitution* and *institution* is key here. The world as constituted is dependent on and makes no sense independent of the constituting subject(s). In contrast, sense as instituted is *encountered*. But it is encountered in the socio-historical field: '[The] inter-subjective or symbolic field ... is our milieu, *our hinge*.'[54] The organisation of existence is sociocultural as well as bodily. Meaning, or form, is encountered by us as something which has been deposited, as a residue of prior engagements; but it is experienced also as something to be *continued* in a way that is open, rather than determined. We find ourselves in a field of culturally mediated objects which we can surpass, but only on the basis of what has been given. Lefort comments: '[I]f institution is openness to, openness is always produced – on the basis of.'[55] We can engage in transformative activity, but only on the condition of our position in an already meaningful world. And the world as instituted suggests the initiation of the new—the invitation to a future. Such an opening, for Merleau-Ponty, is always a collective one, for the 'field' is always 'a double horizon' 'for others and not for me alone.'[56]

Instituted and instituting moments are found in all areas of life. '[There is an] instituted and instituting subject, but inseparably, and *not* a constituting subject ... [this instituted/instituting subject is] exposed to ... an event ...which is productive after it ...which opens a future. The subject [is] that to which such an order of events can advent, field of fields.'[57] 'Sense is deposited ... not as an object left behind ... a residue ... [but] as something to continue ... without it being the case that this sequel is determined.'[58] Instituted meanings will change but these very changes are openings found in them. Complexes of human/non-human life are involved. We find 'a certain variation in the field of existence already instituted, which is always behind us and whose weight, like that of an object in flight, only intervenes in the actions by which we transform it.'[59] This instituted variation has sources which are material/biological and sociohistorical, but are determined by none of these sources. The world, both material and social, which we encounter, 'sediment[s] in me a meaning as the invitation to a sequel, the necessity of a future'[60] What Merleau-Ponty therefore emphasises is the openness of such sequels. Even though each is grounded, he insists on the dimension of difference in the way in which different subjects/times may form a sequel, further institutions which are 'echoes and exchanges'[61] of each other and that which they follow. And on the basis of which new instituting events will take place.

What we take to be nature is here conceived of as a process with non-determining sources which are both material and cultural, and in relation to which individual subjects and social groups are moments, always engaged in creative transition. Creativity is a result of a process which is both instituted and instituting, and the sources or grounds of which are multiple. Creativity is integral to the process of institution itself, as it plays across the individual, the social, and the other elements informing it. We, as subjects, encounter a significance which requires and suggests a sequel to which it must bear an intelligible relation, but does not fix.

Sexed Difference Revisited

If we apply Merleau-Ponty's thinking to the question of biological sexed difference (not something which he did), we find that sexed difference is neither brutely given, nor simply culturally constructed. We also find that a respect for materiality does not privilege any given instituted account of that materiality. The sexed binary, which is currently *instituted*, provides us with an *opening* in relation to which different responses may be possible. It is, of course, unsurprising that in our embodied practices of propagating plants, animals, and ourselves, we have come up with accounts of the biology of sexed reproduction, and that these have led to binary identifications according to perceived roles in this. A genealogy of these accounts, as we have seen, shows the interweaving of material/cultural/technological factors. But currently, we are responding to such an instituted binary with different sets of questions, questions informed by increased knowledge of the variety of biological factors in play, by the experiences of those with intersexed bodies, by experiences of transsexuality and transgendering, by developing technologies of bodily change. It was, in part, the development of surgical technologies, enabling bodily changes, that facilitated the sexed categories of transsexual man or transsexual woman, categories reflecting just this intertwining of the biological, the social and cultural, and the technological. Sexed difference is now something that can change during our lives, legally endorsed in many places by allowing changes from male to female or vice versa on our legal documents. Our application of the categories of male or female to trans people is a consequence of perceived continuities between them and other people categorised as men and women, male or female, continuities anchored in the forms of life in which they participate. In Merleau-Ponty's terms, it is an *instituting* move in our linguistic practices, which brings to expression continuities between peoples rendered invisible by the previously *instituted* practice.

With those instituting changes comes the possibility of our making sense of sexed classification where the link between body and reproductive role has become muddied. Publicity about pregnant men makes this clear. Thomas Beattie, for example, is a transsexual man who retained his womb and carried his child. Afterwards, his wife Nancy breastfed the baby.[62] It would be a mistake to view our practice here in viewing Thomas as male, and as the father of the child, as in some way arbitrary or purely stipulative. Practices require a community for whom the use of the term makes sense. And the making sense here is an intertwining of the material and the cultural.[63]

Conclusion

If we conceive of the natural as that which constrains discourse, which is in a relation with the social and cultural, that which gets transposed in our practices of creating meaning, then we should not expect to be able to disentangle accounts of that nature from the meanings created. As Merleau-Ponty remarks: 'It is impossible to superimpose on man a lower layer of behaviour which one chooses to call "natural", followed by a manufactured cultural or spiritual world. Everything is both manufactured and natural in man, as it were.'[64] It therefore seems mistaken to treat any biological science as if it *had* disentangled the natural and the cultural and presented us with nature disentangled. It itself is just one form of the entanglement: 'The Nature within us must have some relation to Nature outside us, indeed Nature outside us must be revealed to us by the Nature that we are. ... By the nature in us, we can know Nature, and reciprocally it is from ourselves that living beings and even space speak to us ... It is no longer a matter of constructing arguments, but of seeing how all this *hangs together*.'[65]

Notes

1. Fausto-Sterling, A. *Sexing the Body: Gender Politics and the Construction of Sexuality*, (New York: Basic Books, 2000); Cameron, D., *The Myth of Mars and Venus*, (Oxford and New York: Oxford University Press, 2007); Bleir R., *Science and Gender: A Critique of Biology and its Theories on Women*. (New York: Pergamon Press, 1984); Butler, J. *Gender Trouble: Feminism and the Subversion of Identity*. (New York and London: Routledge, 1990).
2. Alaimo, S. and Hekman, S. eds. *Material Feminisms*. (Bloomington, IN: Indiana University Press, 2008), 1.
3. The claim of new materialists that previous feminism has been dominated by constructivist accounts has been disputed. See, for example, Ahmed, Sara. "Some Preliminary Remarks on the Founding Gestures of the New Materialism" *European Journal of Women's Studies* 15, no 1 (2008): 23–39.
4. Toadvine, T. "The Silence of Nature and the Emergence of Philosophy" The Irish Phenomenological Circle Inaugural Conference *Nature, Freedom and History: Merleau-Ponty after 50 Years*, University College Dublin June 2011, 7.
5. Baron-Cohen, S., The *Essential Difference, Men Women and the Extreme Male Brain*. (London: Allen Lane, 2003), 11. Baren-Cohen does, however, accept that sometimes female brains are found in male bodies and vice versa, which raises the question of what makes these *female* brain types?
6. Cameron, D., *The Myth of Mars and Venus*, (Oxford and New York: Oxford University Press, 2007), 2.
7. The accounts offered for these supposed differences currently utilise three, often interwoven, strands of theory. One is evolutionary psychology. The second is research into differences between male and female brains. The third is ethology or animal studies. For discussion, see: Fehr, Carla. "Feminist Philosophy of Biology" in *The Stanford Encyclopedia of Philosophy* (Fall 2011 Edition), Edward N. Zalta (ed.): http://plato.stanford.edu/archives/fall2011/entries/feminist-philosophy-biology/.
8. Baron-Cohen, *The Essential Difference*.
9. Cameron, *The Myths of Mars and Venus*, 43.
10. Fine, C. *Delusions of Gender: The Real Science behind Sex Differences*, (London: Icon Books, 2010), 176.
11. Bleir R. *Science and Gender: A Critique of Biology and its Theories on Women*. (New York: Pergamon Press, 1984), 52.
12. Fausto-Sterling, A. *Sexing the Body: Gender Politics and the Construction of Sexuality*. (New York, Basic Books, 2000), 241.
13. Stone, A. *An Introduction to Feminist Philosophy*. (Cambridge: Polity Press, 2007), 44.

14. Oudshoorn, N. *Beyond the Natural Body: An Archaeology of Sex Hormones.* (London: Routledge, 1994), 13.
15. Fausto-Sterling, *Sexing the Body.*
16. Fausto-Sterling, A. "The Five Sexes: Why Male and Female are Not Enough" *The Sciences*, 33, no. 2 (1993), 20–25. The scientific scepticism of 'binary' sex—that is, the idea that there are men and women and they can be clearly distinguished—started even earlier. In 1968, the *Journal of the American Medical Association* carried an article by biologist Keith L. Moore, listing nine different components of one's sexual identity: external genital appearance, internal reproductive organs, structure of the gonads, endocrinologic sex, genetic sex, nuclear sex, chromosomal sex, psychological sex, and social sex.
17. Butler, J. *Gender Trouble: Feminism and the Subversion of Identity.* (New York and London: Routledge, 1990); Butler, J. *Bodies that Matter: on the Discursive Limits of 'Sex'* (New York and London: Routledge, 1993).
18. Butler, *Gender Trouble*, 8.
19. Butler, *Gender Trouble*, 8.
20. Kirby, V. "Natural Convers(at)ions: or What if Culture was Really Nature all Along?" in eds. Alaimo, S. and Hekman, S. *Material Feminisms.* (Bloomington, IN: Indiana University Press, 2008), 214.
21. Jagger, G. "The New Materialism and Sexual Difference" *Signs* 40, no. 2 (2015).
22. The writings are called *new materialism* to distinguish them both from reductive materialism, which sees scientific facts as determining culture, and from Marxist historical materialism.
23. Alamo, *Material Feminisms*, 98.
24. See: Alcoff, L. "Gender and Reproduction" and Lennon, K. "Biology and the Metaphysics of Sex Difference" in eds. Gonzalez-Arnal, S., Jagger, G., and Lennon, K., *Embodied Selves.* (Basingstoke, Palgrave, 2012).
25. Grosz, E. "Darwin and Feminism: Preliminary Investigations for a possible alliance" in eds. Alaimo, S. and Hekman, S. *Material Feminisms.* (Bloomington, IN: Indiana University Press, 2008), 24.
26. Grosz, "Darwin and Feminism", 28.
27. Grosz, "Darwin and Feminism", 44.
28. Grosz, "Darwin and Feminism", 44.
29. Here, the Marxist insight that humans moved from evolution into history, and its connected insistence that what becomes nature for us is made available within that history, seems lost.
30. Grosz, "Darwin and Feminism", 44.
31. Grosz, "Darwin and Feminism", 44. Also problematically, this sexual differentiation, and the sexual selection with which, for her, it is interwoven, is then invoked to ground racial and other forms of bodily differences.

She quotes approvingly Darwin's anchorage of 'differences between the races of man ... in sexual selection.' Darwin: '[F]or differences between the races of man ... there remains one important agency, namely Sexual Selection, ...It can be shewn that the differences between the races of man, as in colour ... etc., might have been expected [from] ... sexual selection.' Quoted in Grosz, "Darwin and Feminism", 35.

32. Lane, R. "Trans as Bodily Becoming: Rethinking the Biological as Diversity not Dichotomy" *Hypatia* 24 no.3 (2009): 137.
33. Fausto-Sterling, *Sexing the Body*, 108/9.
34. Here, of particular importance are the writings of Danna Haraway (see the following endnote,) and Karen Barad. See "Posthumanist performativity: Towards an Understanding of How Matter comes to Matter" in eds. Alaimo, S. and Hekman, S. *Material Feminisms*. (Bloomington, IN: Indiana University Press, 2008), 120–156.
35. Haraway, D. *Primate Visions: Gender, Race and Nature in the World of Modern Science*. (New York and London: Routledge, 1989); Haraway, D. "Cyborgs at large: interview with Donna Haraway." In eds. C. Penley and A. Ross *Technoculture*, (Minneapolis, University of Minnesota Press: 1991a), 1–25; Haraway, D. *Simians, Cyborgs and Women: the Reinvention of Nature*. (New York and London: Routledge, 1991b); Haraway, D. *Modest_Witness@Second_Millennium.FemaleMan©_ Meets_OncoMouse™: Feminism and Technoscience*. (New York and London: Routledge, 1997); Haraway, D. *The Companion Species Manifesto: Dogs, People, and Significant Otherness*. (Chicago: University of Chicago Press, 2007); Haraway, D. 'Otherworldly Conversations, Terran Topics, Local Terms', in eds. Alaimo, S. and Hekman, S. *Material Feminisms*. (Bloomington, IN: Indiana University Press, 2008).
36. Haraway, D. "Cyborgs at large: interview with Donna Haraway." In eds. C. Penley and A. Ross *Technoculture*, (Minneapolis, University of Minnesota Press: 1991a), 1–25.
37. Haraway, D. 'Otherworldly Conversations, Terran Topics, Local Terms', in eds. Alaimo, S. and Hekman, S. *Material Feminisms*. (Bloomington, IN: Indiana University Press, 2008).
38. See her accounts of contemporary bio-technology in: Haraway, D. *Modest_Witness@Second_Millennium.FemaleMan©_ Meets_OncoMouse™: Feminism and Technoscience*. (New York and London: Routledge, 1997).
39. Haraway provides us with detailed accounts of how particular biological theories emerge. Reflecting in a lecture on the 'enzymes of the electro transport system ... biological catalysts in energy-producing cells,' she concludes, 'Machine, organism and human embodiment all were articulated – brought into particular co-constitutive relations-in complex ways which [were] ...historically specific' (Haraway, "Otherwordly Conversations",

162–163). The agency of the human, manifest in the articulation, narrative and visual, of the process, required the agency (as she terms it, in a use of the term agency without a suggestion of intention) of the organism, and that of the machine, in 'past and present ... socio-technical histories' (Haraway, "Otherwordly Conversations", 163).
40. Merleau-Ponty, M., *Phenomenology of Perception*, trans Donald A. Landes (London and New York: Routledge, 2012), 30.
41. Merleau-Ponty, *Phenomenology of Perception*, 195. This is not simply the point that emotions, for example, are about things, are intentionally directed at a world; it is that the quality of the emotional state is provided by the way in which the world manifests itself.
42. Merleau-Ponty, *Phenomenology of Perception*, 193.
43. Merleau-Ponty, *Phenomenology of Perception*, 200.
44. Merleau-Ponty, M., "Indirect Language and the Voices of Silence", in *The Merleau Ponty Aesthetics Reader* ed. Johnson, G. A. (Evanston: Northwestern University Press, 1993), 104.
45. Merleau-Ponty, *Phenomenology of Perception*, 404–407.
46. Merleau-Ponty, *Phenomenology of Perception*, 405.
47. Merleau-Ponty, *Phenomenology of Perception*, 406. See also the discussion in Hass, L. *Merleau-Ponty's Philosophy* (Bloomington and Indianapolis: Indiana University Press, 2008).
48. Hass, *Merleau-Ponty's Philosophy*, 231.
49. Merleau-Ponty, 'Indirect Language and the Voices of Silence', *The Merleau Ponty Aesthetics Reader,* 112.
50. Merleau-Ponty, 'Indirect Language and the Voices of Silence', *The Merleau Ponty Aesthetics Reader,* 89.
51. Merleau-Ponty, 'Indirect Language and the Voices of Silence', *The Merleau Ponty Aesthetics Reader,* 94.
52. Heidegger, M. "The Origin of the Work of Art" in *Poetry Language Thought*, trans Albert Hofstadter (Harper Collins, New York, 1971).
53. Merleau-Ponty, M. *Institution and Passivity*, trans. Lawlor and Massey, with a foreword by Claude Lefort. (Evanston: Northwestern University Press, 2010).
54. Merleau-Ponty, *Institution and Passivity*, 6.
55. Lefort forward to: Merleau-Ponty, *Institution and Passivity*, xi.
56. Merleau-Ponty, *Institution and Passivity*, 11–12. See the discussion in *Notre Dame Philosophical Reviews* (11).
57. Merleau-Ponty, *Institution and Passivity*, 6.
58. Merleau-Ponty, *Institution and Passivity*, 9.
59. Merleau-Ponty, *Institution and Passivity*, 49–50.
60. Merleau-Ponty, *Institution and Passivity*, 49–50.
61. Merleau-Ponty, *Institution and Passivity*, 15.

62. For images, see http://www.youtube.com/watch?v=Jwk2__Qn3_0& noredirect=1
63. The instituted/instituting framework of linguistic practices is what those insisting that trans women are not real women seem wholly unaware of. For recent debates, see Jenni Murray, http://www.telegraph.co.uk/news/2017/03/05/jenni-murray-transgender-women-not-real-women/, and Chimamanda Ngozi Adichie, http://www.independent.co.uk/arts-entertainment/books/news/chimamanda-ngozi-adichie-transgender-women-channel-four-a7625481.html.
64. Merleau-Ponty, *Phenomenology of Perception*, 195.
65. Merleau-Ponty, M. *Nature: Course Notes from the Collège de France* trans. Dominique Séglard (Evanstan: Northwestern University Press, 2003), 206 (translation modified Toadvine 2011).

Bibliography

Alaimo, S., and S. Hekman, eds. 2008. *Material Feminisms*. Bloomington: Indiana University Press.

Alcoff, L. 2012. Gender and Reproduction. In *Embodied Selves*, ed. S. Gonzalez-Arnal, G. Jagger, and K. Lennon. Basingstoke: Palgrave.

Baron–Cohen, S. 2012. *The Essential Difference, Men, Women and the Extreme Male Brain*. London: Allen Lane.

Bleir, R. 1984. *Science and Gender: A Critique of Biology and Its Theories on Women*. New York: Pergamon Press.

Butler, J. 1990. *Gender Trouble: Feminism and the Subversion of Identity*. New York/London: Routledge.

———. 1993. *Bodies that Matter: on the Discursive Limits of 'Sex'*. New York/London: Routledge.

Cameron, D. 2007. *The Myth of Mars and Venus*. Oxford/New York: Oxford University Press.

Fausto-Sterling, A. 1993. The Five Sexes: Why Male and Female Are Not Enough. *The Sciences* 33 (2): 20–25.

———. 2000. *Sexing the Body: Gender Politics and the Construction of Sexuality*. New York: Basic Books.

Fehr, Carla. 2011. Feminist Philosophy of Biology. In *The Stanford Encyclopedia of Philosophy* (Fall 2011 Edition), ed. Edward N. Zalta. http://plato.stanford.edu/archives/fall2011/entries/feminist-philosophy-biology/

Fine, C. 2010. *Delusions of Gender: The Real Science behind Sex Differences*. London: Icon Books.

Gonzalez-Arnal, S., G. Jagger, and K. Lennon, eds. 2012. *Embodied Selves*. Basingstoke: Palgrave.

Grosz, E. 2008. Darwin and Feminism: Preliminary Investigations for a Possible Alliance. In *Material Feminisms*, ed. S. Alaimo and S. Hekman. Bloomington: Indiana University Press.

Haraway, D. 1989. *Primate Visions: Gender, Race and Nature in the World of Modern Science.* New York/London: Routledge.

———. 1991a. Cyborgs at Large: Interview with Donna Haraway. In *Technoculture*, ed. C. Penley and A. Ross, 1–25. Minneapolis: University of Minnesota Press.

———. 1991b. *Simians, Cyborgs and Women: The Reinvention of Nature.* New York/London: Routledge.

———. 1997. *Modest_Witness@Second_Millennium.FemaleMan©_ Meets_ OncoMouse™: Feminism and Technoscience.* New York/London: Routledge.

———. 2003. *The Companion Species Manifesto: Dogs, People, and Significant Otherness.* Chicago: University of Chicago Press.

———. 2008. Otherworldly Conversations, Terran Topics, Local Terms. In *Material Feminisms*, ed. S. Alaimo and S. Hekman. Bloomington: Indiana University Press.

Hass, L. 2008. *Merleau-Ponty's Philosophy.* Bloomington/Indianapolis: Indiana University Press.

Heidegger, M. 1971. The Origin of the Work of Art. In *Poetry Language Thought* (trans. Hofstadter, A.). New York: Harper Collins.

Jagger, G. 2015. The New Materialism and Sexual Difference. *Signs* 40 (2): 321–342.

Kirby, V. 2008. Natural Convers(at)ions: Or, What if Culture Was Really Nature All Along? In *Material Feminisms*, ed. S. Alaimo and S. Hekman. Bloomington: Indiana University Press.

Lane, R. 2009. Trans as Bodily Becoming: Rethinking the Biological as Diversity Not Dichotomy. *Hypatia* 24 (3): 136–157.

Lennon, K. 2012. Biology and the Metaphysics of Sex Difference. In *Embodied Selves*, ed. S. Gonzalez-Arnal, G. Jagger, and K. Lennon. Basingstoke: Palgrave.

Merleau-Ponty, M. 1993. Indirect Language and the Voices of Silence. In *The Merleau-Ponty Aesthetics Reader*, ed. G.A. Johnson. Evanston: Northwestern University Press.

———. 2003. *Nature: Course Notes from the Collège de France.* Trans. Dominique Séglard. Evanston: Northwestern University Press.

———. 2010. *Institution and Passivity.* Trans. Lawlor and Massey. Evanston: Northwestern University Press.

———. 2012. *Phenomenology of Perception.* Trans. Donald A. Landes. London/New York: Routledge.

Oudshoorn, N. 1994. *Beyond the Natural Body: An Archaeology of Sex Hormones.* London: Routledge.

Stone, A. 2006. *Luce Irigaray and the Philosophy of Sexual Difference.* Cambridge/New York: Cambridge University Press.

———. 2007. *An Introduction to Feminist Philosophy*. Cambridge: Polity.
Toadvine, T. 2011, June. The Silence of Nature and the Emergence of Philosophy. Paper Presented at The Irish Phenomenological Circle Inaugural Conference *Nature, Freedom and History: Merleau-Ponty after 50 Years*, University College Dublin.

PART III

Sex, Violence, and Public Policy

CHAPTER 8

Are Women's Lives (Fully) Grievable? Gendered Framing and Sexual Violence

Dianna Taylor

SEXUAL VIOLENCE/MORAL AMBIVALENCE

In the face of increasing national attention to the prevalence of sexual violence against women in colleges and universities in the United States, the Obama administration launched the "It's On Us" campaign to end campus sexual assault. That campaign, launched in the fall of 2014, provided information to all school districts, colleges, and universities receiving federal funding concerning their legal obligation to prevent and respond to sexual assault; created the White House Task Force to Protect Students from Sexual Assault to collaborate with colleges and universities regarding sexual assault response and prevention best practices; and reviewed existing laws in order to ensure adequate protection of victims.[1] "This is on all of us, every one of us, to fight campus sexual assault," asserted President Obama in 2014. "The entire country is going to make sure that we understand what this is about and that we're going to put a stop to it."[2] Calls to action such as Obama's, however, are made alongside expressions not only of hostility, indifference, and ignorance—both within academia and more broadly—toward women who have experienced sexual violence, but also of sympathy toward perpetrators.[3]

D. Taylor (✉)
John Carroll University, University Heights, OH, USA

© The Author(s) 2018
C. Fischer, L. Dolezal (eds.), *New Feminist Perspectives on Embodiment*, Breaking Feminist Waves,
https://doi.org/10.1007/978-3-319-72353-2_8

147

"I've never experienced anything like it," Poppy Harlow of CNN related to commentator Candy Crowley after witnessing the conviction of two Steubenville, Ohio high school football players, Trent Mays and Ma'lik Richmond, for the rape of an unconscious 16-year-old girl.[4] "It was incredibly emotional – incredibly difficult even for an outsider like me to watch what happened as these two young men that had such promising futures, star football players, very good students, literally watched as they believe their life fell apart."[5]

It is tempting to read Donald Trump's election to the presidency, just over two years after President Obama condemned sexual assault against women, as solidifying the victim blaming and trivialization of sexual violence reflected in Harlow's remarks. Yet as Kelly Oliver points out, neither Trump's election nor a Trump presidency is that simple. In a recent contribution to the *New York Times* philosophy blog, *The Stone*, Oliver reiterates a point that many feminists made in the weeks following the presidential election. "The problem of misogyny and violence against women existed long before this election cycle," she writes. "But the immediate danger that comes with raising an unrepentant misogynist to the nation's highest office is emboldenment; the implicit condoning of degrading or violent behavior against women, and the diminished fear of punishment from authorities."[6]

The following chapter analyzes what it means that two such different responses to sexual violence against women can coexist—how it is, in other words, that the lives of the Trent Mays' and Ma'lik Richmonds throughout the country are mourned as having been ruined, and a man who bragged about committing acts that meet the legal definition of sexual assault can be elected president—whereas the lives of women they rape and assault responses are treated with ambivalence. More specifically, my analysis recasts three questions that underpin Judith Butler's recent work. In *Precarious Life: The Powers of Mourning and Violence*, Butler asks: "Who counts as human? Whose lives count as lives? What *makes for a grievable life?*"[7] Drawing upon Butler's elucidation of these questions in *Frames of War: When Is Life Grievable*, I consider the following: "Do women count as human? Do women's lives count as lives? Are women's lives grievable?"

My assertion is that the ambivalent moral and emotional responses with which sexual violence against women is met within contemporary Western societies such as the United States indicate that women's lives do not (fully) count as lives, with the result that harms against them are not (fully) recognized as harms, and are therefore not (fully) grieved. I begin by providing an overview of Butler's accounts of precariousness, precarity, and the normative cognitive process of framing in order to show how some lives come to be construed as not fully livable and therefore not fully injurable. Next, I present gender as a frame that casts women's lives not fully livable and show that a particular manifestation of women's precarity is their differential exposure to embodied violations such as sexual violence. The third section of the chapter analyzes why, as an embodied violation of a less-than-fully-livable life, sexual violence does not fully register as a harm and is therefore not definitively condemned. I conclude by considering how my own analysis is framed and to what effect, as well as by reflecting upon possibilities for countering the gendered framing that promotes ignoring, minimizing, and excusing sexual violence against women.

Butler on Framing and Grievability

In illustrating how it can be that some lives are not recognized as (fully) livable, Butler invokes the concepts of precariousness and precarity. Precariousness refers to the social (i.e., shared and interconnected) character of human existence. For Butler, sociality necessarily entails "that one's life is always in some sense in the hands of the other. It implies exposure … a dependency on people we know, or barely know, or know not at all."[8] That all human lives and ways of living are not only interconnected but also interdependent means that we have limited control over our actions and their effects. Human beings cannot avoid either "impinging upon" or "being impinged upon by" our "exposure [to] and dependency [upon]" others, or that of others to and upon us.[9]

For Butler, the precarious nature of human existence renders it ambivalent, in the sense that exposure to and dependence upon others is a source of both negative and positive experiences.[10] "The very fact of being bound up with others," Butler contends, "establishes the possibility of being subjugated and exploited … [b]ut it also establishes the possibility of being relieved of suffering, of knowing justice and even love."[11] Fundamental to this ambivalence is human embodiment: it is precisely as bodies that human beings are exposed to and impinge upon one another. "That the body invariably comes up against the outside world is a sign of the general predicament of unwilled proximity to others and circumstances beyond one's control," Butler writes. "This 'coming up against' is one modality that defines the body."[12] As is the case with precariousness generally, the precarious nature of embodiment may, but does not, necessarily generate harmful effects. Eliminating the body's "obtrusive alterity" would cut human beings off from a wide range of experiences and their accompanying affective responses.[13] While we might be protected from torture, humiliation, suffering, and shame, we would also be denied pleasure, surprise, spontaneity, and hope. Our embodied exposure both "raises the possibility of subjugation and cruelty" and "[conditions] ... our desire."[14]

Whereas precariousness is ambivalent, its unequal distribution, which Butler refers to as precarity, is unequivocally harmful. Precarity refers to a "politically induced condition" in which some lives "suffer from failing social and economic networks of support" and are "*differentially* exposed" to harm in the forms of "injury, violence, and death."[15] Precariousness becomes unequally distributed, and precarity in turn gets produced, by means of "framing," a normative cognitive process that Butler describes as occurring on three levels. The first level is recognition, the "active" identification (and accompanying treatment) of someone or something as a life. Second, "recognizability" refers to the "historically articulated and enforced" normative structures that enable recognition and within which it occurs.[16] It is in and through structures of recognizability, in other words, that the livability of lives gets determined. Normative structures of recognizability are themselves "conditioned and produced" by the third level, "schemas of intelligibility," which "establish domains of the knowable."[17] Simply put, to be recognizable and therefore recognized as a (fully livable) life, someone or something must register within a schema of intelligibility. Moving from intelligibility to recognition involves a "delimiting" of one's conceptual field: not everything that is intelligible registers within a framework of recognizability, and not everything that is recognizable is recognized.[18] Framing thus effectively "produce[s] certain subjects as 'recognizable' persons"—as fully livable lives—while making "others decidedly more difficult to recognize" (or simply unrecognizable).[19] For Butler, then, neither the world nor our knowledge of it provides a ground for making normative claims and inquiries; both are, rather, effects of the normative cognitive process of framing.

In addition to producing precarity—casting some lives as not (fully) livable and differentially exposing them to harm—framing is also implicated in the (re)production of conditions under which precarity comes to be seen merely as normal, uncritically accepted, and thus perpetuated. As Butler presents it, like other normative processes, framing is both "iterable" and exclusionary. Frames, she writes, "can only circulate by virtue of their reproducibility."[20] It is through their continual reproduction, in other words, that norms and normative processes are taken up, established, and maintained. The conceptual narrowing that characterizes framing is exclusionary in the sense that anything which fails to fully register within a frame of recognition does not receive (full) ontological, epistemological, or moral consideration.

As early as *Gender Trouble*, Butler has illustrated how the iterable and exclusionary character of norms and normative processes infuses them with normalizing potential in the specifically Foucauldian sense of the term. As Foucault describes it, normalizing norms are those which get reproduced so frequently (and unconsciously) that they come to structure human existence. No longer acknowledged or experienced as norms, they acquire the status of inevitable, ineluctable, and therefore assumed aspects of reality—a status which of course further fixes them within society. Allowing facets of human existence and experience to become entrenched in turn limits possibilities for developing (let alone practicing), or even forecloses, alternatives. In short, by casting prevailing social conditions as necessary conditions, normalizing norms simultaneously stunt critical and creative capacities and cultivate obedience to and conformity with prevailing relations of power.

The normative process of framing as Butler describes it is normalizing: it produces harmful effects, (re)produces the conditions for the possibility of those effects, and inhibits development and exercise of the critical and creative capacities through which those effects and conditions might be identified and countered. In the absence of alternatives, precarity comes to be viewed as a (perhaps) regrettable but nonetheless inevitable fixture, not as a problem of society, but rather one that is specific to and inherent within certain lives. These lives thus continue to be constituted as well as experienced as less than fully livable.

Gender as a Frame of Recognition

Throughout her work, Butler presents gender as a frame of recognition and illustrates how, as a frame, gender both emerges within and in turn reproduces prevailing, normalizing relations of power. It is not merely the case that being gendered makes human beings intelligible in a generic sense; rather, gendering affords intelligibility in particular ways by situating human beings within that schema's normative structures—structures, that is, of recognizability. We constitute, understand, and relate to ourselves and others—we become recognizable—within a dualistic gendered social context that privileges masculinity and devalues femininity, while simultaneously presenting heterosexuality and cisgender as norms. Within this context, human beings gendered as women are constituted, understood, and related to—as well as constitute, understand, and relate themselves—as inferior and subordinate. Butler shows, moreover, that as a normalizing process, gendered framing reproduces normative gender roles to the point where these modes of constituting and relating to oneself and others become naturalized and fixed, such that intelligibility is achieved at the expense of its own potentially multiple forms of expression and recognition. The entrenched and thus intransigent nature of women's ostensible inferiority makes it even more difficult for them to gain recognition as fully livable lives. In sum, because women achieve recognition only as subordinate, devalued, and therefore not fully livable lives, they are not *fully* recognized in the sense that they are denied full access to conditions that promote human flourishing and are therefore differentially exposed to harm.

Ann Cahill, Erinn Gilson, and Debra Bergoffen show that sexual violence is one particular manifestation of the harm to which women are differentially exposed. While they do not use Butler's language of precariousness and precarity, all three thinkers nonetheless conceptualize feminine embodiment as an ambivalent source of exposure to the world and other people, and present sexual violence as the exploitation of this embodied exposure. Cahill conceptualizes the exposure or openness to the world that results from the social and embodied nature of human existence in terms of intersubjectivity. Subjects, she argues, are neither self-contained nor purely intellectual entities. Rather, subjectivity is a "project undertaken … in the course of a variety of relationships … it is only in the context of others and a particular society that the self comes to be."[21] We are selves only relative to other people, as well as to society as whole; our entire mode of existence is characterized by being open to others and the world—we are completely distinct from neither. Moreover, it is in and through our bodies that we constitute, understand, and relate to ourselves, others, and the world. Cahill describes the openness that characterizes embodied intersubjectivity as reciprocal, in the sense that we are open to others and the world, and they are also open to us. This openness, as is the case with precariousness for Butler, is ambivalent: it renders us vulnerable to harm, but also affords us opportunities for developing and exercising capacities that in turn facilitate participation in various kinds of dynamic and positive interactions with both other people and our environment more broadly.

Just as precarity can be seen as the exploitation or negative reduction of the ambivalence of precariousness, sexual violence as Cahill describes it negatively reduces the ambivalent character of embodied intersubjectivity. Such violence, she writes, amounts to "exploitation of the vulnerabilities that an embodied intersubjectivity necessarily entails."[22] The exploitation Cahill refers to is, specifically, destruction of intersubjective reciprocity through the denial of both women's capacities and their ability to exercise them. "The actions of the rapist," Cahill writes, "eclipse the victim's agency in a particularly sexual manner … it renders impossible for that moment the victim's [intersubjectivity]."[23] Bergoffen concurs with Cahill's assertion that in acts of rape, only the perpetrator is exercising capacities and actively engaging; rapists, she contends, appropriate the embodied capacities of their victims for their own purposes.[24] Both Cahill and Bergoffen thus conceptualize rape as a sexual and embodied assault on the sensual and desiring body that destroys intersubjectivity.[25] Insofar as for these two thinkers intersubjectivity is a fundamental condition of "embodied personhood," rape constitutes a "bodily, sexual, assault on a woman's underlying conditions of being."[26]

It is clear from Cahill's description of rape as the *exploitation of vulnerabilities* inherent to intersubjectivity that she does not see vulnerability as merely negative. For her, rather, vulnerability appears to express precisely the ambivalent openness and exposure that intersubjectivity necessarily entails. This is also the case for Gilson, who describes vulnerability as simply "openness … to being affected and affecting in ways that one cannot control."[27] Like Butler and Cahill, Gilson contends that this openness derives from the fact that we share the world with other people, and that our experience of ourselves, others, and the world is characteristically embodied. Moreover, Gilson ties embodiment directly and overtly to sexuality. "[B]eing an embodied, social being means being a sexual being," she writes.[28] Because sexuality is interconnected with embodiment and sociality, it constitutes a key "locus of vulnerability."[29] Sexuality, Gilson argues, "initiates us" as embodied beings "into a particular web of social significances in virtue of which we are especially open … to others."[30]

Within a gendered framework, vulnerability generally but especially sexual vulnerability, while they are effects of *human* sociality, are associated with inferiority and thus coded as feminine. According to Gilson, this coding derives from sexist constructions of feminine embodiment. "If women are typically considered more vulnerable than men," she argues, "it is because of their bodies, which are deemed both weaker and more sexually stimulating ... To be a woman is to inhabit the kind of body that is perceived as inciting lust and thus as inviting sexual attention, whether desired or not."[31] This construction of feminine embodiment in turn effectively "naturalizes [sexual] violence (as an inevitable outcome of male aggression and female violability)."[32] Like Cahill, Gilson conceptualizes sexual violence in terms of the exploitation of the ambivalent openness of human vulnerability, yet also emphasizes the degree to which, for women, vulnerability is always already reduced to a negative sense of being susceptible to (especially sexual forms of) harm.

Gendered Framing and Sexual Violence

Cahill's, Bergoffen's, and Gilson's work illustrates that the gendered framing of women's lives as not fully livable contributes to their precarity, as well as that sexual violence—which exploits a specifically feminine mode of embodied openness to the world and other people—is one particular manifestation of this precarity. A further effect of gendered framing is the fact that the harm of sexual violence is itself not fully recognized. This lack of full recognition illustrates Butler's point that lives which are not fully livable are not fully grievable. As noted previously, Butler contends that all life is precarious: any living thing can die or be killed; it can "be expunged at will or by accident; [its] persistence is in no sense guaranteed."[33] Fully livable lives may be distinguished from those that are not recognized as (fully) livable on the basis of grievability. Grief marks the passing of something meaningful; if life were not valued, it would not be grieved, because its loss, whether through passing or eradication, would not be worth marking. "Only under conditions in which [a] loss would matter does the value of life appear," Butler writes. "Thus, grievability is a presupposition for the life that matters."[34] Analogous to grief marking the loss of meaningful, fully livable lives is unequivocal moral outrage marking violations against or injuries inflicted upon such lives. Fully livable lives are recognized as fully injurable, and therefore, harms they incur are recognized as such and renounced without question. Lives that are not recognized as fully livable, by contrast, are not seen as (fully) injurable, with the result that violations of and harms against them are met with morally equivocal responses. The attenuated grievability of and accompanying ambivalent moral and emotional responses to sexual violence against women are apparent in two ways.

First, sexual violence is not unambiguously considered to be violence. Through contrasting the work of Talal Asad and Michael Walzer, Butler illustrates in *Frames of War* how framing casts some forms of violence as morally legitimate and other forms as morally reprehensible, with the result that the former are uncritically accepted as necessary (or even valorized), while the latter are uncritically denounced. Asad, Butler explains, analyzes the framing of suicide bombing as terrorism not in order to endorse it as a practice, but rather to show how definitions and interpretations function as modes of framing that are not merely descriptive but also normative. Casting suicide bombing as "terrorism" effectively places it outside the realm of critical engagement and analysis, since terrorism is by definition an illegitimate, morally reprehensible form of violence.

Framing suicide bombing as terrorism and thereby making impossible any sort of critical engagement concerning the legitimacy of the practice itself or underlying conditions that give rise to it, Butler argues, is apparent in Walzer's work on just war theory. According to her, in defining what constitutes a just war, Walzer delimits the terms under which analysis of and debate about the justifiable use of certain forms of violence can take place. For Walzer, Butler writes, terrorism (and therefore suicide bombing) is a form of violence that can never be justified, and there is thus no need to debate reasons for its possible use or conditions under which it might legitimately be used. Butler's point here is that by framing certain forms of violence as terrorism, Walzer casts them as "patently unreasonable" and thus open to neither "reflection" nor "debate."[35] His work thus exemplifies the fact that definitions and interpretations "not only carry normative force but also effectively – and without justification – make normative distinctions."[36]

With respect to sexual violence against women, the normative distinction at stake is not so much whether sexual violence is morally acceptable or reprehensible, but rather whether sexual violence is or is not properly violence at all. Gilson's observation that, within the frame of gendered power relations, to be a feminine body is to be sexualized and therefore to invite sexual attention points to the ambiguous status of sexual violence as a violation, let alone a violent one. If simply being embodied as a woman is to "ask for it," then any degree of male sexual attention directed at women cannot by definition be unwanted and, hence, a violation. This in turn calls into question whether such attention can be the sort of forcible and injurious action that constitutes violence. By obfuscating their status as both violation and violence, gendered framing thus casts rape and sexual assault of women as neither definitively morally legitimate nor morally reprehensible. These acts are therefore neither uncritically accepted nor uncritically denounced.

Attenuated grievability and ambivalent moral and emotional responses in the face of violations against women's lives are also apparent in the fact that sexual violence is not unambiguously considered to be a violation, either violent or otherwise. Victim blaming illustrates that sexual violence is not definitively viewed as a violation, and that its status as violence is therefore questioned. Lise Gotell argues that feminist framing of sexual violence in terms of gendered power relations presents it as a social problem that must be addressed through public policy. Such framing has, however, been "replaced with de-gendered and individual policy frameworks."[37] This shift, according to Gotell, reflects neoliberal framing that emphasizes "abstract risk and individuated ... responsibility."[38] She shows that the tension between the ostensibly gender-neutral discourse of neoliberalism, on the one hand, and the gendered nature of sexual violence, on the other, simultaneously and paradoxically masks the gendered nature of sexual violence while at the same time constructing women *qua* women as beings who are both sexually vulnerable and responsible for their own protection. Neoliberal risk management technologies that target individual women's behavior, rather than the gendered social framework that produces sexual violence, construct rape "as a personal problem that each woman herself must solve by limiting her own mobility."[39]

This neoliberal framing produces "bad victims," who do not adhere to prevailing norms of "sexual safekeeping," and "good victims," who practice a kind of "fearful femininity" characterized by self-regulation.[40] In neither case is the injury experienced by the women in question fully recognized. Bad victims are duly and overtly "blamed for the violence they experience."[41] The victim in the Steubenville case, for example, was incapacitated by alcohol (i.e., unconscious) when she was raped. According to Amy Grubb and Emily Turner, studies have found that intoxication in women is viewed negatively in large part because it is perceived as unfeminine. Women who violate gender norms are in turn more likely to be blamed if they are sexually assaulted. They may be seen as receiving deserved punishment for their unfeminine behavior,[42] and the actions of their attackers may be mitigated. "Victims of rape who are intoxicated are held more responsible and more to blame for the rape" than non-intoxicated victims, Grubb and Turner write[43]; conversely, intoxicated perpetrators, are viewed as "less responsible for their actions than sober perpetrators."[44] Contrast, then, reactions to the perpetrators in the Steubenville case, on the one hand, and the young woman they raped, on the other. Ranks were closed around Mays and Richmond, both in the Steubenville community itself[45] and, as the media response expressing indignation over their conviction illustrates, more broadly. The victim in the case, by contrast, was portrayed, both by friends who were with her on the night she was raped and more generally, as sexually promiscuous and therefore a willing participant; she was also subjected to threats not only to her safety but also to her life following the guilty verdict.[46] Holding women responsible, to whatever extent, when they are raped and sexually assaulted while excusing, to whatever extent, their attackers reflects moral ambivalence: doubt (or even flat denial) that a violation has occurred. Through producing ambiguity surrounding the violation itself, such responses reduce the likelihood that the severity of the injury will be recognized and, in doing so, problematize its characterization as violent.

Sexual violence against women who adhere to traditional gender norms and, consistent with neoliberalism, surveil their own behavior and actions may be recognized as a violation and therefore produce a level of moral outrage. That the violation of even "good victims" fails to produce *surprise*, however, illustrates the degree to which sexual violence against women has become uncritically accepted as simply inevitable. A sense of inevitability relative to some phenomenon (an event or the conditions of one's existence, for example) tends to produce complacency or at least resignation in the face of it. These responses, like those of doubt and denial in the case of "bad victims," minimize injury and subsequently mute the moral response to it. Sexual violence is most frequently committed against women, yet, as Cahill points out, focusing on women is often construed as biased because it disregards male victims.[47] Sexual violence against women is prevalent,[48] yet the neoliberal emphasis on the need for women to monitor and restrict their behavior and actions in order to protect themselves leaves unanalyzed and therefore unchallenged the behavior and actions of perpetrators, as well as the conditions that give rise to those behaviors and actions. Framing sexual violence as (individual) women's problem thus reflects, at best, resignation to and, at worst, acceptance or even support of its inevitability.[49] It is, in other words, to frame the prevalence of such violence as a normal or natural, albeit perhaps unfortunate, aspect of human existence or "human nature," as opposed to an effect of human-generated sociopolitical conditions of precarity. Viewing sexual violence against women as a normal occurrence clearly diminishes its status as a violation in the sense that societies view violations (of the law, of social norms, of other people) as at least potential threats to social order and therefore actively seek to correct, curtail, or eliminate (rather than simply require individuals to manage) them. The ambiguity introduced with respect to the status of sexual violence as a violation in turn calls into question whether an injury, let alone one serious enough to be considered violent, could have occurred.

That the frame of gendered power relations casts sexual violence against women as an inevitable aspect of their existence makes clear that no woman's life is recognized as fully livable. The ambivalent moral and emotional responses to sexual violence and women against whom it has been inflicted make clear that women's lives are not fully grievable. This attenuated grievability reflects what Butler refers to as "the politics of moral responsiveness," whereby "[w]hat we feel is in part conditioned by how we interpret the world around us."[50] Framing, which shapes what is interpretable at all as well as particular interpretations, in turn influences the kinds of emotional and moral responses that are called for, deemed appropriate, and therefore experienced. Persons feel "horrified" in the face of some acts of violence and feel not only an absence of horror, but complacency, ambivalence, or even pride in the face of others. Likewise, injury to some lives is readily acknowledged and renounced, whereas in the case of other lives, injury is equivocal or completely unacknowledged because it is not fully or at all recognized. "[P]owerful affective responses are conditioned and structured by interpretations," Butler writes, "and ... these interpretations are formed within taken-for-granted frameworks."[51]

(Self)Critical Feminist Framing and Resistance

My own analysis in this chapter is partially framed by the Steubenville case, which involves the gang rape of a white middle-class teenager in a working-class town in my home state of Ohio. This framing is intentional: the case illustrates how gender functions as a normalizing frame of recognition that constructs women's lives as not fully livable, with the result that sexual violence against women is neither fully recognized as an injury nor fully grieved. But it is also clearly the case that, even within a context of attenuated recognition, different women's lives are more and less recognizable and therefore recognized. The young woman in the Steubenville case achieved recognition only as an inferior life; the affective response to her rape was merely ambivalent. The lives of the 13 women raped and sexually assaulted by Daniel Holtzclaw, formerly of the Oklahoma City police department, by contrast, were scarcely recognized, even as not fully livable.[52] Holtzclaw's victims were African American, and many were socioeconomically disadvantaged and socially marginalized, "with either warrants or suspected of involvement in illegal activities such as prostitution or illegal drug consumption."[53] Holtzclaw forced these women to perform sex acts in order to avoid arrest and incarceration. His case did not receive extensive coverage in the mainstream media.[54] Most worthy of attention seemed to be the question of whether the all-white jury in the case would find Holtzclaw guilty.[55]

My presentation of sexual violence as an embodied violation illustrates Butler's point that it is precisely as bodies that the livability of human lives is or is not recognized. The lack of recognition of, and therefore moral and emotional response to, the violation of the lives of the women of color Holtzclaw raped and sexually assaulted draws into sharp relief Butler's assertion that "certain kinds of bodies will appear more precariously than others, depending on which versions of the body ... support or underwrite the idea of the human life that is worth protecting, sheltering, living, mourning."[56] This chapter endeavors to elucidate sexual violence as a specifically gendered violation; in doing so, it may well risk reproducing the normalizing frames that construct such violence in white middle-class terms. The questions I posed at the outset of this chapter in order to draw attention to and problematize how gendered relations of power frame women's lives as not fully livable themselves raise the question of *which women's lives* are intelligible such that the degree of their recognition can be considered at all.

If emotional and moral responses which might move people to critically analyze, counter, and cultivate alternatives to normalization, as well as scholarly analysis (such as my own) that hopes to invoke such responses, are themselves forged within the normalizing process of framing, it may appear that, in fact, precarity in its myriad harmful manifestations is destined to be a permanent fixture of human existence. It is crucial, however, to recall that, for Butler (like Foucault before her), possibilities for resisting and countering normalization are generated within, not outside, normalizing relations of power. Butler thus identifies possibilities for re- or un-framing, for alleviating precarity, and for critique and creativity within the very characteristics though which frames gain purchase. "Shift[ing] the very terms of recognizability in order to produce more radically democratic results,"[57] she contends, is possible because as iterable, partial, and exclusionary, frames shape but do not determine reality. Like normative processes more broadly, framing is always "in process"; to gain their normative impetus, frames must be continually reproduced. Insofar as this is the case, they need not be reproduced in the same form. Frames "break within themselves in order to install themselves," such that they can be modified—reinstalled or reconstructed in alternative ways—or, indeed, dispensed with altogether.

If frames do not determine reality, then they also do not determine moral and emotional responses in the face of a reality characterized by precarity. Because frames are not all-encompassing, what they exclude is not beyond our cognitive, moral, or emotional grasp. Butler argues that unrecognized injury, as well as the fact of its lack of recognition, can still be *apprehended*, where apprehension is a mode of knowing that is not reducible to recognition. "We can apprehend," Butler asserts, "that something is not recognized by recognition."[58] Apprehending that there are, in fact, phenomena which "exceed the frame," which do not "conform to our established understanding of things," as well as those phenomena themselves, likewise facilitates the cultivation of non- and anti-normalizing alternatives because it "trouble[s] our sense of reality."[59] Such "troubling" or unsettling of prevailing interpretations of the world and ways of being within it provides the basis for critique. It involves revealing a frame and what lies within it as simply one possible way of making sense of the world, rather than objective reality—revealing, in other words, the normative and therefore normalizing function of interpretations. Failure to acknowledge the degree to which interpretations function as judgments produces conditions under which human beings "judge a world we refuse to know," and "our judgment becomes one means of refusing to know that world."[60] An aspect of engaging rather than refusing to know the world thus entails endeavoring to apprehend, and thereby grappling with, the normalizing function of prevailing frames of recognition and, in doing so, questioning interpretations, distinctions (such as that between just wars and terrorism), and ambiguities (such as the status of sexual violence as a violent violation) that present themselves and are widely accepted as natural, necessary, and therefore inevitable.

The questions of whether and which women count as human; whether, which, and to what extent women's lives count as livable; and whether and to what extent any women's lives are grievable are not settled. This fact is discouraging. It reflects the fact that women's lives continue to be differentially characterized by harm, including the exploitation of their embodied precariousness through systemic sexual violence. At the same time, that these questions are unsettled also reflects the fragility of the frames within which they resonate and to which they present a challenge. Our collective task is to identify when and how a frame inevitably "breaks with itself"—indeed, to promote such breakage—and to intervene within these moments in "politically consequential ways."[61] Such intervention includes critically analyzing our own frames and acknowledging the aporetic character of even projects which aim to counter normalization and promote freedom.

Notes

1. https://www.whitehouse.gov/blog/2014/09/19/president-obama-launches-its-us-campaign-end-sexual-assault-campus.
2. Juliet Eilperin, 'Seeking to end rape on campus, White House launches "It's On Us,"' http://www.washingtonpost.com/news/post-politics/wp/2014/09/19/seeking-to-end-rape-on-campus-wh-launches-its-on-us/.
3. See Bogdanich, "Reporting Rape and Wishing She Hadn't," as well as his follow-up article, "Support for a College Student Grows After a Rape Complaint is Dismissed," http://www.nytimes.com/2014/07/22/nyregion/support-for-a-student-grows-as-college-examines-its-sexual-assault-policies.html.
4. Juliet Macur and Nate Schweber, "Rape Case Unfolds on Web and Splits City," http://www.nytimes.com/2012/12/17/sports/high-school-football-rape-case-unfolds-online-and-divides-steubenville-ohio.html.
5. Erik Wemple, "CNN is getting hammered for Steubenville coverage," https://www.washingtonpost.com/blogs/erik-wemple/wp/2013/03/18/cnn-is-getting-hammered-for-steubenville-coverage/.
6. Kelly Oliver, "There's No Such Thing as Nonconsensual Sex: It's Violence," http://www.nytimes.com/2016/11/21/opinion/there-is-no-such-thing-as-nonconsensual-sex-its-violence.html?emc=eta1.
7. Judith Butler, *Precarious Life: The Powers of Mourning and Violence* (New York: Verso, 2004), 20; original emphasis.
8. Judith Butler, *Frames of War: When Is Life Grievable?* (New York: Verso, 2010), 14.
9. Butler, *Frames of War*, 14.
10. Ibid, 61.
11. Ibid.
12. Ibid, 34.
13. Ibid.
14. Ibid, 61.
15. *Frames of War*, 25; my emphasis.

16. Butler describes recognizability as "categories, conventions, and norms that prepare or establish a subject for recognition" and therefore "preceded and make possible the act of recognition itself." See *Frames of War*, 5.
17. *Frames of War*, 6–7.
18. Ibid, 1.
19. Ibid, 6.
20. Ibid, 24.
21. Ann J. Cahill, *Rethinking Rape* (Ithaca, Cornell University Press, 2001), 104.
22. Cahill, *Rethinking Rape*, 132.
23. Ibid.
24. Debra B. Bergoffen, *Contesting the Politics of Genocidal Rape: Affirming the Dignity of the Vulnerable Body* (New York: Routledge, 2012).
25. Bergoffen, *Contesting the Politics of Genocidal Rape*, especially Chap. 2, "Slavery, Torture, Rape: Assaulting the Dignity of the Vulnerable Body."
26. *Rethinking Rape*, 132.
27. Erinn C. Gilson, *The Ethics of Vulnerability: A Feminist Analysis of Social Life and Practice* (New York, Routledge, 2014), 2.
28. Gilson, *The Ethics of Vulnerability*, 151.
29. Ibid, 150.
30. Ibid.
31. Ibid, 152.
32. Ibid, 153.
33. *Frames of War*, 25.
34. Ibid, 14.
35. Ibid, 154.
36. Ibid.
37. Lise Gotell, "Third Wave Antirape Activism on Neoliberal Terrain: The Garneau Sisterhood," Ellizabeth Sheehy, ed., *Sexual Assault Law, Practice & Activism in a Post-Jane Doe Era* (Ottawa, University of Ottawa, 2011), 9.
38. Gotell, "Third Wave Antirape Activism on Neoliberal Terrain," 9.
39. Ibid, 15.
40. Gotell analyzes the situation within Canada specifically, but the neoliberal, anti-feminist framing of sexual violence, as I show, is apparent within a US context as well.
41. "Third Wave Antirape Activism on Neoliberal Terrain," 16.
42. Grubb and Turner cite research that distinguishes between "hostile sexism" and "benevolent sexism." Hostile sexism refers to "the attitude that women should be punished for defying traditional sexual roles" by, for example, "wearing provocative clothes" or "drink[ing] excessively." Benevolent sexism refers to the attitude that "women who are traditionally feminine should be rewarded." See Amy Grubb and Emily Turner, "Attribution of blame in rape cases: A review of the impact of rape myth

acceptance, gender role conformity and substance use on victim blaming," *Aggression and Violent Behavior* 17 (2012), 443–452.
43. Findings by Littleton et al. support the idea that "given the strong stigma against heavy drinking among women," intoxicated victims are viewed as more blameworthy than victims who had not consumed alcohol. Their work also shows that internalized victim blaming appears to be more acute in impaired (i.e., intoxicated) and especially in incapacitated (i.e., unconscious) victims. In addition to engaging in the highest levels of self-blame, incapacitated victims are particularly susceptible to feelings of stigmatization that are unrelated to the external blame they actually experience. In other words, consistent with humiliation, it is the "victim's own perception of [their] experience" that generates "self-blame and ... feelings of stigma." See Littleton et al., "Impaired and Incapacitated Rape Victims: Assault Characteristics and Post-Assault Experiences," *Violence and Victims* 24(4), 439–457.
44. Grubb and Turner, "Attribution of blame in rape cases," 448.
45. See Macur and Nate Schweber, "Rape Case Unfolds on Web and Splits City."
46. Richard A. Oppel, Jr., "Online Comments in Ohio Rape Case Lead to Charges Against Two," http://www.nytimes.com/2013/03/20/us/web-comments-in-ohio-rape-case-lead-to-charges-against-two.html.
47. In the United States, 90 percent of reported cases of sexual violence are committed against women. Cahill describes a conversation she had with a male relative who questioned her focus on sexual violence against women given that men are also victimized. I was similarly confronted by a male panelist at an academic conference when presenting my own work on violence against women. See http://www.bjs.gov/index.cfm?ty=tp&tid=317 and Cahill, *Rethinking Rape*, Chapter Four, "Rape as Embodied Experience."
48. In the United States, it is estimated, based on reported cases, that between 20 and 25 percent of women will experience sexual violence at some point during their lives. See http://www.bjs.gov/index.cfm?ty=tp&tid=317.
49. Support for the inevitability of sexual violence against women is reflected in the attitude of hostile sexism that women who violate norms deserve to be punished. See Grubb and Turner, "Attribution of blame in rape cases."
50. *Frames of War*, 41.
51. Ibid, 159.
52. Media coverage of the case notes that Holtzclaw raped and sexually assaulted "at least" 13 women; the 13 mentioned are those who came forward with allegations. See Matt Ford, "A Guilty Verdict for Daniel Holtzclaw," http://www.theatlantic.com/politics/archive/2015/12/daniel-holtzclaw-trial-guilty/420009/.

53. Treva Lindsey, "The Rape Trial Everyone in America Should Be Watching," http://www.cosmopolitan.com/politics/a49050/daniel-holtzclaw-trial-oklahoma/.
54. The relative lack of coverage is noted by Ford, "A Guilty Verdict for Daniel Holtzclaw." *The Huffington Post* provided comprehensive coverage of the case: http://www.huffingtonpost.com/news/daniel-holtzclaw/.
55. Holtzclaw was sentenced to 263 years in prison. See Ford, "A Guilty Verdict for Daniel Holtzclaw" and Sarah Larimer," Disgraced ex-cop Daniel Holtzclaw sentenced to 263 years for on-duty rapes, sexual assaults," https://www.washingtonpost.com/news/post-nation/wp/2016/01/21/disgraced-ex-officer-daniel-holtzclaw-to-be-sentenced-after-sex-crimes-conviction/.
56. *Frames of War*, 53.
57. Ibid, 6.
58. Ibid, 5.
59. Ibid, 9.
60. Ibid, 156.
61. Ibid, 24.

Bibliography

Bergoffen, Debra B. 2012. *Contesting the Politics of Genocidal Rape: Affirming the Dignity of the Vulnerable Body*. New York: Routledge.

Bogdanich, Walt. 2014a. Reporting Rape and Wishing She Hadn't. *The New York Times*, July 12. https://www.nytimes.com/2014/07/13/us/how-one-college-handled-a-sexual-assault-complaint.html

———. 2014b. Support for a College Student Grows After a Rape Complaint is Dismissed. *The New York Times*, July 21. http://www.nytimes.com/2014/07/22/nyregion/support-for-a-student-grows-as-college-examines-its-sexual-assault-policies.html

Butler, Judith. 2004. *Precarious Life: The Powers of Mourning and Violence*. New York: Verso.

———. 2010. *Frames of War: When is Life Grievable?* New York: Verso.

Cahill, Ann J. 2001. *Rethinking Rape*. Ithaca: Cornell University Press.

Eilperin, Juliet. Seeking to End Rape on Campus, White House Launches "It's On Us,". http://www.washingtonpost.com/news/post-politics/wp/2014/09/19/seeking-to-end-rape-on-campus-wh-launches-its-on-us/

Ford, Matt. 2015. A Guilty Verdict for Daniel Holtzclaw. *The Atlantic*, December 11. http://www.theatlantic.com/politics/archive/2015/12/daniel-holtzclaw-trial-guilty/420009/

Gilson, Erinn C. 2014. *The Ethics of Vulnerability: A Feminist Analysis of Social Life and Practice*. New York: Routledge.

Gotell, Lise. 2011. Third Wave Antirape Activism on Neoliberal Terrain: The Garneau Sisterhood. In *Sexual Assault Law, Practice & Activism in a Post-Jane Doe Era*, ed. Ellizabeth Sheehy. Ottawa: University of Ottawa.

Grubb, Amy, and Emily Turner. 2012. Attribution of Blame in Rape Cases: A Review of the Impact of Rape Myth Acceptance, Gender Role Conformity and Substance Use on Victim Blaming. *Aggression and Violent Behavior* 17: 443–452.

Larimer, Sarah. 2016. Disgraced Ex-cop Daniel Holtzclaw Sentenced to 263 years for On-Duty Rapes, Sexual Assaults. *The Washington Post*, January 22. https://www.washingtonpost.com/news/post-nation/wp/2016/01/21/disgraced-ex-officer-daniel-holtzclaw-to-be-sentenced-after-sex-crimes-conviction/

Lindsey, Treva. 2015. The Rape Trial Everyone in America Should Be Watching. *Cosmopolitan*, November 10. http://www.cosmopolitan.com/politics/a49050/daniel-holtzclaw-trial-oklahoma/

Littleton, H., et al. 2009. Impaired and Incapacitated Rape Victims: Assault Characteristics and Post-Assault Experiences. *Violence and Victims* 24 (4): 439–457.

Macur, Juliet, and Schweber, Nate. 2012. Rape Case Unfolds on Web and Splits City. *The New York Times*, December 6. http://www.nytimes.com/2012/12/17/sports/high-school-football-rape-case-unfolds-online-and-divides-steubenville-ohio.html

Obama Administration White House Website. President Obama Launches the "It's On Us" Campaign to End Sexual Assault on Campus. https://obamawhitehouse.archives.gov/blog/2014/09/19/president-obama-launches-its-us-campaign-end-sexual-assault-campus

Oliver, Kelly. 2016. There's No Such Thing as Nonconsensual Sex: It's Violence. *The New York Times*, November 21. http://www.nytimes.com/2016/11/21/opinion/there-is-no-such-thing-as-nonconsensual-sex-its-violence.html?emc=eta1

Oppel, Richard A., Jr. 2013. Online Comments in Ohio Rape Case Lead to Charges Against Two. *The New York Times*, March 19. http://www.nytimes.com/2013/03/20/us/web-comments-in-ohio-rape-case-lead-to-charges-against-two.html

Wemple, Erik. 2013. CNN is Getting Hammered for Steubenville coverage. *The Washington Post*, March 18. https://www.washingtonpost.com/blogs/erik-wemple/wp/2013/03/18/cnn-is-getting-hammered-for-steubenville-coverage/

CHAPTER 9

Sex Trafficking, Reproductive Rights, and Sovereign Borders: A Transnational Struggle over Women's Bodies

Diana Tietjens Meyers

The aims of this chapter are threefold. First, I draw attention to an overlooked dimension of sex trafficking—namely, its abuse of women's reproductive rights. Second, I diagnose a tension between international anti-trafficking and refugee law, and US anti-trafficking and immigration law. Third, I show that US anti-trafficking and immigration law is enforcing a misguided conception of victims that denies recognition to agentic victims of human rights abuse. Others have already made compelling arguments that women who are citizens of economically disadvantaged states and who have been trafficked into the sex industry in economically advantaged states should be considered candidates for asylum. These arguments cite the sexual violence and forced labor that trafficked women are subjected to, along with their well-founded fear of persecution—stigmatization, social ostracism, and re-trafficking—if they're repatriated.[1] This chapter adds a reproductive rights component to defending the right to asylum for adult women who have been trafficked into the sex industry by transnational criminal organizations.[2]

My line of argument assumes the following reproductive rights, all of which are codified in international human rights treaties:

D. T. Meyers (✉)
University of Connecticut, Storrs, CT, USA

© The Author(s) 2018
C. Fischer, L. Dolezal (eds.), *New Feminist Perspectives on Embodiment*, Breaking Feminist Waves,
https://doi.org/10.1007/978-3-319-72353-2_9

1. The right to marry and found a family,
2. The right to the highest attainable standard of physical and mental health,
3. The right to workplaces that are safe for women in their reproductive years,
4. The right to decide freely and responsibly on the number and spacing of their children and to have access to the information, education, and means to exercise these rights.

Women's reproductive rights guarantee reproductive health and function, together with reproductive freedom and self-determination.[3]

Studies show that transnational sex trafficking organizations abuse all of these rights.[4] In withholding condoms and forcing women to have intercourse with clients, they put women at risk of unwanted pregnancies, and when trafficked sex workers get pregnant, traffickers force them to have abortions. Women trafficked into the sex industry have no reproductive freedom, and their reproductive health is constantly in jeopardy. Forced unprotected sex with strangers exposes women to sexually transmitted diseases (STDs), which when left untreated can lead to infertility. Clients' violent sexual behavior and abortions performed by ill-trained practitioners can damage women's reproductive organs. Except for abortions, sex traffickers provide little or no healthcare for the women they exploit. Consequently, residents of rehabilitation facilities for trafficked women commonly need treatment for STDs and for post-traumatic stress disorder. Moreover, the freedom to marry and found a family eludes many victims of sex trafficking. Some discover that they are infertile after years of forced sex without medical care. Many find that men perceive them as "damaged goods" and consider them ineligible marital partners.[5] In sum, sex trafficking violates women's human right to reproductive health and function while violating their human right to reproductive freedom and self-determination.

Reproductive health and function, and reproductive freedom and self-determination are indisputable human rights that are legally recognized, albeit imperfectly implemented, in destination states where women who have been trafficked into the sex industry are abused. Consequently, it might seem that these women should be candidates for legal protection under asylum law. Yet, they are seldom granted their right to a safe haven, and the first section of this chapter offers an account of the reasons for this failure of protection. I take the tensions between US anti-trafficking and immigration law, on the one hand, and international anti-trafficking and refugee law, on the other, as my case in point and identify two major obstacles to appropriate remedies for victims of sex trafficking. I call them the "smuggled woman" problem and the "crime stopper" problem.

The criminal and legal phenomena I examine add up to a three-way struggle over women's bodily integrity and autonomy. Impoverished women in the Global South seek to migrate to more affluent states in the Global North, where they hope to find economic opportunity. Traffickers take advantage of these women's aspirations and vulnerability to transport them across borders and force them into prostitution when they arrive. Destination states regard most of the trafficked women as criminals, along with their traffickers. Classified as undocumented migrants, the women are deported to their countries of origin, where, the evidence suggests, many of them will be re-trafficked into the sex industry.

There are many lessons to be drawn from this sorry state of affairs. In the second section, I examine the way in which a misconception about victimhood plays out in this vicious, cyclical struggle. US anti-trafficking law rests on a conception of victims as objectified, abject, and devoid of agency. According to this conception, so-called smuggled women who take the initiative and endeavor to migrate disqualify themselves as victims of human rights abuse. As agentic subjects, they are plainly not passive bodies caught up in the schemes of villainous criminals, so they forfeit their rights. Yet, because this conception of a victim is in conflict with established legal doctrine and basic tenets of justice, US and similar anti-trafficking provisions and practices must be reformed.

Asylum Rights and Victims of Sex Trafficking

Protecting people from persecution is the purpose of recognizing refugees and granting asylum to them. The 1951 Geneva Convention Relating to the Status of Refugees defines a refugee as a person who, "owing to well-founded fear of being persecuted for reasons of race, religion, nationality, membership of a particular social group or political opinion, is outside the country of his [sic] nationality and is unable or, owing to such fear, is unwilling to avail himself [sic] of the protection of that country."[6] The convention never defines persecution. However, legal scholar James Hathaway defines persecution as "a sustained or systemic violation of basic human rights demonstrative of a failure of state protection."[7] By definition, sex trafficking organizations violate their victims' rights to liberty and reproductive self-determination. Sometimes called sex slaves—the bodies of women trafficked into the sex industry are under the control of their traffickers and their customers. Moreover, the abusive conditions in which trafficked women are compelled to provide sexual services and the low quality of medical services they receive put their reproductive health and thus their right to found a family in jeopardy. These sustained violations of basic human rights notwithstanding, there are major obstacles to classifying women trafficked into the sex industry as refugees.

Forced sex work is always illegal under international law. The 2000 UN "Protocol to Prevent, Suppress and Punish Trafficking In Persons, Especially Women and Children, Supplementing the United Nations Convention against Transnational Organized Crime," often called the Palermo Protocol, defines trafficking in persons as:

> the recruitment, transportation, transfer, harbouring or receipt of persons, by means of the threat or use of force or other forms of coercion, of abduction, of fraud, of deception, of the abuse of power or of a position of vulnerability or of the giving or receiving of payments or benefits to achieve the consent of a person having control over another person, for the purpose of exploitation.[8]

The protocol goes on to specifically include sexual exploitation. Thus, trafficked sex workers have been tricked or coerced in the recruitment and relocation process, held in debt bondage or imprisoned in brothels at their destinations, or both. Still, most States Parties to the Palermo Protocol and to the Convention on Refugees do not regard women trafficked into the sex industry within their borders as candidates for refugee status and asylum. I'll discuss two of the main reasons why these women's rights are denied.

I call the first obstacle the "smuggled woman" problem. A growing social scientific literature reveals that most adult women trafficked into the sex industry are also economic migrants—that is, they have knowingly availed themselves of trafficking networks in order to be smuggled into more prosperous nations in the hope of economic betterment. According to Dina Haynes, "Victims of human trafficking are people who determined to improve their lives but had that desire exploited."[9] Likewise, Louisa Waugh points out that women in post-trafficking recovery programs think of themselves as "migrants who'd been brutalized because they'd had to resort to desperate measures."[10] Thus, many trafficking scenarios start with a smuggling scenario. The would-be migrants are neither naïve country girls, nor are they duped about their employment prospects abroad.[11] Rather, they are extremely poor women who have no job opportunities sufficient to meet their needs (often family members' needs as well) in their home countries.[12] Seeking a solution, they allow themselves to be recruited by known traffickers in order to obtain fake travel documents and assistance in crossing otherwise closed borders, all the while hoping to escape from poverty. When they reach their destinations, they are forced into prostitution.

In many host countries, however, their cooperation with transnational criminal gangs in the procurement and transport process consigns them to the category "smuggled," a label that excludes them from the category "trafficked." In the USA, for example, the Trafficking Victims Protection Act (TVPA) of 2000 mandates procedures for handling alleged trafficking cases and for providing benefits to individuals certified as trafficking victims. Under the TVPA, qualifying for benefits comparable to those provided to refugees is contingent on being certified as "severely trafficked." But to obtain certification, a female foreign national working in the US sex industry is, for all practical purposes, required to prove that she was kidnapped by, sold to, or deceived by a trafficker at her point of origin.[13] If certified as a victim of severe trafficking, the applicant may apply for a T visa, which can, but does not automatically, lead to permanent residence.[14] Although application numbers and rates of approval for T visas have increased since the program began, it is impossible to say whether women trafficked into the sex industry have benefited because government statistics do not differentiate between their applications and those of individuals trafficked for other types of labor.[15] Moreover, estimates of the number of women trafficked into the sex industry in the USA are much higher than the total number of T visas granted.[16] These figures are unsurprising, for, as we have seen, few of the women doing forced sex work are recruited and relocated through force or fraud. Absent certification as a severely trafficked person, women who have been trafficked into the sex industry and who are subsequently "rescued" by law enforcement officers are relegated to the status of undocumented migrants and processed for deportation despite being forced to perform commercial sexual services in the USA.[17] Consent at any stage of a woman's journey into forced sex work nullifies her claim to be severely trafficked.

I call the second obstacle the "crime stopper" problem. As the title of the United Nations protocol on trafficking implies, international law views trafficking in persons principally as a crime perpetrated by transnational criminals as opposed to an abuse of trafficking victims' human rights. Arresting and prosecuting traffickers are prioritized over rectifying the wrongs done to trafficked victims. In keeping with this focus, international law obliges states to pass anti-trafficking legislation independent of refugee law. One result is that women who claim to have been trafficked into the sex industry are funneled into the criminal law apparatus—in the USA they must agree to cooperate with prosecutors pursuing cases against traffickers—and into a special system of accreditation for extended residence that sets higher criteria for obtaining a T visa than those that asylum seekers must meet.[18] By splitting anti-trafficking law away from human rights law and segregating sex trafficking victims from refugees, the legal system closes off the human rights remedy par excellence—namely, asylum.

A law enforcement gestalt undergirds the smuggled woman problem and the crime stopper problem, and both problems privilege sovereign governance over individual human rights. The crime stopper problem emphasizes prosecuting perpetrators and marginalizes victims except insofar as they can provide incriminating testimony or leads. The smuggled woman problem compounds this marginalization of victims. In all but a few cases, it denies victimhood in the name of defending borders. Once victims of sex trafficking have been classified as malefactors along with traffickers, law enforcement—deporting victims and punishing traffickers—becomes the preeminent objective.

In practice, the law enforcement gestalt creates a presumption against refugee status for women trafficked into the sex industry. We have seen, for example, that US law not only directs women who claim to be sex trafficking victims into the T visa system but also sets more stringent evidential standards for obtaining a T visa than it does for obtaining asylum through regular refugee proceedings. However, this presumption conflicts with US obligations as a signatory and State Party to the Palermo Protocol.[19] Article 14 of the Palermo Protocol states:

> Nothing in this Protocol shall affect the rights, obligations and responsibilities of States and individuals under international law, including international humanitarian law and international human rights law and, in particular, where applicable, the 1951 Convention and the 1967 Protocol relating to the Status of Refugees and the principle of *non-refoulement* as contained therein.

Erecting more restrictive standards for obtaining a safe haven for victims of one type of human rights abuse plainly abrogates the obligations of States Parties to the Refugee Convention and violates the rights of victims under the Convention. The US distinction between a severely trafficked person and a trafficked person is also incompatible with the Palermo Protocol. As Rey Koslowski points out, under the protocol, "a smuggled woman becomes a trafficking victim when she arrives at her destination and is forced into prostitution."[20] Coercion in the recruitment and transport process is not a necessary condition for trafficking. I do not oppose prosecuting transnational sex trafficking organizations. However, deporting women who have been forced to work in the US sex industry in no way deters traffickers with subsidiary businesses in human smuggling.

Implementing the Palermo Protocol requires that a human rights gestalt counterbalance the law enforcement gestalt. In particular, the human rights abuse systematically inflicted on women trafficked into the sex industry must be brought to the fore and redressed. Since reproductive health and function, and reproductive self-determination are both at stake in sex trafficking, justice and law require remedies that respect these human rights. Medical care must be provided to cure STDs and, if possible, to repair damage to trafficked women's reproductive organs. Psychological services must be provided to help victims recover from the trauma they have endured. Insofar as their subjection to sex trafficking rules out marriage and founding a family in their communities of origin, they must be allowed to reside in, be furnished with job training in, and receive employment opportunities in destination countries. In view of more liberal sexual mores in destination states, it is possible that permanent residence and work permits will eventually enable them to recuperate their right to marry and found a family. Alas, very few women trafficked into sex work receive any form of reparative recompense despite the grievous abuse of their reproductive rights.

Summing up, poor, young women who are citizens of states where women and girls are routinely discriminated against in education and employment and/or where law and order have broken down because of social upheaval, widespread poverty, or recent armed conflict often attempt migration to more prosperous states, where they hope to better themselves and perhaps send extra income to their families at home. Transnational criminal gangs that face little or no interference from legal authorities in the countries where women are recruited, or, for that matter, in destination countries, see these women's plight as an opportunity to profit.[21] So they help them to cross borders using counterfeit documents or clandestine routes, sometimes extracting payment for this service, and they sell the women to fellow traffickers, who force them into prostitution at their destinations. No one disputes that the reproductive and other harms resulting from forced work in the sex industry rise to the level of persecution. Still, law enforcement officials in destination states regard these women with suspicion, and domestic law backs up their attitude. Any evidence of a woman's possible complicity in the recruitment or transport process results in her deportation. Moreover, women who are seeking certification as sex trafficking victims must demonstrate the usefulness of the evidence they can furnish to prosecutors if their rights to the protections and benefits of a T visa are to be vindicated.

Women exercising their agency to overcome poverty first land in the crosshairs of trafficking gangsters. Then, if they succeed in escaping from their traffickers, or if authorities raid their traffickers' operations, they land in the crosshairs of immigration police and criminal prosecutors.

An Agency-Denying Victim Paradigm

In my view, two victim paradigms dominate current human rights discourse.[22] The heroic victim paradigm, exemplified by Chinese dissidents Ai Wei Wei and Liu Xiaobo, celebrates the non-violent agency of individuals persecuted for their human rights activism. In contrast, the starving Jews, Roma, and gays and lesbians who were liberated from Hitler's concentration camps at the end of World War II exemplify the pathetic victim paradigm. These Holocaust victims share several characteristics that typify pathetic victims:

1. They were innocent of any wrongdoing relevant to their treatment;
2. They were utterly helpless in the face of insuperable force;
3. Other people subjected them to unspeakable suffering.

Notable as well from the standpoint of the cognizability of these victims, the evidence for this severe, humanly inflicted harm is incontrovertible.

The pathetic victim paradigm frames legal understanding of victims of sex trafficking in the USA. Innocence of wrongdoing that could have provoked the suffering that a victim undergoes is crucial for both paradigms. It is troubling, however, that for apolitical pathetic victims, proof of non-provocation and thus non-complicity has come to require showing that you were subjected to such crushing force that you were reduced to passivity. Helpless and passive—de-agentified—you couldn't be complicit in the harm inflicted on you, so you must be an innocent victim. According to the pathetic victim paradigm, victimization and agency are incompatible.[23]

It is bizarre that de-agentification has come to stand for non-complicity in human rights abuse, for this conception is at odds with familiar legal and customary understandings of the non-responsibility of competent adults for the wrongfully inflicted harms they may suffer. Usually, we invoke force, fraud, or coercion to rule out complicity in abuse and to identify victims of abuse. There is plentiful evidence that international prostitution rings use strategies that combine deception, force, and coercion. To lure targets abroad, traffickers often assure poor women that they will get respectable, well-paid jobs. Afterward, they confiscate their captives' passports, take photographs of them being raped, and threaten to send the pictures to their families.[24] Although traffickers' lies are transparent to many of their targets, their violence and intimidation are highly effective. Consequently, the women they ensnare submit to work in the sex industry, often under abhorrent conditions.

Now, it is worth noting that a broad presumption of innocence in the event of aggression underpins widely accepted understandings about who counts as a victim. There are countless measures you need not take to prevent or halt an attack on your rights, and rights-bearers have a good deal of discretion when it comes to coping with potential or occurring rights violations. For example, residents of neighborhoods where street crime might occur are not required to carry a weapon to defend themselves, and failing to use a weapon or otherwise defend yourself while being mugged does not affect your status as a crime victim. By specifying precautions and risks people aren't obligated to take in order to qualify as victims, conceptions of force, fraud, and coercion delineate action spaces—spheres of freedom and permissible agency. Acting within the bounds of these action spaces ensures that right-holders' non-complicity and innocence are not in question. If they are attacked, they have done nothing to forfeit their status as cognizably innocent victims. If this is correct, the pathetic victim paradigm's de-agentification requirement is far more stringent than standard conceptions of victimization. Indeed, it is far too stringent to make moral or legal sense.

Yet, someone might object, women who knowingly avail themselves of the wiles of traffickers to illegally enter more affluent states are not exercising their agency in a legally permissible way. Since they are acting outside the bounds of legally defined action spaces, they are not acting within their rights. Consequently, they are not innocent victims when they are trafficked into the sex industry, and the states where this industry flourishes owe them nothing.

I have acknowledged that victims of sex trafficking are often economic migrants, as well. Still, I urge, their position is morally complex and by no means clear-cut. They are accomplices in the crime of migrant smuggling, but are also victims of an international economic order in which economic and social human rights are systematically denied. In addition, many women who are being smuggled occupy a liminal position vis-à-vis traffickers, which, in homage to Joseph Heller's masterpiece, *Catch 22*, I'll call "*presque* trafficked." Nevertheless, they are under the effective control of traffickers, and unless border control officers stop them, they soon will be trafficked for sexual exploitation as defined by the Palermo Protocol.

I don't think it's an exaggeration to say that we're discussing a struggle over women's bodies—their desperate migration decisions, transnational sex trafficking organizations' targeting of them, and the Global North's migrant exclusion policies—in the context of an unacknowledged global humanitarian crisis that takes the form of widespread, unrelenting, and severe poverty. There can be no doubt that women who put themselves in harm's way by cooperating with traffickers who facilitate their migration are willing to put their reproductive rights on the line in order to escape from such immiseration. Plainly, they see migration as their only feasible solution. This background suggests that their situation is more ambiguous than the smuggled/trafficked binary embedded in US law acknowledges.

Because women trafficked into the sex industry have defied lawful migration restrictions in the hope of gaining benefits that should be theirs by right, their actions pit law enforcement—specifically, border policing—against the entitlements of social and economic human rights. Although these women are complicit in an illegal migration scheme, their complicity is arguably excusable in light of their acute need for economic betterment and the unavailability of such in sending states. In addition, they are likely to have debts to family members (or other community members) who financed their migration that they can only repay by migrating successfully, or debts to traffickers with side businesses in human smuggling who will track them down and traffic them to recoup their investment.[25] For these women, repatriation is neither a realistic nor a fair option. Not only do they have every reason to fear that if they are deported they will be hunted down and trafficked, but they also have reason to fear that their family members will be harmed unless they surrender themselves to the traffickers. It is not uncommon, we know, for family members to plead with trafficking victims to acquiesce to their traffickers.

Determinations of innocence presuppose moral judgments about the acceptability of various types of agentic initiative in situations that are fraught with multifarious dangers. It is clear, however, that for purposes of human rights, innocence does not entail the absence of all initiative. Accordingly, whether the migration stratagems of women who are subsequently trafficked ought to be countenanced all things considered is a moral and legal question that must reconcile immigration policy with international human rights law. In this connection, it is necessary to bear in mind that human rights priorities and understandings of what constitutes adequate respect for human rights are matters of ongoing debate, negotiation, legislation, and litigation. Correlatively, our understanding of what constitutes wrongful force, fraud, and coercion is not static, nor is our understanding of what measures victims may permissibly take to cope with action spaces demarcated by wrongful force, fraud, or coercion static. There is no way to avoid judging the merit of anyone's claim to be a victim of human rights abuse. Not only must the truthfulness of the claimant's testimony be evaluated, but also it is necessary to assess whether her claim is congruent with a credible interpretation of human rights. These are epistemological and normative questions that cannot be circumvented in good conscience by taking the criterial shortcut of de-agentification and blaming the victims.

Major human rights documents encode civil and political rights; economic, social, and cultural rights; the rights of women; and many more.[26] Although realization of all of these rights is tenuous and incomplete to this day, the framers and States Parties to these covenants intend the human rights enumerated therein to collectively define respect for humanity. To the extent that realizing these rights remains an aspiration, then, respect for humanity remains an aspiration. Still, this persistent injustice must not be used as a pretext for doing nothing or doing as little as possible to address abuses of human rights taking place in our midst. The question that presses upon us is: What can we do in the here and now to respect, as best we can, the rights of women who are victimized first by economic privation and then by traffickers? I have argued that overzealous deportation practices, the invidious distinction between women trafficked into the sex industry and refugees, and the stinginess of reparative benefits available to certified sex trafficking victims compound the dishonor done to their humanity, adding insult to injury.

Notes

1. Binaifer A. Davar, "Rethinking Gender-Related Persecution, Sexual Violence, and Women's Rights: A New Conceptual Framework for Political Asylum and International Human Rights Law" *Texas Journal of Women and the Law* 6 (1997): 241–256; Tala Hartsough, "Asylum for Trafficked Women: Escape Strategies beyond the T Visa," *Hastings Women's Law Journal* 13 (2002): 77–116; Dina Francesca Haynes, "Used, Abused, Arrested, and Deported: Extending Immigration Benefits to Protect Victims of Trafficking and to Secure Prosecution of Traffickers," in *Women's Rights: A* Human Rights Quarterly *Reader*. Ed. Bert B. Lockwood. Baltimore MD. Johns Hopkins University Press (2006); Dina Francesca Haynes, "(Not) Found Chained to a Bed in a Brothel: Conceptual, legal, and Procedural Failures to Fulfill the Promise of the Trafficking Victims Protection Act," *Georgetown Immigration Law Journal* 21 (2007): 337–381.
2. I note the gravity of trafficking children into the sex industry, but I leave it aside, for this topic raises distinct issues that I do not have space to discuss here.
3. See the International Covenant on Civil and Political Rights, the International Covenant on Economic, Social, and Cultural Rights, and CEDAW (accessible at http://www.ohchr.org/EN/ProfessionalInterest/Pages/CoreInstruments.aspx).
4. For analysis of the impact of sex trafficking on reproductive health and function among victims from Eastern Europe, see Cathy Zimmerman, et al., *Stolen Smiles: The Physical And Psychological Health Consequences Of Women And Adolescents Trafficked In Europe*, London School of Hygiene & Tropical Medicine: http://genderviolence.lshtm.ac.uk/files/Stolen-Smiles-Trafficking-and-Health-2006.pdf (2006), 3, 63. A study of Nigerian women trafficked into the sex industry in Europe obtained similar findings. See S. Abdulraheem and A. R. Oladipo, "Trafficking in Women and Children: A Hidden Health and Social Problem in Nigeria," *International Journal of Sociology and Anthropology* 2 (2010): 34–39, 37, 39. A study of the health consequences of sex trafficking in Southeast Asia reports that septic abortions are a major danger faced by trafficked sex workers in Burma and Thailand (Chris Beyrer and Julie Stachowiak, "Health Consequences of Trafficking of Women and Girls in Southeast Asia," *Brown Journal Of World Affairs* 10 (2003): 105–117, 106, 111.
5. I acknowledge the heterosexist assumption underlying this observation. However, heteronormativity remains dominant worldwide and especially so in the states of origin of most women trafficked into the sex industry.
6. http://www.unhcr.org/3b66c2aa10.html (accessed 10/14/2015).
7. James C. Hathaway, *The Law of Refugee Status*, Toronto: Butterworths (1991) 104–105.

8. http://www.unodc.org/unodc/en/human-trafficking/what-is-human-trafficking.html (accessed 9/7/2013).
9. Haynes 2007, 373; also see Wendy Chapkis, "Trafficking, Migration, and the Law: Protecting Innocents, Punishing Immigrants," *Gender and Society* 17, 3 (2003): 923–937, 931–932.
10. Louisa Waugh, *Selling Olga*, xv. Kara notes that in Central and Eastern Europe, seduction, coupled with promises of lifelong romance in the West, is another common ploy to lure women into trafficking schemes: Siddharth Kara, *Sex Trafficking*, 9.
11. Siddharth Kara, Sex *Trafficking: Inside the Business of Modern Slavery*, (New York, NY: Columbia University Press, 2009), 7. Louisa Waugh, *Selling Olga: Stories of Human Trafficking and Resistance*, (London, UK: Orion Books, 2007), xiv, 63.
12. Suzanne Daley, "Rescuing Young Women from Trafficker's Hands," New York Times, October 15, 2010. Siddharth Kara, *Sex Trafficking*, 7, 23–30, 115, 142. Louisa Waugh, *Selling Olga*, 3, 73.
13. Jacqueline Bhabha, "International Gatekeepers?: The Tension between Asylum Advocacy and Human Rights," *Harvard Human Rights Journal* 15 (2002): 155–181,175–176; April Rieger, "Missing The Mark: Why The Trafficking Victims Protection Act Fails To Protect Sex Trafficking Victims In The United States," *Harvard Journal of Law and Gender* 30 (2007): 231–256, 249; Hartsough, 99.
14. Hartsough, 101.
15. http://www.uscis.gov/USCIS/Resources/Reports%20and%20Studies/Immigration%20Forms%20Data/Victims/I914t-I918u_visastatistics_2012-dec.pdf.
16. As Gozdziak and Collett point out, disputed definitions of sex trafficking, not to mention the underground nature of the enterprise, make accurate counts of victims impossible and estimates highly conjectural. Nevertheless, they cite the official US estimate for 2004 of 14,500–17,500. (See Elzbieta M. Gozdziak and Elizabeth A, Collett, "Research on Human Trafficking in North America: A Review of Literature," *International Migration* 43 (2005): 99–127, 107–108, 117.)
17. Rieger, 249.
18. Rieger, 252–253.
19. See https://www.unodc.org/unodc/en/treaties/CTOC/countrylist-traffickingprotocol.html (accessed 10/14/2015).
20. Rey Koslowski, "Response to 'The New Global Slave Trade' by Harold Honfju Koh," in *Displacement, Asylum, Migration: The Oxford Amnesty Lectures 2004*. ed. Kate E. Tunstall. Oxford: Oxford University Press (2006), 259–260. Also see UNHCR "Guidelines on International Protection No. 7: The Application of Article 1A(2) of the 1951 Convention

and/or 1967 Protocol Relating to the Status of Refugees to Victims of Trafficking and Persons At Risk of Being Trafficked". 7 April, 2006 http://www.refworld.org/docid/443679fa4.html (accessed 2/13/2014).
21. Leslie and John Francis show that lack of enforcement of laws prohibiting sex trafficking is not a problem unique to source countries. It is also a failing of destination states, including the USA. See their "Trafficking in Human Beings: Partial Compliance Theory, Enforcement Failure, and Obligations to Victims," in *Poverty, Agency, and Human Rights*, ed. Diana Tietjens Meyers (New York: Oxford University Press, 2014).
22. For detailed treatment of these paradigms, see Chap. 1 of Diana Tietjens Meyers, *Victims Stories and the Advancement of Human Rights*, New York: Oxford University Press (2016).
23. For helpful, related discussion of human dignity and the "simplistic contrast between agency and passivity," see Martha C. Nussbaum, *Upheavals of Thought: The Intelligence of Emotions*, Cambridge: Cambridge University Press (2001), 405–414.
24. For documentation of confiscated passports, see, for example: http://www.nytimes.com/1998/01/11/world/contraband-women-a-special-report-traffickers-new-cargo-arge-slavic-women.html?sec=&spon=&scp=5&sq=trafficking%20victims%20confiscated%20passport&st=cse&pagewanted=all, http://www.nytimes.com/2008/07/10/nyregion/10nurse.html?scp=6&sq=trafficking%20victims%20confiscated%20passport&st=cse, http://www.hrw.org/en/news/2000/02/21/international-trafficking-women-and-children. For evidence of the use of photographs, see: http://www.bloomberg.com/apps/news?pid=20601109&sid=amKSCFA_Fm3s&refer=home, http://www.europarl.europa.eu/workingpapers/libe/pdf/109_en.pdf. p. 13.
25. Liz Kelly points out that many "smuggled" women borrow money from relatives in order to seek their fortunes abroad. If they are deported and return empty-handed, they are unable to repay their debts and feel compelled to submit to re-trafficking in the hope of making good on their debts, if not improving family finances. Thus, the cycle of sexual abuse commonly enters a new iteration. Liz Kelly, "'You Can Find Anything You Want': A Critical Reflection on Research on Trafficking in Persons within and into Europe," *International Migration* 43 (1/2) (2005): 236–265, 248.
26. http://www.ohchr.org/EN/ProfessionalInterest/Pages/CoreInstruments.aspx (accessed 9/14/2014).

Bibliography

Abdulraheem, S., and A.R. Oladipo. 2010. Trafficking in Women and Children: A Hidden Health and Social Problem in Nigeria. *International Journal of Sociology and Anthropology* 2: 34–39.

Beyrer, Chris, and Julie Stachowiak. 2003. Health Consequences of Trafficking of Women and Girls in Southeast Asia. *Brown Journal Of World Affairs* 10: 105–117.

Bhabha, Jacqueline. 2002. International Gatekeepers?: The Tension Between Asylum Advocacy and Human Rights. *Harvard Human Rights Journal* 15: 155–181.

Chapkis, Wendy. 2003. Trafficking, Migration, and the Law: Protecting Innocents, Punishing Immigrants. *Gender and Society* 17 (3): 923–937.

Daley, Suzanne. 2010. Rescuing Young Women from Trafficker's Hands. *New York Times*, October 15.

Davar, Binaifer A. 1997. Rethinking Gender-Related Persecution, Sexual Violence, and Women's Rights: A New Conceptual Framework for Political Asylum and International Human Rights Law. *Texas Journal of Women and the Law* 6: 241–256.

European Parliament, Directorate-General for Research. *Trafficking in Women*. http://www.europarl.europa.eu/workingpapers/libe/pdf/109_en.pdf

Francis, Leslie, and John G. Francis. 2014. Trafficking in Human Beings: Partial Compliance Theory, Enforcement Failure, and Obligations to Victims. In *Poverty, Agency, and Human Rights*, ed. Diana Tietjens Meyers. New York: Oxford University Press.

Gozdziak, Elzbieta M., and Elizabeth A. Collett. 2005. Research on Human Trafficking in North America: A Review of Literature. *International Migration* 43: 99–127.

Hartsough, Tala. 2002. Asylum for Trafficked Women: Escape Strategies Beyond the T Visa. *Hastings Women's Law Journal* 13: 77–116.

Hathaway, C. 1991. *The Law of Refugee Status*, 104–105. Toronto: Butterworths.

Haynes, Dina Francesca. 2006. Used, Abused, Arrested, and Deported: Extending Immigration Benefits to Protect Victims of Trafficking and to Secure Prosecution of Traffickers. In *Women's Rights: A Human Rights Quarterly Reader*, ed. Bert B. Lockwood. Baltimore: Johns Hopkins University Press.

———. 2007. (Not) Found Chained to a Bed in a Brothel: Conceptual, Legal, and Procedural Failures to Fulfill the Promise of the Trafficking Victims Protection Act. *Georgetown Immigration Law Journal* 21: 337–381.

International Covenant on Civil and Political Rights, the International Covenant on Economic, Social, and Cultural Rights, and CEDAW. Accessible at http://www.ohchr.org/EN/ProfessionalInterest/Pages/CoreInstruments.aspx

Kara, Siddharth. 2009. *Sex Trafficking: Inside the Business of Modern Slavery*. New York: Columbia University Press.

Kelly, Liz. 2005. 'You Can Find Anything You Want': A Critical Reflection on Research on Trafficking in Persons Within and into Europe. *International Migration* 43 (1/2): 139–144.

Koslowski, Rey. 2006. Response to 'The New Global Slave Trade' by Harold Honfju Koh. In *Displacement, Asylum, Migration: The Oxford Amnesty Lectures 2004*, ed. Kate E. Tunstall, 259–260. Oxford: Oxford University Press.

Louisa Waugh, Selling Olga: *Stories of Human Trafficking and Resistance*. (London: Orion Books, 2007).

Meyers, Tietjens. 2016. *Diana Victims Stories and the Advancement of Human Rights*. New York: Oxford University Press.

Nussbaum, Martha C. 2001. *Upheavals of Thought: The Intelligence of Emotions*, 405–414. Cambridge: Cambridge University Press.

OHCHR. The Core International Human Rights Instruments and Their Monitoring Bodies. http://www.ohchr.org/EN/ProfessionalInterest/Pages/CoreInstruments.aspx. Accessed 14 Sept 2014.

Rieger, April. 2007. Missing the Mark: Why the Trafficking Victims Protection Act Fails to Protect Sex Trafficking Victims in the United States. *Harvard Journal of Law and Gender* 30: 231–256.

Semple, Kirk. 2008. Nurse Claims Employer Enslaved Her. *New York Times*, July 10. http://www.nytimes.com/2008/07/10/nyregion/10nurse.html?scp=6&sq=trafficking%20victims%20confiscated%20passport&st=cse%20 %20http://www.hrw.org/en/news/2000/02/21/international-trafficking-women-and-children

U.S. Citizenship and Immigration Services. Form I-914 – Application for T Nonimmigrant Status, Form I-918 – Petition for U Nonimmigrant Status Receipts, Approvals, and Denials. https://www.uscis.gov/sites/default/files/USCIS/Resources/Reports%20and%20Studies/Immigration%20Forms%20Data/Victims/I914t-I918u_visastatistics_2012-dec.pdf

UNHCR. 2006. Guidelines on International Protection No. 7: The Application of Article 1A(2) of the 1951 Convention and/or 1967 Protocol Relating to the Status of Refugees to Victims of Trafficking and Persons at Risk of Being Trafficked. April 25. http://www.refworld.org/docid/443679fa4.html. Accessed 13 Feb 2014.

———. Convention and Protocol Relating to the Status on Refugees. http://www.unhcr.org/3b66c2aa10.html. Accessed 14 Oct 2015.

UNODC. Human Trafficking. http://www.unodc.org/unodc/en/human-trafficking/what-is-human-trafficking.html. Accessed 7 Sept 2013.

Waugh, Louisa. 2007. *Selling Olga: Stories of Human Trafficking and Resistance*. London: Orion Books.

Zimmerman, Cathy, et al. 2006. *Stolen Smiles: The Physical And Psychological Health Consequences Of Women and Adolescents Trafficked in Europe*, London School of Hygiene & Tropical Medicine. http://genderviolence.lshtm.ac.uk/files/Stolen-Smiles-Trafficking-and-Health-2006.pdf

CHAPTER 10

Routine Unrecognized Sexual Violence in India

Namrata Mitra

In Delhi, December 2012, a bus conductor and his friends raped and tortured a 23-year-old Hindu, cisgender woman. Subsequently dubbed Nirbhaya (meaning "fearless") by protestors, the woman was attacked so brutally that she died of related injuries within a few days. While this mode of violence was all too common in Delhi, the public outcry, street protests, and constant news coverage that followed this event were unprecedented. Despite the recent outcry and legislative changes, the dominant public rhetoric and courtroom practices in cases of sexual violence continue to function in the service of reifying South Asian patriarchal structures of power. Sexual violence remains routine, quotidian, and depending on the identity of the perpetrator and the victim (such as those from marginalized communities), it is often rendered invisible in the public sphere. South Asian feminists have frequently contested the prevailing rhetoric of sexual violence in which the harms are not framed in terms of trauma, or social ostracism of survivors, but instead in terms of loss of honor for their families, communities, and marriage eligibility.

N. Mitra (✉)
Iona College, New Rochelle, NY, USA

© The Author(s) 2018
C. Fischer, L. Dolezal (eds.), *New Feminist Perspectives on Embodiment*, Breaking Feminist Waves,
https://doi.org/10.1007/978-3-319-72353-2_10

This chapter focuses on some of the ways in which both the event of sexual violence itself and its harms are either rendered invisible in the South Asian public sphere or, when made visible, they are typically articulated in patriarchal terms. For instance, the most prevalent accounts of sexual violence in public circulation are not from survivors, but rather from cisgender men (usually from dominant upper-caste Hindu groups), who not only frame sexual assault against Hindu women in terms of communal dishonor, but represent the orchestrated rape of Muslim or Christian women as justified acts of avenging such dishonor. Consider the following extract from a speech by Yogi Adityanath, the Bharatiya Janata Party appointed Chief Minister of the northern state of Uttar Pradesh. At a political rally in March 2017, he fanned the flames of a commonplace Hindutva (Hindu nationalism) conspiracy called "love jihad" according to which Muslim men purportedly woo and marry Hindu women to convert them to Islam with the alleged aim of dishonoring Hindu men. This conspiracy fulfills a particular political function: it calls upon Hindu men to avenge the purported dishonor by raping Muslim women in order to dishonor Muslim men. "If one Hindu girl marries a Muslim man," Adityanath announced, "then we will take 100 Muslim girls in return. [...] If they [Muslims] kill one Hindu man, then we will kill 100 Muslim men" (Safi 2017). This ideology has been iterated by the state-sponsored "anti-Romeo squads" set up to protect women. However, in practice, the groups harass, attack, shame interreligious couples in public spaces. These squads have been staunchly opposed by feminist groups, who argue that the public rhetoric of sexual violence does not address or curb the widespread sexual violence against women, particularly the routine violence carried out by Hindu-based groups against Dalit and Muslim women as a common means of oppression (Mc Coy 2014). On the contrary, such rhetoric increases the state power to enforce Hindutva ideology (Bhalla 2017).

While the experience of violence and its trauma are frequently erased in dominant political narratives, they live on in the bodies of survivors. According to the Indian nationalist narratives which appear in school curriculums, the nation's history since partition and Independence has been one of peace and "progress," which is sometimes interrupted by occasional bouts of "irrational" violence. Partition violence and riots are frequently represented in ableist tropes of "madness." In contrast, the state's "corrective" violence is framed as sane, rationally motivated, and for the common interest of all. The political investments in these narratives cannot be underestimated, since it legitimizes state-sanctioned violence and domination over marginalized and dissenting groups. Broadly, this chapter presents the genealogy of the gendered scripts of honor, modesty, and nationalist fantasies imprinted on women's bodies which have the effect of either erasing routine sexual violence in the public sphere or rendering it visible only within specific patriarchal terms. Accordingly, this chapter addresses three main areas of inquiry. In the first section, I briefly discuss the partition of British India into the independent countries of India and Pakistan. The two nation-states were ushered in through the rape, torture, and kidnapping of several thousand women, the massacre of nearly 1 million people, and the forced displacement of 12 million. In Muslim-majority areas, Muslim men targeted Sikh and Hindu women, whereas in Sikh- and Hindu-majority areas, the men sought out Muslim women to assault. Attacking the women became the currency by which to shame the communities to which they belonged and thereby reject those communities from the possibility of sharing membership within the same national community. I draw on some interviews with partition survivors, who, in trying to speak of their experience 50 years later, attempt to piece together fragments of memories within a linguistic system that occludes narratives of trauma from sexual violence. My main aim in this section is to draw attention to the chasm between the lived experience and harms of sexual violence as represented by survivors, on the one hand, and public representations of sexual violence in the law, on the other. Accordingly, I briefly draw upon the work of Susan Brison to discuss the embodied experience of trauma and the challenges of its disclosure, and then I turn to Pratiksha Baxi's analysis of courtroom methods and practices which, she argues, structurally exclude narratives of trauma. In the second section, I turn to Judith Butler's *Frames of War* to unpack how the recognizability of persons (also, events and harms) is based not on qualities inherent in them but rather on frames through which they are perceived. I ask about the ways in which norms of gender, nation, and violence render routine sexual violence unrecognizable in the public sphere generally and in the legal sphere more specifically. The third section is aimed at unpacking the genealogy of such unrecognizability in India. I analyze the history of frames in literature and law through which sexual violence has been represented and made visible since India's colonial past. I conclude by briefly discussing a feminist protest against rape and torture by the Indian military stationed in Manipur and how it has since been framed in mainstream news sources. The protest was staged to contest the state's denials of its own violence against marginalized groups. While the protest garnered some support in the media and disrupted some long-standing denials, it nevertheless iterated patriarchal frames of perceiving women's bodies, particularly older women. I end the chapter with a call to imagine bending these frames toward more feminist modes of recognition.

Embodied Violence and Narrative Challenges

While most school history textbooks in South Asia tell the story of August 1947 as the grandiose moment in which the two independent nation-states of India and Pakistan were born, narratives of widespread massacres, sexual violence, mass displacement, and trauma are either omitted or referenced only in passing. As Gyanendra Pandey says, for the survivors, partition *was* the violence; they were not two separate events (2001, p. 7). Fifty years after the event, Ritu Menon and Kamala Bhasin interviewed many women partition violence survivors, many of whom found themselves trying to articulate their experience for the first time. They shared accounts of being physically assaulted, publicly humiliated, and rejected by their families and communities. Many witnessed atrocities or repeated the reports that they heard from others. Commenting on their efforts to record memories of trauma, Menon and Bhasin remarked, "[O]ccasionally, we will reach a point in the story where memory refuses to enter speech" (Menon and Bhasin 1998, p. 18). Taking its cue from them, the main aim of this section is to explore how, on the one hand, the trauma of sexual violence persists in the survivor's body, but, on the other hand, the harms of the violence cannot be easily disclosed in language. I argue that the problem of disclosure for survivors of sexual violence emerges not because the embodied experiences and the medium of linguistic expression are inherently incompatible, but rather because the language of the public sphere is shaped by patriarchal interests. The language of politics and law excludes women's voices and point of view as credible. This exclusion has a direct impact on cultural representations (such as Bollywood, pop music) and on courtroom practices where sexual assault is described from the point of view of the perpetrator. In these contexts, the "objective" difference between sex and rape is made out to be the lack of performed consent rather than the tectonic difference in the experience of the two events from the point of view of the survivor.

During partition, men from majority religious communities (mostly Hindu and Sikh men on the India side of the border and Muslim men on the East and West Pakistan side) sexually assaulted women from minority communities (Hindus and Sikhs in Pakistan, and Muslims in India) specifically to humiliate them, their families, and their communities. Their aim was to shame the other community and mark the minority communities as outsiders to the newly imagined and contested community of the nation. These nationalist aims were executed by raping, naked parading, and mutilating the women of other communities. As Menon and Bhasin point out, "Each one of the violent acts mentioned […] has specific symbolic meaning and physical consequences, and all of them treat women's bodies as territories to be conquered or marked by the assailant" (Menon and Bhasin 1998, p. 43). In many cases, the sexual violence against women involved mutilating their reproductive organs. These attacks were aimed to literally destroy the sites where future generations of the minority communities could be conceived, and to turn the very bodies which were treated as repositories of a community's honor into a site of a community's shame. Many women's bodies were found with messages inscribed on them, such as "Hindustan, Zindabad!" (Long Live Hindustan!) or "Pakistan, Zindabad!" (Long Live Pakistan!) (Menon and Bhasin 1998, p. 43). The specter of such shame was so pervasive across the newly drawn territorial borders that Menon and Bhasin found a common trope in many of their interviews; several survivors spoke of witnessing and one admitted to participating in the killing of one's kinswomen, either as a preemptive measure because they feared their kinswomen may be assaulted or because the women had survived the sexual assault and now signified communal shame. Survivors were not encouraged to articulate their experience, but were instead persuaded to "choose" to "commit suicide," which was subsequently spoken of as acts of valor.

Susan Brison writes about the effects of trauma on the self in the aftermath of sexual assault and the challenges of trying to articulate it. Posttraumatic stress disorder (PTSD) is manifested in the body by the reordering of immediate responses such as a heightened startled response, hypervigilance, terror, loss of control, sleep disorders, and high anxiety, "where fight or flight responses are of no avail" (Brison 2003, p. 40). In the aftermath of her own experience of assault, Brison initially tried to remap her self-relation by appealing to the Cartesian mind-body duality. She sought to restrict the area of assault to her body and identify the mind as her "self" in order to devise a separation between the site of the violence and herself. The experience of trauma, however, called into question the dualism she had previously invoked, as she now found herself having to confront states of nondualism; that is, traditionally classed mental states presented themselves as bodily symptoms, and in turn, her embodied responses became interconnected with her thoughts and affective responses:

> My body was now perceived as an enemy, having betrayed my newfound trust and interest in it, and as a site of increased vulnerability. But rejecting the body and returning to the life of the mind was not an option, since my body and mind had become nearly indistinguishable. My metal state (typically, depression) felt physiological, like lead in my veins, whereas my physical state, (frequently one of incapacity by fear and anxiety), was the incarnation of a cognitive and emotional paralysis resulting from shattered assumptions, about my safety in the world. (Brison 2003, p. 44)

Brison asks why philosophers writing on personal identity are more apt to imagine brain-body transplants, interplanetary beaming of body particles, and other science fiction plots rather than examine the all-too-common experience of PTSD (2003, p. 38). After all, at the heart of experiencing PTSD is suddenly finding that one is no longer the person that one was before the traumatic event. She hints at various possible answers to this question, one of which is that there is not much of a willing audience for narratives of trauma. Brison claims that people who have not experienced trauma do not wish to hear about it because it is an unpleasant subject. She cites Paul Fussell's argument that the challenge to narrativizing the embodied experience of trauma is *not* that it is structurally incompatible with language. Instead, he claims that there are possible ways to arrange words to describe the violence that produces trauma; however, the problem is that the audience is missing. "What speaker wants to be torn and shaken when he doesn't have to be? We have made the *unspeakable* mean indescribable, it really means *nasty*" (Fussell quoted in Brison 2003, p. 51). However, I find Brison's discussion of Primo Levi more compelling who argues that, "our language" "lacks words to express this offense, the demolition of man" (Levi quoted in Brison 2003, p. 50). Neither, I argue, is our language designed to express the "offense" and pain of the specific gendered and sexualized demolition of women, even through it helps execute the destruction everyday. One of the main conditions of possibility of such frequent demolition is that the construction of "woman," particularly women's sexuality, has borne the burden of various patriarchal scripts of purity, honor, and nationalisms.

In what ways are women's bodies inscribed with dominant narratives of purity, modesty, and shame, while their voices are simultaneously excluded from public discourses? Pratiksha Baxi addresses some of the ways in which widespread sexual violence in India can remain a "public secret," by which she means that knowledge of assaults is widely prevalent, but the sexual violence itself and the harms experienced by the survivor is elided in criminal law and courtroom practices. In the courtroom, the survivor is expected to reconstruct the incident as the story of the accused's desire through the "objective" description of events. The accuser must adopt the narrative point of view of the accused and demonstrate that her lack of consent was legible to the accused. The testimony excludes the description of immediate and long-term harm of the sexual assault such as social shaming and exclusion, her lived experience of the event, and the ensuing trauma, which, as we learn from Brison's prior discussion, is already challenging to articulate. The testifying survivor must present the narrative not as one who has lived experience of the violence and its aftermath, but from a third-person perspective, where she is a witness to the violence done to her. The genre of the testimony has troubling resonances to the genre of pornography, since the survivor is expected to reconstruct descriptions of moving body parts and positions, all of which restages the humiliation of the survivor (Baxi 2014, p. 143). Since the event is already being reconstructed from the perspective of the accused, particularly as the story of his desire and actions, it then falls to the defendant to illustrate his innocence by simply pointing to a moment when he was certain of her consent. At this juncture, it is common to draw on patriarchal tropes of gender norms in order to turn a story of violence into one of blaming the victim (Baxi 2014, p. 143). What emerges from Baxi's discussion of the construction of rape in the courtroom is that, while the act of sexual assault is being made visible in one way (pornographic images of moving bodies, the accused's desire as the only possible narrative point of view, legibility of the survivor's consent), it erases the survivor's point of view. "In other words, studies of rape trials explicate the incommensurability of legal fictions with lived experience" (Baxi 2014, p. 143). With the victim erased, there can be no sexual violence. In short, courtroom practices and government rhetoric on rape in India have rendered sexual violence and its harm invisible. In the next two sections, I explore the conditions of possibility for the routine unrecognized sexual violence in India.

The Unrecognizability of Rape in the Law

Perhaps the most unavoidable and frustrating question that arises when working on sexual violence is the following: "*how* does a long history of unrelenting sexual violence that wrecks lives and produces lifelong harms for survivors seem invisible to so many others?" In the context of contemporary India, the mainstream nationalist narrative pushes systemic sexual violence far into the margins rather than reveal how it is a central instrument of social and political oppression. Judith Butler's analysis of frames illustrates how the limits of visible reality get marked by placing some events and people at the center of a frame and others at the edges or outside of it. Accordingly, this section pursues an inquiry into the epistemic conditions that produce these asymmetrical "realities" of sexual violence that circulate within the same social system. As illustrated in the previous section of this chapter, one of the many areas in which this asymmetrical reality manifests is in courtroom practices where the survivor's experience of trauma cannot be disclosed. I then turn to the work of Srimati Basu to unpack the constructions of sexuality and violence through which women's bodies are rendered legible by the law.

In *Frames of War*, Judith Butler argues that the frames through which we apprehend events and people produces our "field of perceptible reality" (2010, p. 64). These frames of perceptible reality shape how we respond to atrocities, and therefore determine whether we grieve or do not grieve the loss of "other" lives, or mourn the harm caused to other lives (Butler 2010, p. 64). For instance, if a particular population is framed as a "war target" by the military, or if the children are framed as their "shields," then those targets and shields are no longer recognized as vulnerable human lives subject to injury and grievable death. Instead, these interpellations turn children made of flesh into shields made of metal, whose elimination becomes necessary for the survival of those peering through the frames (Butler 2010, p. xxvii–xxviii). The recognition of a person is not based on an ontological quality residing in the person which is immediately recognized by others. Rather, the norms of recognizability enable the recognition of a person. To show how this operates, Butler makes a distinction between recognition and recognizability: recognizability refers to the conditions that prepare someone to be recognized as a subject, such that "recognizability precedes recognition" and remains the condition for its possibility. It is on the basis of the norms of recognizability that we determine another as a target, or a shield, or a survivor of sexual violence (Butler 2010, p. 5).

Accordingly, *how* a survivor of sexual of sexual violence is recognized is not based on harms of the violence, such as trauma, persisting within the survivor's body, as though the body is legible outside of norms of recognizability. Rather, the norms of gender, sexuality, shame, honor, and communal and national identity forge the frames of recognizability through which someone is recognized as a survivor.

In the context of contemporary India, the dominant norms of recognizability maintain the interest of upper-caste Hindu men; therefore, any harm experienced by this group is rendered hypervisible, as though it is an attack against the entire public (e.g. the Mumbai bombing by "terrorists" in 1993). The harms of routine state violence against religious minorities (e.g. the military assaults in Kashmir or northeastern regions from 1942 to the present), in contrast, go unrecognized in public discourse every day. In a similar vein, sexual violence against upper-caste Hindu women, in so far as it is perceived as harm to Hindu communal honor, is more readily recognized as sexual violence in mainstream culture. However, the routine rape of religious minorities by Hindutva groups or even state forces during "riots" is rarely recognized as sexual assault. In theory, the laws against sexual assault are accessible to women across religious identities. In practice, however, boarder norms of recognizability which determine who is acknowledged as a rape victim and who is not play a large role in shaping who can and who cannot successfully access the law. There are, however, several identity groups who are formally denied recognition of being a rape victim by the frames of the rape law. Only cisgender unmarried women or cisgender married women under the age of 15 can access the rape law.

In April 2013, in the aftermath of nation-wide protests against the rape and murder of Nirbhaya, the Government of India announced an amendment to the rape law, Indian Penal Code (henceforth IPC) 375, to include nonconsensual penetration by objects and nonconsensual oral sex (*Gazette* 2013, pp. 5–6). However, the law preserved an earlier frame of recognizing survivors of sexual violence by stating that only (cisgender) women are vulnerable to sexual violence if the perpetrator is not her husband. This is made clear by the second exception in the law, which states that "sexual intercourse or sexual acts by a man with his own wife, the wife not being under fifteen years of age, *is not rape*" (*Gazette* 2013, p. 6, emphasis added).

Per IPC 375, only cisgender women can be raped by cisgender men. Moreover, a married woman cannot be raped by her husband.

This particular framing of a rape victim automatically excludes cisgender men and *hijras* (third gender/transwomen). Accordingly, sexual violence against these excluded groups is rendered invisible. In a hideous twist of irony, perhaps the most common target of constant sexual violence and harassment are *hijras*.

How has marital rape remained a lacuna in the law despite decades-long feminist activism on the issue? On 29 April 2015, two years after the nation-wide protests against the assault on Nirbhaya, and amendments to IPC 375, Haribhai Chaudhary, the Minister of State of Home Affairs, made the following statement to explain why marital rape would continue to not be criminalized by the law: "It is considered that the concept of marital rape, as understood internationally, cannot be suitably applied in the Indian context due to various factors, including level of education, illiteracy, poverty, myriad social customs and values, religious beliefs, mindset of the society to treat marriage as a sacrament" (NDTV 2015). Perhaps he means "sacred" and not Christian sacrament to make the case that the "sacrament" is native to India and not shared "internationally"! A year later, this statement was reissued verbatim by the Women and Child Development minister, Maneka Gandhi. According to this statement, either the reality of marital rape is itself called into question because marriage in India, unlike elsewhere, is treated as a "sacrament," or that acts of sexual violence within marriage are excusable because of the "level of education, illiteracy, poverty" of the perpetrators. That husbands beat and rape their wives because the patriarchal system grants them entitlement to their wives' bodies lies outside the frame of recognition of the minister's statement. This official position follows a historical pattern in Indian criminal law of framing marriage as the condition that negates the possibility of sexual assault and renders sexual consent irrelevant. If the harm of sexual violence against women is the loss of honor it brings to the men in her family (her father and brothers if unmarried, or her husband if married), then marital rape becomes a contradiction. The husband loses honor and is shamed if another man takes his wife, who is the repository of the family honor. A husband cannot be dishonored for taking his own wife whenever he wants. According to such a framing of rape, marital rape is an impossibility because there is no harm.

On a subject related to marriage and rape, Srimati Basu examines cases which invoke the fourth clause of IPC 375, according to which a sex act becomes a rape "when the man knows that he is not her husband and that her consent is given because she believes that he is another man to whom she is or believes herself to be lawfully married." Under these terms, if a woman consents because she believes a man to be her husband and he later turns out not to be so, the sex act constitutes rape. This legal clause frames rape as an act of fraud and not of violence; in fact, in this clause rape is entirely removed from violence. Of the various cases that Basu discusses, two stand out in particular. In one case, a young woman's boyfriend had been rejected by her parents on grounds of his caste identity. The young couple decided to elope and get married. The incensed parents brought charges of kidnapping and rape against the groom (Basu 2011, p. 199). In another case, a man accused of rape responded to the charge by offering the judge photos of his wedding with the accuser. The judge then examined and commented on the photos, as though they could provide sufficient evidence to remove the possibility of rape (Basu 2011, p. 196). Consider the legal clause which said that a sex act is rape if the woman gave consent believing the man to be her husband when he was not (which he knew all along).

In instances like the first case discussed, families decide that, since they do not accept a man based on his caste, religious, or ethnic identity as their daughter's husband, they can charge him for raping their daughter. The daughter's consent to the marriage and implied marital sex is irrelevant here and subordinated to the family's withholding of consent to the marriage. Here, the law can recognize the woman as a rape victim. "Legal protections against rape then serve to solidify class and religious hegemonies and to render women's choices moot" (Basu 2011). If we read Basu through Butler, then the first case shows that the recognizability of a rape survivor is framed through norms of caste and communal hierarchies, which in turn design marriage laws and conventions. In the second case, we see that one cannot be a rape survivor if one's husband is said to have committed the act. What we repeatedly see is that women's bodies are overlaid with scripts of sexuality, caste, religious, and gender norms, which then determine if she is eligible to be a victim of sexual assault regardless of her experiences. The body cannot effectively speak for itself or its harms. Rather, bodies are legible based on the existing socio-legal scripts that frame them.

A Brief Genealogy of Past Frames of Sexual Violence in British India

How did we get to the place where the recognition of rape and its harms is based upon norms that conflate cisgender women's sexual purity with communal and national honor? Consider the law cited for molestation, IPC 354, which frames molestation as "assault or criminal force to woman with intent to *outrage her modesty*." While I have thus far examined the manifestation of these norms in the case of the law and courtroom practices in India, they are equally pervasive in literary and media representations. In this section, I present a brief genealogy of political investments in women's sexuality in India's past in order to explore previous frames of sexual violence in nineteenth-century British India which the current frames of sexual violence frequently cite and reproduce.

The legitimacy of the British Empire in India in the latter half of the nineteenth century was forged through images of white men saving modest, white, upper-class British women and subordinated brown women from predatory and domineering brown men. Jenny Sharpe argues that this cultural trope emerged as a response to political uncertainties within the Empire (1993). These images functioned to shift the legitimacy of colonization before and after the failed First War of Independence (more commonly called the "Sepoy Mutiny"). Before the war, the British government claimed that its presence was invited by the natives, who welcomed the civilizing knowledge of modernity, particularly of modern government and of science. However, once the eruption of the revolt showed that not to be the case, the justification for imperial rule shifted to the English duty of saving native women from practices of "suttee" (widow burned alive on the husband's cremation) and other forms of patriarchal oppressions (Sharpe 1993). Narratives of Englishmen rescuing distressed, native young women from "sati/suttee" became a common trope in European fiction, such as in Jules Verne's *Around the World in Eighty Days*. In this novel, the young woman falls in love with her rescuer and flees to freedom with him. Lata Mani shows how the practice of sati became a flashpoint of debate in letters and public treatises by English and Indian writers in nineteenth-century British India. If proponents of imperialism in Britain used Orientalist accounts of sati to justify the civilizing mission of colonization, then South Asian nationalists framed sati as an issue of native social reform to justify social and political autonomy. Either way, native women were framed as "repositories of tradition" who either as "abject victims or heroines [...] frequently represented both shame *and* promise" (Mani 1990, p. 118–19).

From the late nineteenth century until after the 1947 partition, turning women's bodies into repositories of communal honor (if sexually pure) and communal shame (if sexually tainted) set the sociopolitical conditions, whereby attacks against the women's bodies or "repositories of communal honor" would become a common means of attacking the politically oppositional community. This frame was one of the cultural conditions of enacting sexual violence on women's bodies during the three partitions in South Asia (1905, 1947, 1797). During the rise of Indian nationalist movements in late colonial British India, the abstract idea of the nation was often cast in the image of a woman, particularly a Hindu Goddess exhorting her sons to fight for freedom. The political investment in representing the nation as a woman was not driven by feminist concerns, but rather to provide certainty and a specific image of masculine national membership whose task was to fight for and rescue their mother and eroticized Goddess from British servitude. The symbolic construction of the abstract concept of the nation into the "magnified sexuality" of a goddess turned women's bodies into a canvas upon which masculine national fantasies could be inscribed, contested, and ultimately destroyed (Das 2007, p. 45–46).

The narratives of honor and violence made attacks against some women hypervisible in the nineteenth century; however, sexual violence enacted as a form of caste-based oppression or colonial entitlement was invisible in the public sphere and easily deniable. Only those images of sexual violence which could be turned into a political metaphor and mobilized to justify continued colonialism or national independence were widely circulated. These narratives of women's racialized sexuality written by colonialists and Indian nationalists were then imprinted on women's bodies. While women's bodies were made into sites of proxy war by men, nationalists and imperialists, South Asian and British women's voices were routinely silenced or ignored in the political sphere.

In the genre of adventure-romance novels from the late nineteenth until the early twentieth century, British women's bodies were portrayed as under imminent threat of rape by Indian men and who therefore had to be prevented and punished by the English. In the immediate aftermath of the 1857 revolt, when dissenting voices in the English public demanded an explanation for the continuation of colonization, English newspapers published stories describing native Indian men sexually assaulting and brutally cutting off the noses of white English women to shame them (Chakravarty 2005, p. 37). While these reports were never corroborated despite efforts by the imperial government in India, Sharpe argues that they did nevertheless fulfill an important function in quelling doubts about the justification for the continuation of the Empire (1993). While Sharpe's argument has been influential in South Asian studies on the construction of race, gender, and sexuality in the making of the Empire, and though the rape of white women by brown men was very likely to be believed in the law courts, which were set up for that very purpose in British India, I would like to pause at the problematic implication that the lack of reports signifies the lack of sexual violence against white women. The total lack of judicial evidence for rape of white British women by Indian men should not be taken as an indication that white British women were never victimized or that they were otherwise considered credible in the English court of law. Feminist accounts of courtroom practices within the English common law in eighteenth-century England demonstrate its hostility to the survivors, whose demeanor and character were subject to impossible scrutiny in order to dismiss the rape charges as "malicious prosecutions" and "exhortation" attempts (Eldestein 1998). Instead, accounts of rape were commonly framed by the defense and in public discourse as acts of normative white male sexual desire.

While the British claimed that their rule in India was necessary to save Indian women from the Islamic law, under which rape prosecution was almost impossible, an examination of nineteenth-century British Indian court cases in which Indian men were tried for sexual violence against Indian women revealed that it was the accuser's character that was examined to determine the verdict (Kolsky 2010, p. 1113–14). While the evidentiary rules of the Islamic law excluded women as reliable witnesses altogether, British practices placed the credibility and the character of the accuser in the forefront of judging rape cases. Over the course of the nineteenth century, the British Indian law gradually replaced Islamic law. In 1837, Thomas Macaulay and the Indian Law Commission drafted the IPC, which was passed in 1860 and to this day governs all sex laws (Kolsky 2010, p. 1098), such as those discussed earlier in this chapter and IPC 377, which criminalizes "carnal acts against the order of nature" and to this day is used as means to criminalize acts of same-sex desire. So intense was the fear of false accusations in British Indian courts, particularly the worry that women would consent to sex and, then to save their virtue, would lie about it later, that Kolsky says this was the reason that it was far more likely for girls (below the age of consent at 8) to be believed, whereas the testimony of married women (seen as potential covering for an adulterous act) was treated with far greater suspicion. Since colonial India, ideas of modesty and credibility have always been inscribed differently on women's bodies based on their caste, class, and religious identity.

That women across different identities are made into bearers of modesty, sexual purity, and familial and communal honor in different ways has a long legacy in India. The metaphorical inscriptions of these abstract ideas on the bodies of women are drawn from gendered constructions of caste, class, and religious identity. Upper-caste Hindu and Muslim women's sexual purity is conflated with communal order, whereas Dalit and Adivasi (indigenous) women are left out of such a frame altogether. This is one of the main conditions that allows for the recognition of rape only of unmarried, cisgender, and upper-caste women, whereas the routine assaults on Dalit, poor religious minorities, and married women are rarely covered in the news or reaches the courtroom. To reiterate one of the main arguments of this chapter, the public recognition of sexual violence survivors and the harms of violence is based not on the experiences of survivor, the aftermath of trauma, or even the fact of the event, but instead on broader norms of recognizability that precede the recognition of a rape survivor.

Resisting Routine Unrecognized Sexual Violence in India

While this chapter has focused on some of the ways in which norms of honor, sexuality, gender, and nationalism render routine sexual violence against women, especially those from marginalized communities, unrecognizable in law and in the public sphere, I conclude this chapter by briefly focusing on a protest against the rape of a Manipuri woman by a group of Indian soldiers. While the protest did not result in major legislative changes, it did challenge the dominant frames through which women's bodies are represented and circulated.

The Indian military, protected by the Armed Special Forces Act, which gives them impunity to enact violence, has for years abducted, raped, and tortured women in parts of the North East and in Kashmir. On 11 July 2004, soldiers of the Assam Rifles regiment arrested 32-year-old Thangjam Manorama from her home, gang raped her, shot her in the vagina, dumped her in the fields, and then publicly called her an insurgent (Human Rights

Watch, HRW). On 15 July, a group of older Manipuri women activists called Meira Paibi, or "Torch Bearers," protested naked outside the Assam Rifles headquarters. They held a banner on which was inscribed in red, "Indian Army Rape Us." The women chanted, "We mothers have come. Drink our blood. Eat our flesh. Maybe this way you can spare our daughters" (HRW). While the state forces had sought to rape and torture Manorama and then erase the embodied violence from public record, the members of Miera Paibi entered the narrative of the violence in public record through an embodied protest that disrupted the official discourse of sexual violence. Now, the rest of the nation-state was invited to imagine the violence which we collectively deny as a nation-state. This protest has since received some national and international attention, yet no one has been identified or tried for the rape and torture in the last 15 years. Some journalists seeking to be allies to the protesters have written about the atrocity and its ensuing protest recently. However, while the reporters try to present the "facts" of the violence and the protests, they still frame the protestors through patriarchal norms of recognition. Consider the following extracts from different articles written in the last two years. The first journalist frames the women protesters through norms of feminized "modesty" when he says that "[g]iving up their modesty for justice, the women stripped themselves naked" (Bhoopesh), while another newspaper article frames the protests through sexist ageist tropes when she says, "[t]heir nakedness, old, haggard, was indescribably sacred" (Bhonsle). While the protesters presented their naked bodies in the public sphere to disrupt the invisibility of the widely prevalent sexual violence, the journalists iterated the patriarchal frames and denied feminist frames of the protest. Imagining alternative feminist frames through which to recognize women's bodies remains an urgent task. Certainly, in the area of literature, fiction writers such as Mahasweta Devi and Shashi Deshpande, and nonfiction writers such as Nivedita Menon and Arundhati Roy have for decades challenged the dominant frames through which women of different castes have been repeatedly represented. A lot remains at stake in drawing on those literary representations to disrupt the continuous reproduction of the dominant frames of sexual violence.

Bibliography

Basu, S. 2011. "Sexual Property" Staging Rape and Marriage in Indian Law and Feminist Theory. *Feminist Studies* 37 (1): 185–211.

Baxi, P. 2014. Sexual Violence and Its Discontents. *The Annual Review of Anthropology*. 43 (1): 139–154. https://doi.org/10.1146/annurev-anthro-102313-030247.

Bhalla, N. 2017. India's "Anti-Romeo Squads' Accused of Harassing Couples, Shaming Young Men. *Reuters*. Available from www.reuters.com [5 April 2017].

Bhonsle, A. 2016. *Indian Army, Rape Us: The Fascinating and Moving Story Behind the Unique Protest in 2004 by 12 Imas in Imphal Manipur....* Available from Outlook.com [10 February 2016].

Bhoopesh, NK. 2016. Twelve Years After 'Indian Army Rape Us' Strike, AFSPA Continues to Shield Violators. *Narada News*. Available from naradanews.com [15 July 2016].

Brison, S.J. 2003. *Aftermath: Violence and the Remaking of a Self*. Princeton: Princeton University Press.

Butalia, U. 1998. *The Other Side of Silence: Voices from the Partition of India*. New Delhi: Penguin.

Butler, J. 2010. *Frames of War: When Is Life Grievable?* New York: Verso.

Chakravarty, G. 2005. *The Indian Mutiny and the British Imagination*. Cambridge: Cambridge University Press.

Das, V. 2007. *Life and Words: Violence and the Descent into the Ordinary*. Berkeley: University of California Press.

Edelstein, L. 1998. An Accusation Easily to Be Made? Rape and Malicious Prosecution in the Eighteenth-Century England. *American Journal of Legal History* 42 (4): 351–390.

Human Rights Watch. 2017. *The Killing of Thangjam Manorama Devi*. Available from https://www.hrw.org/reports/2008/india0908/3.htm#_ftn66 [1 August 2017].

Kolsky, E. 2010. The Rule of Colonial Indifference: Rape on Trial in Early Colonial India, 1805–87. *The Journal of Asian Studies* 69 (4): 1093–1117. https://doi.org/10.1017/S0021911810002937.

Mani, L. 1990. Contentious Traditions: The Debate on *Sati* in Colonial India. In *Recasting Women: Essays in Indian Colonial History*, ed. Kumkum Sangari and Sudesh Vaid, 88–127. New Brunswick: Rutgers University Press.

"Marriage Sacred in India, So Marital Rape Does Not Apply," *NDTV*, Available from www.ndtv.com [30 April 2015].

Mc Coy, T 2014. India's Gang Rapes – And the Failure to Stop Them. *The Washington Post*. Available from www.washingtonpost.com [30 March, 2014].

Menon, R., and K. Bhasin. 1998. *Borders and Boundaries: Women in India's Partition*. New Delhi: Kali for Women.

Ministry of Law of Justice. 2013. The Criminal Law (Amendment) Act 2013. *The Gazette of India*. Available from http://indiacode.nic.in/acts-in-pdf/132013.pdf [2 April 2013].
Pandey, G. 2001. *Remembering Partition: Violence, Nationalism and History of India*. New York: Cambridge University Press.
Peer, B. 2014. The Armed Forces Special Powers Act: A Brief History. *Al-Jazeera*. Available from www.america.aljazeera.com [8 March 2014].
Safi, M. 2017. Controversial Hindu Priest Chosen as Uttar Pradesh Chief Minister. *The Guardian*. Available from www.guardian.com [19 March 2017].
Sharpe, J. 1993. *Allegories of Empire: The Figure of Woman in the Colonial Text*. Minneapolis: Minnesota University Press.

PART IV

Pregnancy and Reproductive Technology

CHAPTER 11

Performing Pregnant: An Aesthetic Investigation of Pregnancy

EL Putnam

Introduction

In 2011, artist Marni Kotak presented *The Birth of Baby X*, a durational performance piece that culminated in the live birth of her son, Ajax. For this work, she transformed the Microscope Gallery in Brooklyn, NY into a birthing centre, including various personal, practical, and symbolic items, such as an inflatable birthing pool, a kitchenette, and two ten-foot trophies—one for Baby X for being born and the other for Kotak for giving birth. She also incorporated snapshots from her pregnancy and baby shower that were made into wallpaper, rugs, sheets, blankets, and a serving tray, turning the room into an immersive photographic album. Interspersed throughout the installation, there were a number of family relics, such as her grandmother's bed and her mother's rocking chair, fleshing out this collection to contain the traces of her genealogy. On October 25, 2011, she gave birth to Ajax with the assistance of a midwife and a doula in front of a restricted audience of about 15 people.

EL Putnam (✉)
Dublin Institute of Technology, Dublin, Ireland

© The Author(s) 2018
C. Fischer, L. Dolezal (eds.), *New Feminist Perspectives on Embodiment*, Breaking Feminist Waves,
https://doi.org/10.1007/978-3-319-72353-2_11

Unlike the videos and photographs of live births that have come to populate the Internet, Kotak's performance manifested as a multisensory event. This piece, along with other works Kotak has created in conjunction with her pregnancy and post-partum experiences, explicitly manifests the idea that pregnancy is a creative process. Her merger of art and life through the act of giving birth in a gallery challenges the norms of delivery while framing her actions in the context of contemporary art and aesthetics. This performance is significant because it blurs the distinction between bodily pregnancy and creative production. Consistent with Amy Mullin's interpretation of some examples of feminist body art, Kotak undermines the assumption that bodily pregnancies are "to be valued only because and only when they lead to the birth of children."[1] Instead of treating pregnancy as a state to be endured, physical pregnancy can function as a source for intellectual growth and creative exploration. Performances by pregnant artists, including Kotak, Cathy Van Eck, and Sandy Huckleberry, counter the containment of maternal subjectivity through the medicalisation of pregnancy as well as challenge a questionable legacy of representations of pregnancy in art, which historically have been dominated by images of the Virgin Mary. In their performances, where art is treated as a realm for corporeal exploration, pregnancy becomes the impetus for aesthetic experience.

In this chapter, I explore how the aesthetics of pregnancy and childbirth in art persists as a controversial topic that also offers a platform for exploring the pregnant body in the cultural consciousness by building on Iris Marion Young's phenomenological understanding of pregnancy and Martin Heidegger's treatment of the essence of technology as *Gestell* (enframing). Young argues that advances in antenatal technology in association with the increased medicalisation of pregnancy have progressively alienated the mother-to-be from reproductive processes and the birthing experience. According to Young, emphasis is transferred from the lived-body experience of the pregnant subject to medical discourse, which tends to standardise this process while also minimising the presence of the mother-to-be as a subject. The impact of technology on pregnancy is examined using Martin Heidegger's definition of enframing, or the understanding that technology reduces pregnant women to mere resources. I argue that enframing is not just restricted to medical discourse, but can be found in the visual arts. Julia Kristeva describes how in many works of art, particularly in depictions of the Virgin Mary, the artist reduces the pregnant woman to a sign—an image that comes to replace her experience.

She is silenced through these imaginary, visual presentations that perpetuate idealised, patriarchal ideas regarding the maternal.

In order to counteract the alienation of the pregnant subject, Young proposes that pregnancy can be experienced from an aesthetic perspective. Moreover, the pregnant body becomes a site of interest, curiosity, and wonder, as opposed to a collection of symptoms that make the body inadequate, abnormal, and estranged. I build upon Young's proposal by suggesting that pregnancy does not just allow for a reflexive intrasubjectivity, but as a liminal bodily experience, it also involves intersubjective relationships between the pregnant woman, the foetus, and others. Through performance, artists draw attention to the experience of pregnancy as itself a process of transformation, as opposed to treating it as a state to be endured that is only valued when resulting in the birth of a child.

Performance artists who merge the experience of pregnancy with art facilitate the ability to consider pregnancy in aesthetic terms, as they welcome the type of reception that people bring to an artistic encounter to the sensorial perception of pregnancy. Moreover, aesthetic in this context means that pregnancy is perceived in the manner a person would treat a work of art or theatre event. Emphasis is placed on the experience, as opposed to the outcome. Perception is treated as synaesthetic, incorporating the visual and sonic, as well as "physical sensations of the entire body."[2] German theatre scholar Erika Fischer-Lichte focuses on the role of perception in shaping the dynamic of a performance, where the conditions for perception are informed by the spatial arrangements or staging of a work as well as certain types of embodiment.[3] Perception also functions as a mode of relation that involves the interplay of various subjects, which in these cases include the pregnant woman, the foetus, and observers—an intersubjective exchange that unfolds in real time and space. The immediacy of the performance encounter opens a potentiality absent in other forms of artistic production. When performing, artists respond to the audience in a cognitive, physical, and emotional manner, both intentionally and unintentionally. The unfinished and incomplete qualities of performance art allow the event to be directly informed by audience presence. At the same time, performance art involves the merging of the roles of the artist, the artwork, and the pregnant woman, offering an opportunity to consider subjectivity in pregnancy that other media do not offer so explicitly.

Fischer-Lichte emphasises how performance encapsulates a distinctive type of aesthetic experience—an aesthetics of the performative:

[The aesthetics of the performative] identifies performances not as the allegory and image of human life but both as human life in itself and simultaneously as its model. The lives of all participants are entwined in performance, not just metaphorically but in actual fact. [...] The reenchantment of the world is accomplished through the linkage of art and life, which is the aim of the aesthetics of the performative.[4]

The "reenchantment of the world" that Fischer-Lichte describes is the transformative potential of performance as a liminal experience where art and life merge.[5] In these moments, according to Marvin Carlson in his analysis of Ficher-Lichte, there is "sudden deeper insight into the shared process of being in the world."[6] In the works to be discussed, artists Marni Kotak, Cathy Van Eck, and Sandy Huckleberry use pregnancy as the impetus for shared, embodied aesthetic experiences, providing the potential for transformation through performance in a manner that counters the restricted treatment of the pregnant subject as perpetuated in medical discourse and art history. Art becomes a way of communicating the phenomenological changes of the pregnant body, a means of reasserting the woman's presence as a subject in both pregnancy and delivery, and an opportunity to explore the maternal in the cultural imagination.

Pre-conceptions of the Maternal

With the *Birth of Baby X*, Kotak invited spectators to appreciate the act of giving birth as an aesthetic experience. Framing the performance within the conventions of the gallery context welcomes attendees to not restrict their perception of pregnancy to medical definitions, but to engage with it as one would a work of art. As Fischer-Lichte notes, "[P]erformance induces an extraordinary state of permanently heightened attention in the spectator, thus transforming what has been ordinary into components of aesthetic experience."[7]

Admittedly, Marni Kotak's act of giving birth in a gallery comprises an intersection between art and pregnancy that can be challenging for some audiences to appreciate. Unsurprisingly, *The Birth of Baby X* received a range of responses in the US media even prior to its presentation, evoking popular debates regarding the perceived ethical implications and possible safety concerns associated with Kotak's actions. While some bloggers, including one for the *Washington Post*, noted that the work is not so controversial in today's Facebook and YouTube society, where the public display of images of births have become commonplace, other commentators labelled Kotak as self-absorbed and narcissistic.[8] Additionally, some people questioned whether the piece could be considered art. In a comment to the *Village Voice* interview with Kotak, one person states: "Art requires talent/skill. Motherhood, while requiring much more hard work, does not require either of these. This is not art. It's exploitation. Poor Baby X will be scarred for life from its inception."[9] Commentators vented judgemental expressions on the numerous blogs and news sites reporting the work, condemning Kotak as an artist, woman, and mother.[10] As people attempted to shame Kotak, this digital simulacrum of a debate on websites and social media reveals how perceptions of pregnancy and childbirth remain a contested terrain in the twenty-first century. These comments and popular observations, many of which come with disparaging sentiments about what it means to give birth and become a mother, reveal more about people's attitudes regarding motherhood and cultures of mother-blaming, or the tendency to judge a mother's actions when it comes to raising children,[11] than offering insight into the work itself. Female reproduction, which extends beyond pregnancy and the act of giving birth to the abortion debate and contraception, is regulated and heavily contested in the United States, Ireland, and other nations, where political authorities, religious doctrine, and medical science dominate discourse, cultural attitudes, and legislation. Ironically, the controversy that Kotak's work evoked online emphasises the necessity of artistic interventions in order to reveal how understandings of pregnancy can be so structured and restrained.

Pregnancy and birth, like performance art, constitute a series of unfolding events that are unstable and can be unpredictable. During pregnancy, the woman's body transforms—biologically, psychically, socially, and culturally. In conjunction with these growth processes, her identity morphs through complex exchanges of individual agency, and institutional and social influences. As Sandra Matthews and Laura Wexler point out: "Even a desired, 'natural' pregnancy is a complicated physical, psychological and social passage, both intensely private and unavoidably public. [...] Pregnancy links the most intimate aspects of a woman's body with ideas about the wellbeing of the social body."[12] The pregnant woman is doubled and decentred, with bodily boundaries blurring through a phenomenological process of growth and transformation. In her reconsideration of the female body through the lens of Maurice Merleau-Ponty, Carol Bigwood describes the human body as a living or phenomenological body that "is not fixed but continually emerges anew out of an ever changing weave of relations to earth and sky, things, tasks, and other bodies."[13] With a shifting body schema, a pregnant woman can become both aware and estranged from her own body through an uncanny corporeal relationship. Iris Marion Young explores this process in her essay, "Pregnant Embodiment: Subjectivity and Alienation." For Young, these changes make a woman hyper-aware of her body and how it moves. Starting from Julia Kristeva's treatment of pregnancy as a splitting of the subject, Young describes how during pregnancy the body changes in conjunction with the growth of the foetus, whose movements make the mother-to-be attuned to a doubling of the subject. These motions are both connected to the female body and independent of the woman's actions. As Young notes: "[T]he fetus's movements are wholly mine, completely within me, conditioning my experience and space. Only I have access to these movements from their origin, as it were."[14] As such, pregnancy interrupts the integration of bodily experience, blurring the boundaries and disrupting the distinction between the internal (what is mine) and the external (what is other). In turn, the pregnant woman poses a threat to understandings of the subject as a unified or stable whole.

The Question Concerning Antenatal Technology

Young stresses how "at a phenomenological level the pregnant woman has a unique knowledge of her body processes and the life of the fetus."[15] However, she argues that advances in antenatal technology contribute to the progressive alienation of the mother-to-be from pregnancy and birth. She states: "[T]he use of instruments provides a means of objectifying the pregnancy and birth that alienates a woman because it negates and devalues her own experience of those processes."[16] Technology, including the foetal Doppler monitor and the ultrasound, externalises the presence of the foetus, so that a woman's intimate knowledge of her pregnancy is no longer required, as it is "replaced by more objective means of observation."[17] For example, ultrasound images focus on the foetus, visually circumventing the woman, with the womb functioning as a shadowed container. While the diagnostic purpose of the imagery is to measure the growth and development of the foetus, these images externalise internal processes, making the pregnant woman's embodied observations unnecessary. Ultrasound imagery has earned a place in numerous cultures as providing the first images of the child.[18] In her analysis of the use of foetal medical images by the anti-choice organisation Operation Rescue, Peggy Phelan states: "Fetal imagery locates reproductive visibility as a term and an image independent of the woman's body [...] [i]n making the fetus the focus of the visible spectacle of the demonstrations, Operation Rescue subtly erases the pregnant woman herself."[19] Through their public performances, Operation Rescue appropriates these images in order to present the foetus as an autonomous subject in need of salvation. In addition, Barbara Katz Rothman emphasises how there is an increased tendency to treat foetuses as separate patients within medically managed pregnancies,[20] with the language used in this context—that is, the use of the phrase "being delivered" and as opposed to "giving birth"—further contributing to the erasure of the maternal subject.[21]

The impact of technology on the medical understanding of pregnancy can be examined using Martin Heidegger's definition of *Gestell*. In "The Question Concerning Technology," Heidegger explores humanity's relationship to the essence of technology. He argues that technology is "a mode of revealing. Technology comes to presence in the realm where revealing and unconcealment take place, where *alēthia*, truth, happens."[22] He describes the essence of technology as *Gestell*, or enframing:

> Enframing means the gathering together of the setting-upon which sets upon man, i.e., challenges him forth, to reveal the real, in the mode of ordering, as standing-reserve. Enframing means that way of revealing which holds sway in the essence of modern technology and which is itself nothing technological.[23]

This challenging forth is problematic for Heidegger. Challenging forth is what causes the mode of ordering that Heidegger refers to as standing-reserve, or the tendency to treat the world as merely an energy resource for production and consumption.[24] When something is allocated to standing-reserve, it becomes disposable.

It is important to emphasise that Heidegger is more interested in examining the essence of technology as opposed to limiting his discussion to its mechanics. According to Gregory Ulmer, "From Heidegger's point of view, the danger of technology is that its rigid cause-and-effect enframing order might blind humanity to alternative orders. It is not the technology itself, but this blindness to its enframing, that must be confronted."[25] This essence of technology concerns Heidegger, since it blocks other forms of revealing, including *poiēsis*.[26] When defining *poiēsis*, Heidegger states:

It is of utmost importance that we think bringing-forth in its full scope and at the same time in the sense in which the Greeks thought it. Not only handicraft manufacture, not only artistic and poetical bringing into appearance and concrete imagery, is a bringing-forth, *poiēsis*.[27]

In other words, Heidegger does not limit *poiēsis* to the act of artistic production, but extends it to encompass the unconcealment of truth— *alēthia*.[28] Moreover, when considering Heidegger's definition of technology, technology is not inherently problematic, but rather how it is utilised: whether it is used for the challenging forth of enframing or the bringing forth of *poiēsis*. Heidegger emphasises this point when he refers to Friedrich Hölderlin's poetic verse: "But where the danger is, grows / The saving power also."[29] That is, if enframing, the essence of technology, is what poses the supreme danger, then it "must harbour in itself the growth of the saving power."[30] Therefore, the medical apparatuses that have come to dominate understandings of pregnancy in the twentieth century, which Young is quick to point out as leading to the alienation of pregnant women, are not inherently the problem. Rather, it is how these technologies are used, along with the political legislation and religious agendas that draw from scientific findings to regulate pregnancy, that turns women into standing-reserve, delegating them into a resource and placing their subjectivity under erasure.

In the performance *Double Beat*, Dutch sound artist and composer Cathy von Eck creates a scenario that challenges the alienation of pregnant women through the creative repurposing of a consumer Doppler machine. For this work, von Eck connects one Doppler to measure her heartbeat and another to her unborn baby. The audio output from these devices is fed into her computer, which is connected to loudspeakers so that it is audible to the audience. The sounds are processed depending on the volume of her blowing air into a bag. As the work progresses, the heartbeats transition from being in a pure state to gaining pitches and becoming cords through electronic processing. In the culmination of the performance, the heartbeats are slowly transformed into musical chords, "derived from the Cold Genius's solo in the 'Frost Scene' of the opera *King Arthur* (1691) by Henry Purcell, a piece that is dealing with death."[31] Through this performance, von Eck uses her breath as the driving force that converts her heartbeat and that of her unborn daughter's into a musical composition—a performance that merges life with its antecedent and death. A consumer, medical device that Young describes as contributing to the alienation of mothers-to-be is repurposed by a pregnant woman through live performance. In Heidegger's terms, the mode of revealing in this performance is *poiēsis*, which brings something forth into being, in contrast to the challenging forth of enframing that treats pregnant women as merely a resource.[32] At the same time, this creative act allows Cathy von Eck to connect with her pregnancy as an embodied and phenomenological experience through the aesthetic event of live performance.

Artistic Legacies

While medicalisation has facilitated the alienation of mothers-to-be from the embodied and phenomenological aspects of pregnancy, this process did not begin with modern medical technology. Rather, it encompasses an attitude that is detected in earlier visual representations of pregnant women in art, specifically images depicting the Virgin Mary. For example, according to Brendan Cassidy, in some early Byzantine iconographic images of the Madonna, Jesus is presented in a medallion placed on her breast. In some Northern European renditions of Mary's visitation to Elizabeth, artists offer a view inside the womb to allow spectators to catch a glimpse of the unborn Christ. Later Tuscan illustrations of the pregnant virgin, referred to as *Madonna del Parto*, offer a more naturalistic vision of pregnancy, though are still laden with symbolic imagery to emphasise the presence of Christ.[33] In a fresco painting by Piero della Francesca (ca. 1457), the Madonna stands erect as two hieratically scaled angels part curtains decorated with the images of pomegranates, a symbol of fertility. Some art historians interpret this tent as the tabernacle, which Mary also symbolises, with her functioning as the container for Jesus.[34] The parting duplicates the stretched material of her maternity dress, placing emphasis on her stomach area while also alluding to the parting of the vaginal lips in birth. When the fresco first appeared, it was a focus of devotion for local women, though it is unclear whether it was thought that the image could cure infertility or lead to a successful pregnancy. Historian James R. Banker emphasises the distinctive, naturalistic presence of Mary in this painting when he states: "Few images of Mary by Piero or other fifteenth-century painters possess the gravity of this young woman. The image seems to belong to no other narrative than that of a young woman managing her pregnancy with grace and poise."[35] In contrast to other depictions of Mary created in his time, Piero presented an idealised model of pregnancy that focused on Mary's body. However, this initial use was undermined as

Catholic authorities drew attention away from the painting, admonishing its affiliated fertility cults in the sixteenth and seventeenth centuries.[36] Emphasis is shifted from Mary's bodily experience of pregnancy, delegating her role to a vessel containing Christ.

Additionally, depictions of the Virgin Mary eradicate a pregnant woman's sensuality through claims of immaculate conception, resulting in what Michelle Bolous Walker refers to as "the impossible dilemma of femininity under patriarchy. She is appropriated as a vessel for divine productivity, and is represented as both virtuous and asexual."[37] Julia Kristeva describes how in many works of art, the artist "speaks where she [the pregnant woman] is not, where she knows not," reducing her to a sign, an image that comes to replace her experience.[38] Bolous Walker notes in her reading of Kristeva: "The mother, reduced to an imaginary maternal body, is spoken for by the male artist/son. She herself never speaks. This great debt to motherhood, owed by Western art, is never repaid by recognising her right to speak for herself."[39] These representations of pregnancy, embodied in the religious figure of the Virgin Mary, reveal the maternal in an unattainable way—pregnancy without sexual intercourse—while placing the pregnant woman in what Heidegger refers to as standing-reserve, delivering the ideology of Christianity through the iconography of the bump. It is this legacy that certain artists, such as Kotak and Von Eck, are challenging by presenting the experience of pregnancy as an aesthetic encounter.

From Art to Aesthetics

In 1995, performance artist Sandy Huckleberry attended the opening of the exhibition *Neo-Dada: Redefining Art 1958–1963* at the Aidekman Gallery in Tufts University. Sipping on club soda and mingling with other attendees, Huckleberry partook in the various activities affiliated with this sort of social gathering, except she was in her ninth month of pregnancy and completely nude. In her recollections of the experience, Huckleberry describes how she performed the typical behaviours associated with gallery openings without acknowledging her state of undress. She engaged with other attendees through face-to-face conversations and was fascinated by the conflicting tension that arose as they expressed desire to look at her body, but did not want to appear inappropriate.[40] Nudity created an opportunity for others to gaze upon a heavily pregnant body, to examine the various external physical changes that accompany pregnancy so close to delivery, which included glimpses of her unborn son's gestures on the surface of her abdomen. Young describes how in pregnancy, it is possible for a pregnant woman to relate to her body through "innocent narcissism." She states:

> As I undress in the morning and evening, I gaze in the mirror for long minutes, without stealth or vanity. I do not appraise myself, ask whether I look good enough for others, but like a child take pleasure in discovering new things in my body. I turn to the side and stroke the taut flesh that protrudes under my breasts.[41]

During pregnancy, the body can become a site of fascination and exploration. Breasts become larger and more tender; the body retains fluid; a woman's pace slows as her centre of gravity shifts and the overall body schema transforms; hormonal changes lead to alterations (at times drastic) in emotional responses; fatigue sets in easily; breathing becomes shallow and can be more difficult; and so on. These are only some of the common changes associated with pregnancy, which as Young points out, lead to sensations of defamiliarisation in one's own body—an uncanny state of corporeal existence as the body itself becomes foreign. Bigwood emphasises how these changes extend the physical limits of the female body, as they become intertwined with a "mother's personal and cultural life."[42] She is enmeshed in an ever-shifting state of becoming:

> In pregnancy, a woman actively and continually responds to the fresh 'phusical' (from the Greek phusis, commonly translated as 'nature') upsurge that independently runs through her body with a life of its own. She creatively takes up the profound changes of her body, constantly readjusting her body image and weaving subtle relations to the phusical pulse that has emerged from elsewhere.[43]

Even though there are some commonalities between pregnant women, there is no certainty as to what changes actually occur and when they take place, making this time both unpredictable and unstable. Pregnancy is a whole-body—a whole-being—experience.

In Huckleberry's performance, she took Young's gestures of innocent narcissism out of the privacy of the bedroom and the reflective surface of the mirror, creating a collective experience that allowed viewers an opportunity to partake in this privileged act of looking. The simultaneous gestures of Huckleberry and her unborn son make both their presences evident, allowing the viewer to shift between them, resulting in an intersubjective encounter between the mother, the foetus, and the observer. Through performance, an artist does not just create an object for the reception of the audience. Instead, presentation and reception are merged as the artist presents herself as the work of art. As such, she occupies the position of creator-subject and art object, which for Fischer-Lichte, transforms her and her audience into co-subjects, where the subject-object relationship is no longer dichotomous, but oscillatory.[44] Subjects relate to each other through co-presence, perception, and response.[45] Perception is multifaceted and varies depending on the position of the subject. As the pregnant woman, Huckelberry experiences the movements of her unborn child through internal haptic interactions, while the audience can visually perceive the trace of a gesture through her abdomen. An intersubjective exchange occurs between the various participants, whose experience of the moment will differ depending on sensory stimuli and positionality. The performance takes place between the subjects, whose actions and reactions inform and respond to each other in what Fischer-Lichte refers to as a feedback loop.[46]

Even though performance artists are producing artistic events, it is possible to extend the aesthetic appreciation of pregnancy beyond the context of art. Young emphasises how the phenomenological changes of pregnancy may be disconcerting, but they do not have to be alienating. Instead, they can be experienced from an aesthetic perspective. Young's analysis emerges from Sally Gaddow's proposal that it is possible to build an intra-subjective relationship with the body that involves aesthetic immediacy where the "self recognises the body as another manifestation of selfness."[47] Even though Gaddow specifically refers to the body that transforms as the result of illness and ageing, Young applies her theories to pregnancy. By appreciating the body from an aesthetic perspective that is characterised as a "complex balance of form and freedom,"[48] it is possible to build a dialectical relationship with the changing body, its sensations, and shifting boundaries as a "fullness rather than a lack."[49] Instead of treating pregnancy from the medical perspective, or even that of an *expectant* mother, but treating it aesthetically, it can become a source of haptic curiosity, with proprioceptive and corporeal boundaries shifting and distending. Rather than fearing or loathing these changes, treating them as a source of discomfort to be endured, they become a temporary state of bodily transformation to be explored through a position of embodied perception, inside and out. Performance art is an effective impetus for inviting this awareness, as it can transform how people perceive the ordinary.[50]

It is possible to expand upon Young's interpretation of pregnancy by adding that it does not just allow for reflective intrasubjectivity, but, as a liminal bodily experience, also involves intersubjective relationships between the pregnant woman, the foetus, and others. Francine Wynn encourages this approach in her call for a "bodily intervolvement of mother-to-be and the baby-in-the-womb."[51] Moreover, Wynn breaks from the presumption that intercorporiality begins with birth, arguing that "during pregnancy both mother-to-be and her pre-infant are modified through their intertwining and spreading away."[52] As with Young and Rothman, Wynn challenges the increasingly dominant position of the foetus in pregnancy put forth by medical technology, arguing that these flattened presentations have come to replace the fullness of corporeal shared experience. However, unlike Young, Wynn shifts from a woman's self-conscious experience of the body to incorporate the multifaceted, and more challenging to pinpoint, duality of the pregnant woman and the foetus: "[Young] leaves unexplored the emerging and chiasmic relationship between mother and her pre-infant, who remains at the level of a possession or object."[53] Wynn critiques this "possessiveness," arguing for a phenomenological understanding of pregnancy that does not reside solely in treating either the pregnant woman or the foetus as a subject at the expense of the other. In this fashion, Huckleberry's performance extends the shared subjective experience beyond the pregnant woman and her unborn child to include others in a non-confrontational manner.

Conclusion

How others relate to the pregnant body plays a major role in shaping understandings of subjectivity in pregnancy, whether this discourse has religious, scientific, or public policy connotations. Many constructs and images have perpetuated an aesthetics of pregnancy that leaves little room for consideration of the pregnant woman's subjectivity, either by removing her from the picture entirely, as in ultrasound imagery; speaking in her place, as with the long history of male artists representing pregnant women in art; or emphasising an unattainable role for the maternal, as with the predominance of the Virgin Mary as the iconic image of pregnancy. At the same time, these images reinforce the notion that pregnancy is to be treated as a period when a woman merely awaits the arrival of her child. To return to Mullin's point, there is a tendency to consider pregnancies "solely in terms of whether or not they end in the birth of children," without fully appreciating the significance this experience has on a woman's life, whether a pregnancy is wanted or not.[54] In the hands of some artists, including Kotak, von Eck, and Huckleberry, the corporeal transformations of pregnancy become the source of an aesthetic experience, opening up intersubjective relations between the pregnant woman, the foetus, and others. Countering the alienation of pregnant subjects that Young describes, these artists place emphasis on the experience of pregnancy, drawing attention to the bodily changes that can be appreciated in their own right, as opposed to where they may lead. Collapsing the dichotomies of subject and object in art, along with those between art and reality, these artists open up rich sites for aesthetic encounters to manifest, while offering mothers-to-be opportunities to share the distinctive embodied and phenomenological characteristics of what it means to be pregnant.

Notes

1. Amy Mullin, "Pregnant Bodies, Pregnant Minds," *Feminist Theory* 3, no. 1 (2002): 28.
2. Erika Fischer-Lichte, *The Transformative Power of Performance: A New Aesthetics*, trans. Saskya Iris Jain (London and New York: Routledge, 2008), 32.
3. Ibid., 59.
4. Ibid., 206.
5. Ibid., 190.
6. Marvin Carlson, "Perspectives on Performance: Germany and America" in *The Transformative Power of Performance: A New Aesthetics*, ed. Erika Fischer-Lichte (London and New York: Routledge, 2008), 9.
7. Fischer-Lichte, *The Transformative Power of Performance: A New Aesthetics*, 168.
8. Maura Judkis, "Live Birth Performance Artist Marni Kotak Gives Birth to Healthy Baby Boy," http://www.washingtonpost.com/blogs/arts-post/post/live-birth-performance-artist-marni-kotak-delivers-healthy-baby-boy/2011/10/26/gIQAsUxoIM_blog.html.
9. Araceli Cruz, "Marni Kotak, Artist, Will Give Birth at Microscope Gallery, for Real," http://blogs.villagevoice.com/runninscared/2011/10/marni_kotak_gives_birth.php.
10. For example, see Hannah Roberts, "It's a Labour of Love: Pregnant Woman Who Will Give Birth on Stage," Daily Mail, http://www.dailymail.co.uk/news/article-2046814/Marni-Kotak-Pregnant-performance-artist-birth-stage.html; Stefanie Wilder-Taylor, "Childbirth as Performance Art? Top 10 Reasons This Is a Bad Idea," http://www.today.com/parents/

childbirth-performance-art-top-10-reasons-bad-idea-1C7398092?franchis eSlug=todayparentsmain.
11. Mother-blaming is not a new phenomenon. As the mother tends to be the primary caretaker of a child, she is commonly held responsible when something goes wrong, even if she has no influence on the child's actions. In the twenty-first century, with the advent of social media, the ability to judge a mother's decisions in raising a child has reached a larger public audience, with stories being shared rapidly and people are able to add their opinions through exhaustive comment sections. For more information about mother-blaming, please refer to Beverly Birns and Niza ben-Ner, "Psychoanalysis Constructs Motherhood," in *The Different Faces of Motherhood*, ed. Beverly Birns and Dale Hay (New York: Springer, 2013), and Denise Sommerfeld, "The Origins of Mother Blaming: Historical Perspectives on Childhood and Motherhood," *Infant Mental Health Journal* 10, no. 1 (1989).
12. Sandra Matthews and Laura Wexler, *Pregnant Pictures* (New York and London: Routledge, 2000), 2.
13. Carol Bigwood, "Renaturalizing the Body (with the Help of Merleau-Ponty)," *Hypatia* 6, no. 3 (1991): 62.
14. Iris Marion Young, "Pregnant Embodiment: Subjectivity and Alienation," in *On Female Body Experience: "Throwing Like a Girl" and Other Essays* (Oxford: Oxford University Press, 2005), 49.
15. Ibid.
16. Ibid., 58.
17. Ibid.
18. Numerous feminists have argued that the increased prominence of foetal imagery has led to visual and discursive undermining of maternal subjectivity at the expense of the increased recognition of foetal personhood. See Barbara Duden, *Disembodying Women: Perspectives on Pregnancy & the Unborn*, (Cambridge, MA: Harvard University Press, 1993); Alice Elaine Adams, *Reproducing the Womb: Images of Childbirth in Science, Feminist Theory, and Literature*, (Ithaca: Cornell University, 1994); Margarete Sandelowski, "Separate, but less unequal: fetal ultrasonography and the transformation of expectant mother/fatherhood," *Gender and Society*, 8 (1994): 230–245; Marilyn Maness, "Fetal attractions: the limit of Cyborg theory," *Women's Studies*, 29, no. 2 (2000): 177–194; Julie Palmer, "The Placental Body in 4D: Everyday Practices of Non-Diagnostic Sonography," *Feminist Review* 93 (2009): 64–80.
19. Peggy Phelan, "White Men and Pregnancy: Discovering the Body to Be Rescued," in *Unmarked: The Politics of Performance* (London and New York: Routledge, 1996), 132.

20. In Ireland, the treatment of the foetus as a separate patient is legally institutionalised, as it is written into the nation's constitution. According to the Eighth Amendment of the Constitution Act, 1983: "The State acknowledges the right to life of the unborn, with due regard to the equal right to life of the mother, guarantees in its laws to respect, and, as far as practicable, by its laws to defend and vindicate that right."
21. Barbara Katz Rothman, "Laboring Now: Current Cultural Constructions of Pregnancy, Birth, and Mothering," in *The Body Reader*, ed. Lisa Jean Moore and Mary Kosut (New York and London: New York University Press, 2010), 48.
22. Martin Heidegger, *The Question Concerning Technology and Other Essays*, trans. William Lovitt (New York: Harper Perennial, 1977), 13.
23. Ibid., 20.
24. Ibid., 19.
25. Gregory Ulmer, *Applied Grammatology: Post(E)-Pedagogy from Jacques Derrida to Joseph Beuys* (Baltimore and London: The John Hopkins University Press, 1985), 15.
26. Heidegger, *The Question Concerning Technology and Other Essays*, 26.
27. Ibid., 10.
28. Ibid., 11–12.
29. Ibid., 28.
30. Ibid.
31. Cathy Von Eck, "Double Beat—for Plastic Bags, Two Heart Beats, Breath and Electronics," http://www.cathyvaneck.net/gallery/double-beat-for-plastic-bags-two-heart-beats-breath-and-electronics/.
32. Heidegger, *The Question Concerning Technology and Other Essays*, 10.
33. Brendan Cassidy, "A Relic, Some Pictures and the Mothers of Florence in the Late Fourteenth Century," *Gesta* 30, no. 2 (1991): 91.
34. Naomi Haskell, *Piero Della Francesca*, 2nd ed. (Maidstone: Crescent Moon, 2008), 47.
35. James Banker, *Piero Della Francesca: Artist and Man* (Oxford: Oxford University Press, 2014), 102.
36. Ibid., 101.
37. Michelle Boulous Walker, *Philosophy and the Maternal Body: Reading Silence* (London and New York: Routledge, 1998), 136.
38. Julia Kristeva, "The Maternal Body (1975), from 'Motherhood According to Bellini'," in *The Portable Kristeva*, ed. Kelly Oliver (New York: Columbia University Press, 2002).
39. Boulous Walker, *Philosophy and the Maternal Body: Reading Silence*, 118.
40. Sandy Huckleberry (performance artist) in discussion with the author, September 2014.
41. Young, "Pregnant Embodiment: Subjectivity and Alienation," 53–54.

42. Bigwood, "Renaturalizing the Body (with the Help of Merleau-Ponty)," 68.
43. Ibid.
44. Fischer-Lichte, *The Transformative Power of Performance: A New Aesthetics*, 17.
45. Ibid., 32.
46. Ibid., 38.
47. Sally Gadow, "Body and Self: A Dialectic," *The Journal of Medicine and Philosophy* 5, no. 3 (1980): 181.
48. Ibid., 183.
49. Young, "Pregnant Embodiment: Subjectivity and Alienation," 51.
50. Fischer-Lichte, *The Transformative Power of Performance: A New Aesthetics*, 179.
51. Francine Wynn, "The Early Relationship of Mother and Pre-Infant: Merleau-Ponty and Pregnancy," *Nursing Philosophy* 3 (2002): 4.
52. Ibid., 5.
53. Ibid., 9.
54. Mullin, "Pregnant Bodies, Pregnant Minds," 40.

Bibliography

Adams, Alice Elaine. 1994. *Reproducing the Womb: Images of Childbirth in Science, Feminist Theory, and Literature*. Ithaca: Cornell University.
Banker, James. 2014. *Piero Della Francesca: Artist and Man*. Oxford: Oxford University Press.
Bigwood, Carol. 1991. Renaturalizing the Body (with the Help of Merleau-Ponty). *Hypatia* 6 (3): 54–73.
Birns, Beverly, and Niza Ben-Ner. 2013. Psychoanalysis Constructs Motherhood. In *The Different Faces of Motherhood*, ed. Beverly Birns and Dale Hay, 47–70. New York: Springer.
Boulous Walker, Michelle. 1998. *Philosophy and the Maternal Body: Reading Silence*. London/New York: Routledge.
Carlson, Marvin. 2008. Perspectives on Performance: Germany and America. Trans. Saskya Iris Jain. In *The Transformative Power of Performance: A New Aesthetics*, ed. Erika Fischer-Lichte, 1–10. London/New York: Routledge.
Cassidy, Brendan. 1991. A Relic, Some Pictures and the Mothers of Florence in the Late Fourteenth Century. *Gesta* 30 (2): 91–99.
Cruz, Araceli. Marni Kotak, Artist, Will Give Birth at Microscope Gallery, for Real. http://blogs.villagevoice.com/runninscared/2011/10/marni_kotak_gives_birth.php
Fischer-Lichte, Erika. 2008. *The Transformative Power of Performance: A New Aesthetics*. Trans. Saskya Iris Jain. London/New York: Routledge.

Gadow, Sally. 1980. Body and Self: A Dialectic. *The Journal of Medicine and Philosophy* 5 (3): 172–185.
Haskell, Naomi. 2008. *Piero Della Francesca*. 2nd ed. Maidstone: Crescent Moon.
Heidegger, Martin. 1977. *The Question Concerning Technology and Other Essays*. Trans. William Lovitt. New York: Harper Perennial.
Judkis, Maura. *Live Birth Performance Artist Marni Kotak Gives Birth to Healthy Baby Boy*. http://www.washingtonpost.com/blogs/arts-post/post/live-birth-performance-artist-marni-kotak-delivers-healthy-baby-boy/2011/10/26/gIQAsUxoIM_blog.html
Kristeva, Julia. 2002. The Maternal Body (1975), from "Motherhood According to Bellini". In *The Portable Kristeva*, ed. Kelly Oliver. New York: Columbia University Press.
Matthews, Sandra, and Laura Wexler. 2000. *Pregnant Pictures*. New York/London: Routledge.
Mullin, Amy. 2002. Pregnant Bodies, Pregnant Minds. *Feminist Theory* 3 (1): 27–44.
Phelan, Peggy. 1996. White Men and Pregnancy: Discovering the Body to Be Rescued. In *Unmarked: The Politics of Performance*. London/New York: Routledge.
Roberts, Hannah. 2011. It's a Labour of Love: Pregnant Woman Who Will Give Birth on Stage. *Daily Mail*. http://www.dailymail.co.uk/news/article-2046814/Marni-Kotak-Pregnant-performance-artist-birth-stage.html
Rothman, Barbara Katz. 2010. Laboring Now: Current Cultural Constructions of Pregnancy, Birth, and Mothering. In *The Body Reader*, ed. Lisa Jean Moore and Mary Kosut, 48–65. New York/London: New York University Press.
Sommerfeld, Denise. 1989. The Origins of Mother Blaming: Historical Perspectives on Childhood and Motherhood. *Infant Mental Health Journal* 10 (1): 14–24.
Ulmer, Gregory. 1985. *Applied Grammatology: Post(E)-Pedagogy from Jacques Derrida to Joseph Beuys*. Baltimore/London: The John Hopkins University Press.
Von Eck, Cathy. 2013. *Double Beat—For Plastic Bags, Two Heart Beats, Breath and Electronics*. http://www.cathyvaneck.net/gallery/double-beat-for-plastic-bags-two-heart-beats-breath-and-electronics/
Wilder-Taylor, Stefanie. 2011. *Childbirth as Performance Art? Top 10 Reasons This Is a Bad Idea*. http://www.today.com/parents/childbirth-performance-art-top-10-reasons-bad-idea-1C7398092?franchiseSlug=todayparentsmain
Wynn, Francine. 2002. The Early Relationship of Mother and Pre-infant: Merleau-Ponty and Pregnancy. *Nursing Philosophy* 3: 4–14.
Young, Iris Marion. 2005. Pregnant Embodiment: Subjectivity and Alienation. In *On Female Body Experience: "Throwing Like a Girl" and Other Essays*. Oxford: Oxford University Press.

CHAPTER 12

The Metaphors of Commercial Surrogacy: Rethinking the Materiality of Hospitality Through Pregnant Embodiment

Luna Dolezal

INTRODUCTION

Terminology, particularly in medical or scientific contexts, is almost always metaphorically loaded and, as a result, value-laden.[1] The words we choose, or adopt, directly influence how we conceive of new technologies, shaping our ethical intuitions, along with behaviour, practice and policy. Emily Martin's seminal work on metaphor and women's reproduction has demonstrated that the language that is used to articulate reproduction, pregnancy and childbirth shapes the logics through which we perceive women and their social roles.[2] In the context of the third-party reproduction practice commonly referred to as 'commercial surrogacy,' the dominant metaphoric landscape has had concrete consequences in terms of practice, policy, ethics and, more fundamentally, how we conceive of women, kin relationships and the pregnant body.[3] The aim of this chapter is to consider some of the metaphors that have shaped, and continue to determine, how we understand 'commercial surrogacy,'[4] or that which is commonly understood to be the practice where a woman undergoes fertilization and

L. Dolezal (✉)
University of Exeter, Exeter, UK

© The Author(s) 2018
C. Fischer, L. Dolezal (eds.), *New Feminist Perspectives on Embodiment*, Breaking Feminist Waves,
https://doi.org/10.1007/978-3-319-72353-2_12

221

subsequently gestates a foetus, ultimately relinquishing the resulting child to the intended parent or parents, who financially compensate her for the pregnancy.[5]

Since the advent of in vitro fertilization (IVF), commercial gestational surrogacy (where the surrogate has no genetic ties to the foetus) has become a feasible alternative to adoption. However, it is still often a last resort for couples or individuals who wish to have a child but may be physically unable to carry a foetus to term themselves. Increasingly, international cross-border arrangements, frequently with surrogates in developing countries, are pursued in order to avoid legal restrictions and for reasons of dramatically reduced costs. As a result, in recent times, a global industry of commercial surrogacy has rapidly expanded, where parents from high-resource countries are contracting surrogates from low-resource countries to carry pregnancies to term.[6] While some developing countries, such as Thailand and India, have made recent attempts to ban commercial gestational surrogacy, reproductive medical tourism remains a multi-billion-dollar global industry, with commercial gestational surrogacy playing a central role in the global medical market.[7]

Surrogacy is a highly contested terrain within assisted reproductive practices. Recent controversies demonstrate that it is a practice riddled with philosophical, moral, legal and ethical questions regarding the competing and conflicting rights and responsibilities of the parties involved in surrogacy arrangements. These questions concern the exploitation of vulnerable women, the alienation of reproductive bodily functions, 'baby selling,' transnational citizenship rights, eugenics and selective parenting, and the legal, social and existential status of motherhood, paternity and kin relationships—or who counts as a child's 'real' family and parents.

While surrogacy is a practice that is mired in controversy, the terms that have been deployed tropologically to describe the agents, practices, biological processes and social relationships within commercial surrogacy arrangements have shaped the landscape of the practice and the logics of its permissibility and ethicality in certain contexts, not to mention the manner by which women in these arrangements are conceptualized and treated. The aim of this chapter is to examine aspects of the metaphoric landscape of commercial surrogacy, with particular emphasis on the recent use of 'hospitality' as a metaphor to describe the role pregnant women play within surrogacy arrangements.

Hospitality is a concept that has been extensively theorized within philosophy, through thinkers such as Kant, Levinas and Derrida. It is central to a multitude of philosophical issues, such as the constitution of subjectivity, the character of social relations and questions concerning the nation-state, private property and borders. However, standard philosophical accounts of hospitality have been subject to feminist critique, especially when considering the long-standing associations between femininity, domesticity and 'hosting,' which are uncritically reproduced in many philosophical discourses on hospitality. Furthermore, feminist theorists have recently appropriated the concept of hospitality, not only to critique dominant gender-essentialising tendencies within Western thought, but also as a productive means to conceptualize female embodiment when considering the experiences of pregnancy, gestation and maternal-foetal relations. With particular focus on Levinas' account of hospitality as central to subjective constitution, I will explore how hospitality is implicated in maternity. I will commence by examining how the common metaphors of 'production' and 'the container' in pregnancy have served as a justificatory ground for commercial surrogacy practices. I will then turn to examine how 'hospitality' has been taken up as a metaphor by clinics, regulating bodies and theorists to describe a pregnant woman's role in gestational commercial surrogacy, particularly in transnational contexts. Considering the recent work of the feminist scholar Irina Aristarkhova,[8] my aim is to bring new feminist conceptions of *embodied hospitality* into dialogue with the various discourses of commercial surrogacy which deploy the metaphor. I will ultimately argue that pregnancy is a *human* and *maternal* process that has *constitutional* status, involving complex subjective affects and roles through relations of care and nurturing. As a result, the gestating mother, who creates space for and welcomes the 'other,' should not be effaced or forgotten.

The Foundational Metaphors of Surrogacy: Production and the Container

Metaphors are tropological by nature; they entail a 'displacement,' as Vivian Sobchack contends.[9] A metaphor takes 'a nominative term from its mundane (hence literal, nonfigural) context and [places it] elsewhere to illuminate some other context through its *refiguration*.'[10] By using a metaphor, we take something that is familiar and then refigure it through understanding it in terms of something else. Metaphors are pervasive in everyday thought and language, and the dominant metaphors within a linguistic community shape our understandings and intuitions. This section will outline two of the central metaphors of pregnancy that shape how we commonly conceive of women's social role in reproduction: production and the container metaphor. As will be demonstrated, the already dominant metaphors of pregnancy have served as a foundational logic for gestational commercial surrogacy, providing a conceptual ground from which this third-party reproductive practice is not only permissible, but can be construed as ethical.

Production

A central metaphor in pregnancy is that of 'labour.' Since the fifteenth century, the same English word 'labour' has been used to describe both what women do in order to birth their children and what paid workers do to produce goods for use and exchange in the home and market.[11] The conflation of these two distinct concepts means that reproduction has been commonly conceived of as a type of production: the woman, as Emily Martin notes, is conceived of as 'a "labourer", whose "machine" (uterus) produces the "product", babies.'[12] Underpinning this logic is the 'machine imagery' for the human body, which, as Mary Midgley notes, started to pervade our thought in the seventeenth century and remains a potent metaphor in the present day.[13] Under the machine metaphor, we 'tend to see ourselves, and the living things around us, as pieces of clockwork: items of a kind that we ourselves could make.'[14] In pregnancy, women are construed as both *being* and *containing* reproductive machines that perform a specialized type of mechanistic constructive labour. Understood through these metaphoric constraints, the discourses of pregnancy become enthralled to what Lakoff and Johnson identify as a 'resource' logic: Labour 'can be *quantified* fairly precisely (in terms of time); can be assigned a *value* per unit; serves a *purposeful* end; is *used up* progressively as it serves it purpose.'[15] Conceived through these parameters, pregnant women, as specialized labourers, should be able to be compensated for their time and for the products they produce.

It is clear that conceiving of pregnancy as productive labour serves the conceptual bedrock of commercial surrogacy practices, which, in the present day, are governed primarily by service or employment contracts.[16] Understanding the 'costs' of carrying a child to term for another through quantifying possible 'physical [and] psychological health burdens'[17] means that pregnant women can ultimately be compensated for their 'labour' through an economic or altruistic transaction. In essence, commercial surrogacy involves the purchase of 'reproductive labour' from a third party.[18] Arising from the central metaphor of pregnancy as 'labour,' coupled with the contemporary neoliberal tendency to frame all aspects of life in economic terms according to a market agenda,[19] terms such as 'costs,' 'factories,' 'contracts,' 'outsourcing,' 'commissioning,' 'compensation,' 'services' and 'renting,' among others, are ubiquitous in the discourses that surround gestational surrogacy, and it is almost impossible to theorize or even speak about surrogacy without leaning heavily on these sorts of metaphors. The ubiquity and acceptability of labour as a central metaphor in pregnancy has been central to shaping ethical intuitions about commercial surrogacy and, hence, its social and legal permissibility. As many bioethicists argue, if pregnancy is merely a specialized type of labour, or work—comparable to bodily work done by athletes or professional dancers—then contracted pregnancy is no different from other types of physical work that can be governed by employment contracts.[20]

Container

In recent decades, as a result of the rise of imaging technologies, such as routine ultrasound examinations, the container metaphor has become central to how pregnancy is conceived in the present day. As Barbara Rothman notes, from 'a time of "expecting" a baby,' pregnancy has transformed into 'a time of containing a foetus.'[21] The now iconic images of the disembodied foetus from Lennart Nilsson's 1966 *Life Magazine* feature heralded this important cultural shift in how pregnancy is construed within medical and social discourses. These striking images of a foetus floating in a celestial-like black space, accompanied with captions such as 'the drama of life before birth' and 'a thumb to suck, a veil to wear,' allowed the expression of a previously unarticulated foetal subjectivity.[22]

Without imaging technology, the foetus is manifested only through the swelling pregnant belly of its mother; without technologically mediated visibility, as a separate entity, it exists only as an imagined projection.[23] However, through visibility, the unborn has been interpellated as human—a baby, son or daughter—and has been endowed with interests, rights and, in the present day, specialized medical care.[24] At the same time as presenting the foetus as an independent subjectivity, foetal imagery also presents the womb as a generalized container-like space.[25] This container space is alienated from the pregnant woman's subjectivity, one 'whose particular embodied experience' would '[warrant] consideration.'[26] In fact, since

Nilsson's *Life Magazine* foetus was depicted floating in a disembodied space, with the maternal body—on which it would have been entirely dependent—nowhere in sight, images of disembodied wombs containing baby-like foetuses are part of the standard visual discourse of pregnancy and gestation.[27]

In surrogacy arrangements, container metaphors abound, where gestational mothers are described as 'hosts,' 'vessels' and 'carriers' who can 'rent' their wombs, as one would rent a house or other temporary dwelling place. Images of largely disembodied pregnant bellies, decontextualized and depersonalized in white clinical spaces, are ubiquitous in the promotional material and websites of fertility clinics worldwide, which offer commercial gestational surrogacy as one of their services.[28] In fact, along with the idea that pregnancy is labour, the underpinning logic of commercial surrogacy positions pregnant women as fungible and indifferent containers to foetuses, who are, in turn, conceived as independent subjectivities.[29] In short, surrogate mothers are rendered 'human incubators,'[30] who act as mere 'carriers' or containers for the 'real' parents.[31]

Hospitality

While production and container metaphors continue to powerfully structure how we understand pregnancy and surrogacy practices, a leading intuition among many is that it is reductive and dehumanizing to conceive of pregnancy as merely a form of labour or work. As Martin argues, the dominant metaphors of production and 'labour' are limiting, inherently concealing other aspects of experience: '[W]omen lose ... by having a complex process that interrelates physical, emotional and mental experience treated as if it could be broken down and managed like other forms of production.'[32] Pregnancy is a complex embodied and affective experience with a unique life-generating and kinship-generating capacity that arguably transcends any attempt to be quantified as a form of production.[33] As a result, many bioethicists, practitioners, policy-makers and feminist theorists have profound ambivalences and anxieties regarding surrogates being contracted for their reproductive capacities, or wombs. Many argue that these practices are inherently dehumanizing, leading to exploitation, objectification and an intensification of gender inequality, reducing women to a mere 'breeder class.'[34]

In order to assuage the ethical and social problems of conceiving of surrogacy as merely a contractual economic transaction—a logic that gets us dangerously close to 'baby selling'—more palatable metaphors have been adopted by regulating bodies, bioethicists and fertility clinics, among others, in part to 'soften the pecuniary image of commercial surrogacy.'[35] For instance, the metaphor of 'the gift' has been frequently used in order to characterize the exchange between the surrogate and the intended parents as a relation of altruism.[36] The gift metaphor alleviates concerns about exploitation and potential coercion as a result of financial need on the part of the surrogates: the baby is not sold, but instead is given; the surrogate not paid, but instead is 'compensated.' Furthermore, the gift metaphor invokes an essentialized feminine altruism where the idea is that women 'naturally' want to help each other.[37]

While the gift metaphor has been invoked to describe the relationship between the surrogate and the intended parents,[38] the metaphor of 'hospitality' has recently been taken up by regulating bodies, clinics, ethicists and others, as a means to describe the relationship between the surrogate and the foetus she is gestating. While again invoking an inherent sense of generosity through welcoming, a further aim of this metaphor is to mitigate concerns that the surrogate has any claims to kinship or 'motherhood.'[39] Commercial surrogacy clinics explicitly refer to gestational surrogates as 'hosts,' invoking a relation of temporary dwelling with no kinship ties.[40] In fact, the metaphor of the gestational mother as an 'innkeeper' who provides a welcoming space for her 'guest' has been used in Israeli courts to define surrogacy practices.[41] In transnational arrangements, the surrogate, additionally, serves as an international host—the long-standing cultural discourses of the importance of hospitality for the 'stranger' or foreigner invoking a national welcoming through the maternal body. Understanding women as sites of hospitality not only reiterates the idea of an essential feminine altruism, reinforcing a long-standing association between 'hosting,' domesticity and femininity, but also reinforces the container logic that justifies a property rights discourses: women own their bodies and they are free to rent or loan them to guests of their choosing.

Hospitality in Philosophy and the Maternal

Hospitality is a concept within philosophy that is often thought to have the status of universality. In other words, it is seen to be something essential not only to the human condition, but also to how societies organize themselves with respect to the 'other' or the 'outsider.' As Judith Still notes, 'Hospitality is a topic that has consistently been considered important over long periods of time, over wider tracks of the globe ... hospitality is traditionally defined as universal (even *the* universal) human virtue.'[42] Despite differing rituals or practices of hospitality within certain cultures or historical periods, it is posited that hospitality is an essential and enduring practice, fundamental to the human condition and social relations. We (as individuals and collectively) are constituted by the impulse to welcome and host the stranger, even if this relationship can become fraught or be subverted by hostility, scapegoating or antagonism.

It is precisely this conception of hospitality, as *essential* to the human condition and to human relations, that underpins Emmanuel Levinas' philosophical project of an ontological ethics; his work has been described by Jacques Derrida as an 'immense treatise of hospitality.'[43] In fact, the reception of Levinas' conception of hospitality has been strongly influenced by Derrida's reading that brings Levinas' ontological description of the impulse to welcome the other to the realm of international hospitality and justice in the questions that underpin contemporary cosmopolitanism. As Derrida's reading contends, in contrast to Kant's premise that war and hostility are 'natural' impulses to be overcome by acts of hospitality,[44] Levinas radically proposes that welcoming the other is at the foundation of subjectivity and, therefore, of social and political life. Levinas conceptualizes the ground of ethics not in virtues or moral law, but instead in a phenomenological and ontological relation of openness and welcoming towards the 'other.' Prior to any hostility or antagonism, the ethical call of the other is at the heart of our ontological constitution. I do not have the scope here to do justice to the entirety of Levinas' account, which traverses the ontological, ethical, social, and political and involves an unresolvable aproetic tension at its heart—pure hospitality is ultimately an impossibility, being both unconditional and conditional. For Levinas, hospitality concerns not only primary relations between human subjects (originary and unconditional), but also the private domestic sphere, welcoming someone into one's home, and the public political sphere, nations welcoming immigrants,[45] the latter practices governed by laws and rules (and, therefore, conditional).[46] Putting to one side the aporetic tensions in conditional hospitality, my aim is to focus on the ontological and constitutional aspects of Levinas' account, where his tropological use of the feminine is instrumental in theorizing a primary hospitality between subjects as the condition for human subjectivity and human relations.

Access to the other, Levinas contends, is 'straightaway ethical.'[47] This relation is characterized by an asymmetry in the encounter with another, where the other's insurmountable otherness, or alterity, results in an infinite and *inescapable* responsibility to the other.[48] This responsibility is prior to any duty or obligation; it is 'for a debt contracted before any freedom and before any consciousness and any present.'[49] The absolute asymmetry of the I-other relation implies that I am hostage to the other in a necessary and absolute sense at the originary moment of the metaphysical founding of subjectivity. On this metaphysical level, there is no way to eliminate or ignore the bond to the other. As Levinas argues: '[A]t no time can one say I have done all my duty.'[50] I am *always* in relation to the other, through my unceasing responsibility to host and welcome the other, who holds me hostage; this is, according to Levinas, 'the essential, primary and fundamental structure of subjectivity.'[51] Our a priori responsibility to the other and others, as Levinas understands it, is that which makes responsibility and hospitality, in the usual sense of constituted through choices, duties and actions (along with sociality and politics), possible.[52]

Through positioning an openness and welcoming to the other at the heart of the human condition, Levinas portrays the human subject as radically relational, vulnerable and dependent—in contrast to the self-contained, rational and autonomous Kantian subject. Hospitality, for Levinas, is about this inherent openness to the other (and to otherness) that is at the heart of our subjective constitution. As Rosalyn Diprose notes, 'Hospitality is not a footnote to human existence: this responsiveness, this welcome, this openness *is* subjectivity; it *is* dwelling; it *is* the political.'[53] In this way, hospitality traverses subjectivity, sociality and the political. It is characterized, on all these levels, by welcoming, receptivity, intimacy, recollection and a feeling of being at 'home.'[54]

Interestingly, for Levinas, hospitality is explicitly and intimately connected to femininity. The feminine is tropologically invoked in his account as the foundation, or pre-condition, for any hospitality. Levinas writes: '[T]he other whose presence ... with which is accomplished the primary hospitable welcome ... is the Woman.'[55] The 'feminine being' is the 'welcoming one par excellence, welcome in itself.'[56] Feminine alterity, he contends, opens up 'the dimension of interiority,'[57] the dwelling place or 'home,' which is the condition of existence in the first place. Levinas concludes: 'To exist henceforth means to dwell,'[58] and this dwelling (read existence) is made possible by the 'feminine being,' or 'Woman.' Derrida takes up Levinas' idealized femininity in his own reading of hospitality.

He writes: 'The absolute, absolutely originary welcome, indeed, the pre-original welcome, the welcoming par excellence, is feminine; it takes place in a place that cannot be appropriated, in an open "interiority" whose hospitality the master or owner receives before himself then wishing to give it.'[59]

While it seems obvious that the spatial metaphors, along with the association of the feminine with the site of original relationality (fleshed out by both Levinas and Derrida as the idea that one is *constituted by the other* and has *infinite responsibility* for the other), are a reference to the maternal, neither Levinas nor Derrida acknowledge the figure of the mother, or the processes of pregnancy and gestation, as a site of original welcoming. Instead, they distance the 'feminine' and the 'Woman' from empirical flesh-and-blood women, using these gendered terms in what they contend is merely a figurative capacity.[60] The feminine is always idealized, connected to spatial (container) metaphors—home, house, interiority—in order to figure the site where the masculine subject or 'master' can receive his guest. The dematerialized and idealized feminine silently creates the space, or 'interiority,' for hospitality (or subjective and ethical constitution) to be able to occur between male subjects, but the female is effaced and silenced in its creation.[61] Levinas' use of the feminine in this context has, not surprisingly, been criticized by feminist scholars at length, so I will not dwell on the obviously problematically patriarchal tendencies at play here.[62] However, it is clear that this patriarchal reading of hospitality does, in part, reinforce the logic of many transnational commercial surrogacy practices, where (often subaltern) women are conceived as merely passive vessels for the realization of hospitality for those with the (social and economic) capital to claim fully human status.

However, as Irina Aristakhova, in her recent book *Hospitality of the Matrix*, notes, the non-empirical feminine in Levinas' and Derrida's accounts is inextricably 'haunted by the maternal imaginary.'[63] While pregnancy, nursing and the materiality of empirical female bodies do not figure at all in their conceptualization of hospitality and the originary moments of self-other relations, it is virtually impossible not to see the womb as the first dwelling place, or 'first home,' when this metaphysical account is extrapolated into the realm of the material.[64] In other words, Aristarkhova argues that 'an underlying confusion of the feminine and the maternal in Levinas and Derrida'[65] renders the (empirical rather than figurative) female body as the originary ground for the constitution of subjectivity and self-other relations. Aristarkhova argues that admitting a connection between hospitality and the maternal would move the feminine out of the merely conceptual realm and address the experience and condition of *actual women*, positioning gestation and motherhood at the centre of all philosophical thinking about subjectivity, ethics and politics, something, it is clear, that male theorists have long been at pains to avoid.[66]

Recent feminist scholarship has sought to 'materializ[e] hospitality,'[67] rendering 'women's pregnant flesh' the 'original home and ground of human sociality.'[68] Following Frances Gray, the idea is that 'pregnant flesh' is the 'prototype (and archetype) of hospitality … [where] hospitality as a social function in the human world is secondary to the relationships we find embodied in pregnant flesh.'[69] Notably, Irina Aristarkhova takes up this refiguring of hospitality as a maternal relation, situating hospitality in the material, namely at the biological origins of life, considering the reproductive space of the maternal body as the original site for the very possibility of welcoming/hosting the 'other.' Returning to the etymological roots of the term, Aristarkhova figures the 'matrix' as a generative space, signifying the womb, pregnancy and the maternal. The matrix is conceived both literally and figuratively as the space and *possibility* of hospitality. Reconceiving of the matrix in this way destabilizes the dominant production and container metaphors deployed in pregnancy. Aristrarkhova writes: '[The] conflation of space and mother by way of their role (mother … as a receptacle that contains and generates all) is one of the foundations of our cultural, philosophical and scientific imagery. The problem with this conflation … is that it "reduces" mother to space without acknowledging that she is more than "just" a sacrificial receptacle, a "bag of tissue" for the child.'[70] Refiguring the matrix as the site where the *generation* of space is made possible (rather than merely being a passive space) means that there 'is no space available for the other unless the mother makes it.'[71] To use Aristarkhova's formulation, hospitality, then is rendered, 'the concrete practice of "making-space" for the other through accommodation, expectation-expectancy, and nursing and nourishing.'[72]

Positioning this reading of hospitality at the centre of generative processes means that reproduction cannot be conceived as merely a biological process where the maternal body is conceived as some sort of 'container' or 'receptacle,' which could be indifferently outsourced to another's body. Instead, pregnancy is a *human* and *maternal* process that has *constitutional* status, involving complex subjective affects and roles through relations of care and nurturing. The gestating mother, who creates space for and welcomes the 'other,' cannot be effaced or forgotten, but instead is central in the drama of subjective constitution, on an ontological level, and human reproduction, on a material level.[73] She welcomes 'the guest' in an act of absolute hospitality. Conceiving of surrogacy as a radical act of hospitality means that it is not merely about 'making-space' for the other, through loaning the space of one's womb; instead, hospitality invokes the ongoing constitutive maternal-foetal relationship through a relation of giving and receiving, and this envelopes and involves the pregnant woman's whole being.[74]

However, Aristarkhova is at pains to avoid any essentialism in her thinking, reiterating that her arguments 'are not tied to some essentialized notions of the feminine or the maternal.'[75] And this is an important point: the social and cultural variation in experiences of pregnancy overwhelms any physiological sameness.[76] As Debra Satz is right to point out, arguing that there is some sort of 'maternal instinct' or 'sacrosanct bonding' between a mother and her child-to-be is a troubling line of reasoning, as 'not all women bond with their foetuses. Some women abort them.'[77] As long as hospitality is read 'as not a mere biological state or process, but as a metaphor for conscious, living, pregnant flesh,' then the variation of women's experiences and subjective states—whether a pregnancy is wanted or unwanted—is neither trivialized or effaced.[78] While it is important not to essentialize or sentimentalize women's experiences of pregnancy, it also seems obvious that recognizing the constitutional aspects of pregnancy is not irrelevant within surrogacy debates, especially when considering transnational gestational surrogacy, where 'donor-and-surrogacy amnesia'[79] is common practice. In fact, until pregnancy is adequately theorized, and the complexity of *embodied* hospitality is honoured within the discourses of commercial surrogacy, the ethical ground of surrogacy will not be clearly delineated, nor can the question of who is 'real' kin be addressed.

Conclusion

Harking back to historical legacy of patriarchy in defining familial relationships and kinship, the location of paternity is still traditionally found in the 'seed,' which continues to trump all other embodied or caring relationships.[80] Under this patriarchal understanding of kinship, the 'ownership' of a baby, and who are the 'real' parents, is not a result of pregnancy, gestation, birth or an embodied maternal relationship, but results from, as Rothman remarks, 'those who produced (or indeed in these days simply purchased) the genetic material.'[81] Although this patriarchal privilege has been extended to the 'seeds' of women, the understanding of kin or 'of who is and is not "really" related' renders, in the context of surrogacy, pregnancies somehow marginal and without significant kinship-generating capacity.[82] As a result, commissioning parents have no obligation to maintain a connection with the surrogate who will carry their child to term, nor any obligation to inform the child of the identity of their surrogate mother. The pregnant woman, as a subjectivity whose embodied and affective experience warrants consideration and as an individual who has the embodied capacity to generate and sustain life, remains conspicuously absent in the dominant logic that governs surrogacy arrangements. She is figured as the silent but affable host, welcoming and then discharging her guest. Not only does this superficial understanding of hospitality efface the complex and constitutional status of pregnancy and gestation, or the 'hospitality of the matrix,' to deploy Aristarkhova's terminology, but it also occludes social class and intersections of dubious political legacies that have fed into the practices of sex-specific reproductive 'labour,' such as racial slavery, gender segregation and global inequalities, among others.[83]

Following this new feminist reading of embodied hospitality destabilizes the dominant understanding of hospitality as it is deployed in the discourses of commercial surrogacy, while also giving a relational and embodied, rather than mechanistic, reading of 'labour' as it might be thought of in commercial surrogacy arrangements. The hospitality of pregnant women's bodies, as we have seen, does not merely involve a biological or physiological process, but is instead a complex affective state of interrelationality. A new subjectivity, with the capacity for meaningful action, is produced through the relationality and communication that necessarily occurs in utero.[84] In fact, when considering what constitutes kinship, parenting and relatedness, taking emphasis away from the 'seed' and putting it towards blood ties and a sharing of origins,[85] then it starts to seem reasonable to assign a type of kinship status to gestational mothers who provide the primary months of care and nurturing through pregnancy. This kinship would be based on social and intercorporeal ties arising from the initial maternal-foetal relation established through gestation, rather than on any genetic link. This should be the case even if the surrogate mother does not share a genetic bond with the child she has carried or if she does not continue to play any parental role after the child's birth. In light of this, a proposal made by Mary Shanley and Sujatha Jesudason that would allow children born through surrogacy to learn the identity of the surrogate and any gamete donor, could redress some of the injustices, resulting from common donor and surrogate 'amnesia,' inherent to current commercial surrogacy arrangements.[86] Modelled on practices in adoption, this proposal would allow the formation of new family relationships and, at least, acknowledge the key role that surrogates play in generating new life. This is a role that cannot be and should not be effaced through an economic transaction or governed entirely by a contract.

Hospitality as a metaphor for commercial surrogacy in fact problematizes the idea that 'pregnant flesh' is merely an affable, albeit indifferent, container to the 'other.' In fact, if we are to take this metaphor seriously, we see that the principle of hospitality is the ground for human sociality and ethics, and that in the case of the surrogacy arrangement, the pregnant body provides the materialization of that principle for those parties involved in the arrangement.[87] While, in some contexts, a superficial reading of hospitality may be an apt metaphor for pregnant women's experiences of surrogacy, where kin relations may prompt altruism,[88] what is clear is that the manner by which metaphor is currently deployed in transnational commercial arrangements has the potential to occlude a range of injustices and social equalities that, it should be remembered, affect only women. As Aristarkhova notes, 'Hosting is a culturally organized way of relating to others, and there is little about it that happens by itself. It is especially important and radical because it is difficult and takes time and effort.'[89] The materiality of embodied hospitality, actual physical responses of care, sustenance and nurturing, must be acknowledged meaningfully.

My aim is not to argue that commercial surrogacy should be unqualifiedly considered morally and legally impermissible. Instead, my hope is to unsettle some of the concepts which underpin contemporary manifestations of this reproductive service, especially when considering transnational arrangements, or those that occlude substantial economic and social inequalities between contracting parties and surrogates. The aim is to do some work towards reframing the metaphorical landscape that informs the discourses, ethics and legislative frameworks that govern surrogacy arrangements, with the view that these practices have the potential, if they are to continue, to be less exploitative and dehumanizing. In other words, the 'labour' performed by commercial surrogates should be considered relational, embodied and with kinship-generating potential, rather than a mechanistic service governed in totality by service contracts and economic transactions. To reiterate, pregnancy is a *human* and *maternal* process that has *constitutional* status, involving complex subjective affects and roles through relations of care and nurturing. The gestating mother, who creates space for and welcomes the 'other,' cannot be effaced or forgotten.

The very concept of surrogacy is 'metaphorically structured,'[90] and following Lakoff and Johnson, it is clear that when we deploy a metaphor 'that allows us to comprehend one aspect of a concept in terms of another,' we will necessarily conceal or deemphasize 'other aspects of the concept,'[91] a practice that is common when considering the discourses of assisted reproduction.[92] There is a lot at stake in how pregnancy and the gestating woman are portrayed within commercial surrogacy arrangements. In effect, the manner through which pregnancy and gestational motherhood are conceived and theorized shapes the ethical landscape, delineating what is acceptable and unacceptable in terms of common practices, where potential injustices fall largely on (already underprivileged) women's shoulders. Rethinking hospitality as an *embodied* phenomenon has the potential to problematize taken-for-granted ideas that may be sustaining ethically dubious practices with respect to gestational commercial surrogacy.

Notes

1. John D. Loike, "Loaded Words," *The Scientist*, 1 December 2014.
2. Emily Martin, *The Woman in the Body: A Cultural Analysis of Reproduction* (Boston: Beacon Books, 2001).
3. As Beeson et al. point out, there are terminological issues even in the use of the term 'surrogate' in describing third-party reproductive practices where a woman gestates a foetus on behalf of another. See Diane Beeson, Marcy Darnovsky, and Abby Lipman, "What's in a Name?: Variations in Terminology of Third-Party Reproduction," *Reproductive BioMedicine Online* 31 (2015).
4. I have written about commercial surrogacy elsewhere in order to demonstrate how pregnancy, as an embodied and existential experience, is often effaced in dominant discourses. This chapter is a further development of these themes. See Luna Dolezal, "Phenomenology and Intercorporeality in the Case of Commercial Surrogacy," in *Body/Self/Other: The Phenomenology of Social Encounters*, ed. Luna Dolezal and Danielle Petherbridge (Albany: SUNY Press, 2017). Also see "Considering Pregnancy in Commercial Surrogacy: A Response to Bronwyn Parry," *Medical Humanities* 41, no. 1 (2015).
5. Traditionally, in commercial surrogacy, the surrogate mother is the genetic parent and the sperm comes from a donor or the intended father. However, with the advent of in vitro fertilization (IVF), genetic ties to the gestating

surrogate are now completely elective, as embryos are created and implanted into the womb of the surrogate, without her needing to have any genetic ties to the foetus she will gestate. While gametes may often come from what are referred to as the 'commissioning parents,' creating a genetic link between the child and its intended parents, they may also simply be purchased by the commissioning parents, meaning that it is possible for there to be no genetic link between the child and its intended parents.

6. See France Winddance Twine, *Outsourcing the Womb: Race, Class and Gestational Surrogacy in a Global Market* (London: Routledge, 2011).
7. Ibid., 17.
8. See Luna Dolezal, "Review of Hospitality of the Matrix: Philosophy, Biomedicine and Culture, Irina Aristarkhova (2012)," *Hospitality & Society* 2, no. 3 (2012).
9. Vivian Sobchack, "A Leg to Stand On: Prosthetics, Metaphor, and Materiality," in *The Prosthetic Impulse: From a Posthuman Present to a Biocultural Future*, ed. Marquard Smith and Joanne Morra (London: MIT Press, 2006), 21.
10. Ibid.
11. Martin, 66.
12. Ibid., 57.
13. Mary Midgley, *The Myths We Live By* (London: Routledge, 2011), 1.
14. Ibid.
15. George Lakoff and Mark Johnson, *Metaphors We Live By* (Chicago: The University of Chicago Press, 1980), 66.
16. For a discussion of the philosophical underpinnings of the contract model in surrogacy, see Rosalyn Diprose, *The Bodies of Women: Ethics, Embodiment and Sexual Difference* (London: Routledge, 1994), 2–17.
17. Jeffrey Kirby, "Transnational Gestational Surrogacy: Does It Have to Be Exploitative," *The American Journal of Bioethics* 14, no. 5 (2014): 28.
18. Twine, 15.
19. See Wendy Brown, *Undoing the Demos: Neoliberalism's Stealth Revolution* (New York: Zone Books, 2015), 10.
20. For example, see Bronwyn Parry, "Narratives of Neoliberalism: 'Clinical Labour' in Context," *Medical Humanities* 41, no. 1 (2015).
21. Barbara Katz Rothman, "Laboring Now: Current Cultural Constructions of Pregnancy, Birth and Mothering," in *The Body Reader: Essential Social and Cultural Readings*, ed. Lisa Jean Moore and Mary Kosut (New York: New York University Press, 2010), 50.
22. See Lennart Nilsson and Lars Hamberger, *A Child Is Born* (Delacorte Press, 2003). See also Jane Lymer and Fiona Utley, "Hospitality and Maternal Consent," *Law Text Culture* 17 (2013): 262–63.
23. Catherine Mills, "Images and Emotions in Abortion Debates," *The American Journal of Bioethics* 8, no. 12 (2008): 62.

24. Deborah Lupton, *The Social Worlds of the Unborn* (Basingstoke, Hampshire: Palgrave Macmillan, 2013), 35–38.
25. This of course has had profound consequences within the debates surrounding abortion and foetal rights. It has been well-theorized in the literature, where it is argued that the emotive effect of 'this capacity to see the fetus [sic] ... performing activities normally associated with babies' has led to an intensification of the anti-abortion position. Catherine Mills, "Technology, Embodiment and Abortion," *Internal Medicine Journal* 35 (2005): 427. Mills argues that 'taking the possibility of a "visual bioethics" seriously requires that more attention is paid to the emotive and affective impact of images on ethical intuitions.' See "Images and Emotions in Abortion Debates," 61.
26. Lymer and Utley, 265. See also Myra J. Hird, "The Corporeal Generosity of Maternity," *Body & Society* 13, no. 1 (2007): 15.
27. See, for example, Clare Hanson, *A Cultural History of Pregnancy* (Basingstoke, UK: Palgrave Macmillan, 2004), 154–61.
28. For instance, see the All Things Surrogacy website: http://allthingssurrogacy.org.
29. Melinda Cooper and Catherine Waldby, *Clinical Labor: Tissue Donors and Research Subjects in the Global Bioeconomy* (Durham, NC: Duke University Press, 2014), 85.
30. Amrita Pande, "This Birth and That: Surrogacy and Stratified Motherhood in India," *PhiloSophia* 4, no. 1 (2014): 60.
31. Gillian Goslinga-Roy, "Body Boundaries, Fiction and the Female Self: An Ethnography of Power, Feminism and the Reproductive Technologies," *Feminist Studies* 26, no. 1 (2000).
32. Martin, 66.
33. See Dolezal, "Phenomenology and Intercorporeality in the Case of Commercial Surrogacy."
34. Pande, 50.
35. "Transnational Commercial Surrogacy in India: Gifts for Global Sisters?," *Reproductive BioMedicine Online* 23 (2011): 620.
36. Rosalyn Diprose, *Corporeal Generosity: On Giving with Nietzsche, Merleau-Ponty, and Levinas* (Albany: SUNY Press, 2002), 52.
37. Wendy Lynne Lee, *Contemporary Feminist Theory and Activism: Six Global Issues* (Peterborough, Ontario: Broadview Press, 2010), 67. See also Pande, "Transnational Commercial Surrogacy in India: Gifts for Global Sisters?," 620.
38. It should also be noted that 'the gift' is also used metaphorically to discuss maternal-foetal relations, where the pregnant women is seen to give the 'gift' of life. See, for example, Hird.

39. In fact, as Kelly Oliver notes, the terminological shift between 'what used to be called *surrogate mothers*, now called *gestational carriers*' is also very telling when considering shifting ideas of who counts as 'real' kin. See Kelly Oliver, *Technologies of Life and Death: From Cloning to Capital Punishment* (New York: Fordham University Press, 2013), 52.
40. For example, see http://www.drpadmajafertility.com/surrogacy/ (accessed 8th January 2015).
41. Elly Teman, *Birthing a Mother: The Surrogate Body and the Pregnant Self* (Berkeley: University of California Press, 2010), 58.
42. Judith Still, "Figures of Oriental Hospitality: Nomads and Sybarites," in *Mobilizing Hospitality: The Ethics of Social Relations in a Mobile World*, ed. Jennie G. Molz and Sarah Gibson (Surrey: Ashgate, 2007), 194.
43. Jacques Derrida, *Adieu to Emmanuel Levinas*, trans. Pascale-Anne Brault (Stanford: Stanford University Press, 1999), 21.
44. Immanuel Kant, *Perpetual Peace*, trans. Mary Campbell Smith (New York: Cosimo, 2005), 17–18.
45. Derrida identifies the aporetic tension at the heart of hospitality as central to the question of cosmopolitanism, or the question of nations welcoming immigrants or 'strangers.' While cosmopolitanism is a theme that is clearly relevant to the question of transnational surrogacy, as a practice which crosses national borders and involves nationalities traversing human bodies, I do not have the scope to explore the theme in this chapter. See Jacques Derrida, *On Cosmopolitanism and Forgiveness*, trans. Mark Dooley and Michael Hughes (London: Routledge, 2001).
46. See Jacques Derrida and Anne Dufourmantelle, *Of Hospitality: Anne Dufourmantelle Invites Jacques Derrida to Respond*, trans. Rachel Bowlby (Stanford, California: Stanford University Press, 2000), 83.
47. Emmanuel Levinas, *Ethics and Infinity: Conversations with Phillip Nemo*, trans. Richard A. Cohen (Pittsburgh: Duquesne University Press, 1985), 85.
48. *Entre Nous: Thinking-of-the-Other*, trans. Michael B. Smith (New York: Columbia University Press, 1998), 147.
49. *Otherwise Than Being or Beyond Essence*, trans. Alphonso Lingus (Pittsburgh: Duquesne University Press, 1998), 12.
50. *Ethics and Infinity: Conversations with Phillip Nemo*, 105.
51. Ibid., 95.
52. See also Derrida and Dufourmantelle, 83.
53. Rosalyn Diprose, "Women's Bodies between National Hospitality and Domestic Biopolitics," *Paragraph* 32, no. 1 (2009): 69.
54. Emmanuel Levinas, *Totality and Infinity: An Essay on Exteriority* trans. Alfonso Lingus (Pittsburgh: Duquesne University Press, 1969).
55. Ibid., 155.

56. Ibid., 157.
57. Ibid., 155.
58. Ibid., 156.
59. Derrida, *Adieu to Emmanuel Levinas*, 44.
60. Ibid., 40, 44. See also Adriaan Peperzak, *To the Other: An Introduction to the Philosophy of Emmanuel Levinas* (West Lafayette, IN: Purdue University Press, 1993), 157.
61. Lisa Guenther, *The Gift of the Other: Levinas and the Politics of Reproduction* (Albany: SUNY Press, 2006), 60.
62. See, for example, Diane Perpich, "From the Caress to the Word: Transcendence and the Feminine in the Philosophy of Emmanuel Levinas," in *Feminist Interpretations of Emmanuel Levinas*, ed. Tina Chanter (Penn State University Press, 2001). See also Guenther, 58–73. Guenther's critique is particularly relevant for the themes of this chapter, focusing on the maternal body in order to restore it to the status of human 'subjectivity.' And Tina Chanter, *Time, Death and the Feminine: Levinas with Heidegger* (Stanford: Stanford University Press, 2001), 241–62. Also see Stella Sandford, "Levinas, Feminism and the Feminine," in *The Cambridge Companion to Levinas*, ed. Simon Critchley and Peter Osborne (Cambridge, UK: Cambridge University Press, 2002).
63. Irina Aristarkhova, *Hospitality of the Matrix: Philosophy, Biomedicine and Culture* (New York: Columbia University Press, 2012), 41. And Lisa Guenther makes much of Levinas' passing comments regarding the 'maternal body' and bearing responsibility for the other in one's own flesh. See: Guenther, 96.
64. Aristarkhova, 44.
65. Ibid., 42.
66. See Andrew Parker, *The Theorist's Mother* (Durham, NC: Duke University Press, 2012). Parker notes: 'The mother is seldom included among the customary topoi of philosophy, even as philosophers rely heavily in their discourses on the tropes of maternity' (p. 1).
67. Aristarkhova, 29.
68. Frances Gray, "Original Habitation: Pregnant Flesh as Absolute Hospitality," in *Coming to Life*, ed. Sarah La Chance and Caroline Lundquist (New York: Fordham University Press, 2012), 71. Hannah Arendt, in fact, makes this conceptual move, making political natality dependent on the fact that women give birth. See Hannah Arendt, *The Human Condition* (Chicago: The University of Chicago Press, 1998).
69. Gray, 82–83.
70. Aristarkhova, 3.
71. Ibid.
72. Ibid., 9.

73. For example, see Jane Lymer, "Merleau-Ponty and the Affective Maternal-Foetal Relation," *Parrhesia* 13 (2011).
74. Sarah Jane Toledo and Kristin Zeiler, "Hosting for the Others' Child?: Relational Work and Embodied Responsibility in Altruistic Surrogate Motherhood," *Feminist Theory* (forthcoming).
75. Aristarkhova, 169.
76. Rothman, 63.
77. Debra Satz, *Why Some Things Should Not Be for Sale: The Moral Limits of Markets* (Oxford: Oxford University Press, 2010), 122.
78. Gray, 85.
79. Anne Phillips, *Our Bodies, Whose Property?* (Princeton: Princeton University Press, 2013), 96.
80. Barbara Katz Rothman, "The Legacy of Patriarchy as Context for Surrogacy: Or Why Are We Quibbling over This?," *American Journal of Bioethics* 14 (2014): 36.
81. Rothman, ibid.
82. Rothman, ibid., 37.
83. See Twine.
84. Dolezal, "Phenomenology and Intercorporeality in the Case of Commercial Surrogacy."
85. See Amrita Pande, "'It May Be Her Eggs but It's My Blood': Surrogates and Everyday Forms of Kinship in India," *Qualitative Sociology* 32 (2009): 380.
86. Mary Lyndon Shanley and Sujatha Jesudason, "Surrogacy: Reinscribed or Pluralizing Understandings of Family," in *Families – Beyond the Nuclear Ideal: For Better or Worse?*, ed. Daniela Cutas and Sarah Chan (London: Bloomsbury Academic, 2012).
87. Gray, 71–72. I explore the theme of pregnancy as the ground of human sociality and subjectivity further in other writing. See Luna Dolezal, "Feminist Reflections on the Phenomenological Foundations of Home," *Symposim: Canadian Journal of Continental Philosophy* 21 (2017): 101–120.
88. See, for example, Toledo and Zeiler.
89. Aristarkhova, 43.
90. Lakoff and Johnson, 5.
91. Ibid., 10.
92. Beeson, Darnovsky, and Lipman. See also Amrita Pande, "The Power of Narratives: Negotiating Commercial Surrogacy in India," in *Globalization and Transnational Surrogacy in India: Outsourcing Life*, ed. S. Das Gupta and S. Das Dasgupta (New York: Lexington Books, 2014).

Bibliography

Arendt, Hannah. 1998. *The Human Condition*. Chicago: The University of Chicago Press.

Aristarkhova, Irina. 2012. *Hospitality of the Matrix: Philosophy, Biomedicine and Culture*. New York: Columbia University Press.

Beeson, Diane, Marcy Darnovsky, and Abby Lipman. 2015. What's in a Name?: Variations in Terminology of Third-Party Reproduction. *Reproductive Biomedicine Online* 31: 805–814.

Brown, Wendy. 2015. *Undoing the Demos: Neoliberalism's Stealth Revolution*. New York: Zone Books.

Chanter, Tina. 2001. *Time, Death and the Feminine: Levinas with Heidegger*. Stanford: Stanford University Press.

Cooper, Melinda, and Catherine Waldby. 2014. *Clinical Labor: Tissue Donors and Research Subjects in the Global Bioeconomy*. Durham: Duke University Press.

Derrida, Jacques. 1999. *Adieu to Emmanuel Levinas*. Trans. P.-A. Brault. Stanford: Stanford University Press.

———. 2001. *On Cosmopolitanism and Forgiveness*. Trans. M. Dooley and M. Hughes. London: Routledge.

Derrida, Jacques, and Anne Dufourmantelle. 2000. *Of Hospitality: Anne Dufourmantelle Invites Jacques Derrida to Respond*. Trans. R. Bowlby. Stanford: Stanford University Press.

Diprose, Rosalyn. 1994. *The Bodies of Women: Ethics, Embodiment and Sexual Difference*. London: Routledge.

———. 2002. *Corporeal Generosity: On Giving with Nietzsche, Merleau-Ponty, and Levinas*. Albany: SUNY Press.

———. 2009. Women's Bodies Between National Hospitality and Domestic Biopolitics. *Paragraph* 32 (1): 69–86.

Dolezal, Luna. 2012. Review of Hospitality of the Matrix: Philosophy, Biomedicine and Culture, Irina Aristarkhova (2012). *Hospitality & Society* 2 (3): 321–324.

———. 2015. Considering Pregnancy in Commercial Surrogacy: A Response to Bronwyn Parry. *Medical Humanities* 41 (1): 38–39.

———. 2017. Phenomenology and Intercorporeality in the Case of Commercial Surrogacy. In *Body/Self/Other: The Phenomenology of Social Encounters*, ed. Luna Dolezal and Danielle Petherbridge, 311–336. Albany: SUNY Press.

———. 2017. Feminist Reflections on the Phenomenological Foundations of Home. *Symposium: Canadian Journal of Continental Philosophy* 21 (2): 101–120.

Goslinga-Roy, Gillian. 2000. Body Boundaries, Fiction and the Female Self: An Ethnography of Power, Feminism and the Reproductive Technologies. *Feminist Studies* 26 (1): 113–140.

Gray, Frances. 2012. Original Habitation: Pregnant Flesh as Absolute Hospitality. In *Coming to Life*, ed. Sarah La Chance and Caroline Lundquist, 71–87. New York: Fordham University Press.

Guenther, Lisa. 2006. *The Gift of the Other: Levinas and the Politics of Reproduction*. Albany: SUNY Press.

Hanson, Clare. 2004. *A Cultural History of Pregnancy*. Basingstoke: Palgrave Macmillan.

Hird, Myra J. 2007. The Corporeal Generosity of Maternity. *Body & Society* 13 (1): 1–20.

Kant, Immanuel. 2005. *Perpetual Peace*. Trans. M. Campbell Smith. New York: Cosimo.

Kirby, Jeffrey. 2014. Transnational Gestational Surrogacy: Does It Have to Be Exploitative. *The American Journal of Bioethics* 14 (5): 24–32.

Lakoff, George, and Mark Johnson. 1980. *Metaphors We Live By*. Chicago: The University of Chicago Press.

Lee, Wendy Lynne. 2010. *Contemporary Feminist Theory and Activism: Six Global Issues*. Peterborough: Broadview Press.

Levinas, Emmanuel. 1969. *Totality and Infinity: An Essay on Exteriority*. Trans. Alfonso Lingus. Pittsburgh: Duquesne University Press.

———. 1985. *Ethics and Infinity: Conversations with Phillip Nemo*. Trans. R. A. Cohen. Pittsburgh: Duquesne University Press.

———. 1998a. *Entre Nous: Thinking-of-the-Other*. Trans. M. B. Smith. New York: Columbia University Press.

———. 1998b. *Otherwise Than Being or Beyond Essence*. Trans. A. Lingus. Pittsburgh: Duquesne University Press.

Loike, John D. 2014. Loaded Words. *The Scientist*, 1 December.

Lupton, Deborah. 2013. *The Social Worlds of the Unborn*. Basingstoke/Hampshire: Palgrave Macmillan.

Lymer, Jane. 2011. Merleau-Ponty and the Affective Maternal-Foetal Relation. *Parrhesia* 13: 126–143.

Lymer, Jane, and Fiona Utley. 2013. Hospitality and Maternal Consent. *Law Text Culture* 17: 240–272.

Martin, Emily. 2001. *The Woman in the Body: A Cultural Analysis of Reproduction*. Boston: Beacon Books.

Midgley, Mary. 2011. *The Myths We Live By*. London: Routledge.

Mills, Catherine. 2005. Technology, Embodiment and Abortion. *Internal Medicine Journal* 35: 427–428.

———. 2008. Images and Emotions in Abortion Debates. *The American Journal of Bioethics* 8 (12): 61–62.

Nilsson, Lennart, and Lars Hamberger. 2003. *A Child Is Born*. New York: Delacorte Press.

Oliver, Kelly. 2013. *Technologies of Life and Death: From Cloning to Capital Punishment*. New York: Fordham University Press.

Pande, Amrita. 2009. 'It May Be Her Eggs but It's My Blood': Surrogates and Everyday Forms of Kinship in India. *Qualitative Sociology* 32: 379–397.

———. 2011. Transnational Commercial Surrogacy in India: Gifts for Global Sisters? *Reproductive Biomedicine Online* 23: 618–625.

———. 2014a. The Power of Narratives: Negotiating Commercial Surrogacy in India. In *Globalization and Transnational Surrogacy in India: Outsourcing Life*, ed. S. Das Gupta and S. Das Dasgupta, 87–105. New York: Lexington Books.

———. 2014b. This Birth and That: Surrogacy and Stratified Motherhood in India. *Philosophia* 4 (1): 50–64.

Parker, Andrew. 2012. *The Theorist's Mother*. Durham: Duke University Press.

Parry, Bronwyn. 2015. Narratives of Neoliberalism: 'Clinical Labour' in Context. *Medical Humanities* 41 (1): 32–37.

Peperzak, Adriaan. 1993. *To the Other: An Introduction to the Philosophy of Emmanuel Levinas*. West Lafayette: Purdue University Press.

Perpich, Diane. 2001. From the Caress to the Word: Transcendence and the Feminine in the Philosophy of Emmanuel Levinas. In *Feminist Interpretations of Emmanuel Levinas*, ed. Tina Chanter, 28–52. University Park: Penn State University Press.

Phillips, Anne. 2013. *Our Bodies, Whose Property?* Princeton: Princeton University Press.

Rothman, Barbara Katz. 2010. Laboring Now: Current Cultural Constructions of Pregnancy, Birth and Mothering. In *The Body Reader: Essential Social and Cultural Readings*, ed. Lisa Jean Moore and Mary Kosut, 48–65. New York: New York University Press.

———. 2014. The Legacy of Patriarchy as Context for Surrogacy: Or Why Are We Quibbling over This? *American Journal of Bioethics* 14: 36–37.

Sandford, Stella. 2002. Levinas, Feminism and the Feminine. In *The Cambridge Companion to Levinas*, ed. Simon Critchley and Peter Osborne, 139–160. Cambridge, UK: Cambridge University Press.

Satz, Debra. 2010. *Why Some Things Should Not Be for Sale: The Moral Limits of Markets*. Oxford: Oxford University Press.

Shanley, Mary Lyndon, and Sujatha Jesudason. 2012. Surrogacy: Reinscribed or Pluralizing Understandings of Family. In *Families – Beyond the Nuclear Ideal: For Better or Worse?* ed. Daniela Cutas and Sarah Chan. London: Bloomsbury Academic.

Sobchack, Vivian. 2006. A Leg to Stand On: Prosthetics, Metaphor, and Materiality. In *The Prosthetic Impulse: From a Posthuman Present to a Biocultural Future*, ed. Marquard Smith and Joanne Morra, 17–41. London: MIT Press.

Still, Judith. 2007. Figures of Oriental Hospitality: Nomads and Sybarites. In *Mobilizing Hospitality: The Ethics of Social Relations in a Mobile World*, ed. Jennie G. Molz and Sarah Gibson, 193–210. Surrey: Ashgate.

Teman, Elly. 2010. *Birthing a Mother: The Surrogate Body and the Pregnant Self.* Berkeley: University of California Press.

Toledo, Sarah Jane, and Kristin Zeiler. forthcoming. Hosting for the Others' Child?: Relational Work and Embodied Responsibility in Altruistic Surrogate Motherhood. *Feminist Theory.*

Twine, France Winddance. 2011. *Outsourcing the Womb: Race, Class and Gestational Surrogacy in a Global Market.* London: Routledge.

Index[1]

A
Abortion, 168, 178n4, 207, 236n23, 237n25
Abuse, 58, 74, 167–170, 172, 173, 175, 177, 180n25
Addams, Jane, 89, 97n23, 97n28
Aesthetics, 11, 12, 47, 203–216
Affect, 2, 7, 12, 70, 83–89, 95, 104, 172, 223, 231, 234
Affect theory, 7, 86, 97n19
Agency, 111, 130, 132, 153, 169, 174–177, 207
Agency (of matter), 90, 94
Ahmed, Sara, 85, 96n12, 119n5, 138n3
Ai Wei Wei, 174
Alaimo, Stacy, 8, 85, 86, 88, 89, 91–94, 96n7, 96n16, 97n21, 97n27, 98n36, 98n37, 99n50, 99n51, 99n52, 99n58, 99n59, 99n61, 99n62, 138n2, 139n20, 139n25, 140n34, 140n35, 140n37

Alēthia, 209, 210
Arendt, Hannah, 62, 239n68
Aristarkhova, Irina, 12, 223, 230–234, 236n8, 239n63, 239n64, 239n67, 239n70, 240n75, 240n89
Aristotle, 6, 19, 21, 22, 24
Art, 204–207, 211–216
  See also Performance art
Asad, Talal, 154, 155
Asylum, 2, 10, 167–174

B
Banker, James R., 211, 218n35
Barad, Karen, 8, 85–89, 91, 93, 94, 97n26, 98n34, 98n36, 98n37, 99n38, 99n49, 140n34
Bartky, Sandra, 44, 45, 52n23
Basu, Srimati, 190, 192, 193
Baxi, Pratiksha, 10, 185, 189

---
[1] Note: Page numbers followed by 'n' refer to notes.

246 INDEX

Bergoffen, Debra, 3, 13n3, 28–30, 32n33, 32n35, 32n36, 32n37, 152–154
Bhasin, Kamala, 186, 187
Bigwood, Carol, 207, 213, 217n13, 219n42
Bindel, Julie, 106
Biopolitics, 6, 43, 46, 238n53
Birth, 62, 118n1, 119n11, 128, 203–209, 211, 215, 224, 225, 232, 233
Body, 1, 17, 37–50, 61, 83, 106, 125, 149, 186, 204, 221
Body image, 38, 40, 42, 43, 45, 47–49, 52n15, 213
Body schema, 38, 39, 42, 43, 52n15, 208, 213
Bohr, Niels, 89, 90, 94, 99n49
Boulous Walker, Michelle, 212, 218n37
Brandom, Robert, 87
Brison, Susan, 10, 185, 187–189
Britain, 194
Butler, Judith, 4, 9, 10, 13n4, 13n6, 26, 28–30, 32n30, 32n32, 37, 51n1, 52n17, 53n31, 57–61, 73, 74, 75n2, 75n3, 75n7, 75n8, 75n9, 75n10, 75n13, 76n14, 76n15, 76n16, 76n17, 76n18, 76n19, 76n20, 76n21, 76n22, 78n72, 85, 87, 90, 95, 106, 107, 120–121n28, 129, 138n1, 139n17, 139n18, 139n19, 148–155, 158–160, 161n7, 161n8, 161n9, 162n16, 185, 190, 193

C

Cahill, Ann, 152–154, 157, 162n21, 163n47
Cárdenas, Micha, 117, 122n49, 122n50
Carlson, Marvin, 206, 216n6
Cartesianism, 187
    See also Mind/body dichotomy or mind/body dualism

Cassidy, Brendan, 211, 218n33
Caste, 184, 191, 193, 195, 197, 198
Catholicism, 212
Cavarero, Adriana, 7, 58, 61, 62, 67, 68, 70, 76n23, 76n25, 76n26, 76n27
Cavell, Stanley, 59, 65, 66, 69–72, 77n41, 77n42, 77n43, 77n44, 77n58, 77n60
Childbirth, 11, 204, 207, 221
Children, 11, 66, 168, 170, 190, 204, 207, 215, 224, 233
Cisgender, 103–106, 109, 114, 118, 152, 183, 184, 191, 192, 194, 197
Class, 4, 20, 42, 108, 110, 158, 159, 193, 194, 197, 226, 233
Coetzee, J.M., 7, 58, 63, 65, 66, 68, 69, 72, 73, 75n6, 76n28, 76n29, 76n30, 76n31, 76n32, 76n36, 76n37, 76n39, 77n40, 77n45, 77n46, 77n47, 77n48, 77n49, 77n51, 77n52, 77n53, 78n76
Cognition, 84, 86, 95
Colonization, 194, 195
Community, 20, 41, 67, 115, 116, 137, 157, 173, 176, 183, 185–187, 195, 197, 223
Consent, 170, 171, 186, 189, 192, 193, 196, 197
Container metaphor, 224–226, 230 231
Crowley, Candy, 148
Culture, 2, 5, 8, 9, 38, 39, 83, 84, 86–90, 94, 95, 105, 106, 115, 125–137, 191, 207, 208, 228
Currah, Paisley, 118, 122n47, 122n51

D

Darwin, Charles, 88, 89, 131, 132, 139n25, 139n26, 139n27, 139n28, 139n30, 139–140n31
Darwinism, 88, 89, 93

de Beauvoir, Simone, 23, 31n16, 31n17, 114
Deleuze, Gilles, 46, 53n24
Delhi, 183
Derrida, Jacques, 11, 222, 228–230, 238n43, 238n45, 238n46, 238n52, 239n59
Descartes, René, 19, 21, 31n8, 31n9
Deshpande, Shashi, 198
Devi, Mahasweta, 198
Dewey, John, 3, 7, 83–95
Diamond, Cora, 59, 64, 65, 69–71
Diprose, Rosalyn, 229, 236n16, 237n36, 238n53
Disability, 12, 52n12, 103
Discipline, 39, 43, 46, 48, 85, 116
Discourse, 4, 5, 7, 11, 38, 69, 86, 90, 107–114, 133, 137, 156, 174, 189, 191, 196, 198, 204, 206, 207, 215, 223–227, 232–235
Discourse analysis, 113
Dualisms, 2, 3, 24, 30, 84, 86, 88–90, 93, 129, 132, 152, 187

E
Embodiment, 1–12, 17, 25, 26, 29, 30, 37–40, 42, 43, 49, 50, 85, 86, 103–118, 130, 133, 135, 149, 150, 152–154, 205, 208, 221–235
Emotion, 22, 30, 83–88, 148, 154, 156, 158–160, 188, 205, 213, 226
Empathy, 40, 51n7, 64, 67
Empire, British, 194
Empiricism, 133
Enframing, 5, 11, 204, 209–211
Environment, 40, 41, 45, 84, 88, 91–94, 128, 152
Epistemology, 61, 74, 84, 88, 90, 91, 93, 151, 177
Essentialism, 8, 86, 88, 109, 232
Ethics, 3–7, 17–23, 25, 27, 28, 30, 57–61, 87, 221, 228, 231, 234

Experience, 4–7, 11, 19, 29, 30, 40–42, 49, 50, 57, 58, 60, 62, 70, 71, 87, 104, 106, 108–115, 117, 118, 151, 153, 156, 163n43, 184–190, 204–206, 208, 211–216, 225, 226, 231, 233

F
Fallibilism, 84, 93, 94
Fanon, Frantz, 6, 24, 25, 30, 114
Feeling/cognition dichotomy, 5, 21, 29, 37, 38, 43, 63–65, 67, 84, 86–89, 95, 105, 109, 111, 112, 119n7, 158, 163n43, 229
Feminism, 1, 6–8, 84, 86–89, 91, 93–95, 106, 115–118, 125
Feminist theory, 1–3, 5–8, 12, 85–87, 89, 91, 104, 107–109, 125
Fischer-Lichte, Erika, 205, 206, 214
Flesh, 3, 12, 26, 27, 63, 65, 108, 113, 114, 190, 198, 213, 230–232, 234
Foetal imagery, 225
Foetus, 11, 205, 208, 209, 214–216, 222, 225–227
Foucault, Michel, 3, 6, 13n5, 30, 39, 43–48, 52n19, 52n20, 52n23, 53n25, 53n29, 151, 159
Foundationalism, 87, 88
Frames, 4, 7, 9, 10, 40, 61, 74, 92, 149–151, 157–161, 174, 184–186, 190–198, 225
Frank, Adam, 70, 77n59, 77n61, 86, 96n17
Freud, Sigmund, 22, 23, 31n12
Fussell, Paul, 188

G
Gaddow, Sally, 214
Garber, Marjorie, 75n6, 109, 110, 120n27
Gender (gender as frame), 9, 149, 151, 153, 158

248 INDEX

Gender binary, 106, 118
Gender identity, 105, 108, 111, 119n11
Genealogy, 10, 17–31, 113, 128, 136, 185, 194–197, 203
Geneva Convention Relating to the Status of Refugees, 169
See also Human rights; Law
Gestell, see Enframing
Gift, the, 11, 227
Gift metaphor, 227
Gilson, Erinn, 75n8, 152–154
Glissant, Édouard, 50, 53n33
Gotell, Lise, 156, 162n37, 162n38, 162n40
Governmentality, 6, 45, 46
Grievability, 9, 149–154, 156, 158
Grosz, Elizabeth, 17, 31n1, 31n2, 89, 97n18, 98n33, 98n36, 130–132, 139n25, 139n26, 139n27, 139n28, 139n30, 139–140n31
Grubb, Amy, 156, 162n42, 163n44, 163n49

H

Habit, 38, 40–42, 44, 46, 85, 93, 94
Habituation/habitualization, 44
Haraway, Donna, 132, 140n34, 140n35, 140n36, 140n37, 140n38, 140–141n39
Harlow, Poppy, 148
Harm, 9, 10, 26, 27, 109, 148–150, 152, 154, 160, 174–176, 183–186, 189–194, 197
See also Violence
Hathaway, James, 169, 178n7
Hausman, Bernice, 109, 110, 121n29, 121n30, 121n31, 121n33, 121n40
Haynes, Dina, 170
Heidegger, Martin, 11, 114, 135, 141n52, 204, 209–212, 218n22, 218n26, 218n32

Hekman, Susan, 86, 96n7, 96n16, 97n21, 97n27, 98n37, 138n2, 139n20, 139n25, 140n34, 140n35, 140n37
Heller, Joseph, 176
Hemmings, Clare, 85, 95n1, 96n12
Hindutva (Hindu nationalism), 184, 191
Hölderlin, Friedrich, 210
Holocaust, 63, 174
Holtzclaw case, 159
Home, 64, 117, 158, 171, 173, 192, 197, 224, 228–231
Honour, 10, 232
Hospitality, 2, 11, 12, 221–235
Huckleberry, Sandy, 11, 204, 206, 212, 213, 215, 216, 218n40
Human rights, 2, 5, 9, 28, 167–170, 172–177
See also Law; Reproductive rights
Humiliation, 28, 150, 163n43, 189
Husserl, Edmund, 6, 40, 41, 45, 51n6, 51n8, 51n9, 51n10, 52n11, 111, 112, 114, 121n43

I

Identity, 8, 10, 26, 38, 105, 108, 111, 115–117, 119–120n11, 130, 183, 187, 188, 191, 193, 197, 207, 233
See also Gender identity
Identity politics, 8, 115
Immigration, 167, 169, 174, 177
See also Law
India, 132, 183–198, 222
Intellectualism, 133
Intelligibility, 61, 74, 118, 150–152
Intercorporeality, 25, 71
International Criminal Tribunal for the Former Yugoslavia (ICTY), 28, 30
Intersectionality, 8, 115
Intersex, 110, 114, 119n10, 130

Intersubjectivity, 71, 152, 153
Intra-action, 85, 89, 90, 93, 94
Irigaray, Luce, 22, 31n13, 31n14, 31n15

J
James, William, 84, 95n5, 98n28
Jeffreys, Sheila, 106, 116, 120n13, 120n14, 120n15, 120n16, 121n31

K
Kant, Immanuel, 19, 25, 222, 228, 238n44
Kinship, 12, 226, 227, 232–234
Kirby, Vicki, 87, 97n21, 139n20
Kittay, Eve Feder, 27, 28, 32n31
Koslowski, Rey, 173, 179n20
Kotak, Marni, 11, 203, 204, 206, 207, 212, 216, 216n8, 216n9
Kristeva, Julia, 204, 208, 212, 218n38

L
Labour, 224–226, 233, 234
Language, 5, 65, 70, 84–87, 90, 94, 106, 107, 111, 114, 131, 133, 152, 186, 188, 209, 221, 223
Law
  immigration law, 167, 169
  Indian Penal Code, 191
  international human rights law, 172, 177
  law and sexual violence, 5, 147, 158, 167, 185, 186, 189, 190, 191, 192, 194, 196, 197
Law enforcement, 9, 10, 172–174, 176
Leib, 114
Levi, Primo, 188
Levinas, Emmanuel, 25–27, 32n26, 32n27, 32n28, 32n29, 60, 114, 222, 223, 228–230, 238n47, 238n54, 239n62, 239n63

Linguistic turn, 86–88
  See also Post-linguistic turn
Literature, 10, 46, 51n11, 58, 170, 185, 198, 237n25
Liu Xiaobo, 174

M
Mani, Lata, 194, 195
Manipur, 185
Manorama, Thangjam, 197, 198
Marcano, Donna-Dale, 20, 24, 31n6, 31n7
Markula, Pirkko, 50, 53n32
Marriage, 173, 183, 192, 193
Martin, Emily, 221, 224, 235n2
Mary (Virgin Mary), 11, 204, 211, 212, 215
Massumi, Brian, 84–86, 96n9, 97n20
Materialism, 95, 133, 139n22
  See also New materialism
Materiality, 7, 8, 84–88, 90–92, 94, 105, 107, 108, 114, 116, 120n11, 125, 136, 221–235
Maternity/the maternal, 12, 211, 223
  See also Motherhood
Matrix, the, 12, 230, 231, 233
Matter, 60, 71, 83–95, 105, 107, 109, 111, 113, 114, 117, 130, 137, 154, 177
Matthews, Sandra, 207, 217n12
Medicalization, 2, 40, 204, 211
Memory, 131, 186
Menon, Nivedita, 186, 187, 198
Menon, Ritu, 186
Merleau-Ponty, Maurice, 3, 8, 9, 25, 32n22, 32n23, 38, 51n2, 51n7, 70, 71, 77n63, 78n68, 113, 114, 125–137, 207
Metaphor, 2, 5, 12, 92, 132, 195, 221–235
#MeToo, 9
Midgley, Mary, 224, 236n13

Military, 43, 59, 185, 190, 191, 197
Mind/body dichotomy or mind/body dualism, 3, 24, 84
Modesty, 185, 189, 194, 197, 198
Motherhood, 1, 11, 207, 212, 222, 227, 231, 235
Mullin, Amy, 204, 215, 216n1, 219n54

N

Namaste, Viviane, 104, 108, 109, 115, 116, 119n7, 120n24, 120n25, 120n26, 121n28, 121n33, 122n46
Nationalism, 10, 184, 188, 197
Naturalism, 88, 89, 94
Nature/culture dichotomy, 2, 8, 126, 130
Neoliberal/neoliberalism, 1, 2, 4–7, 39, 45–49, 156, 157, 225
New materialism, 2, 3, 7, 8, 83–95, 125, 130
Nietzsche, Fredrich, 32n38
Nirbhaya (fearless), 183, 191, 192
Normalization, 1, 4, 7, 37–50, 61, 74, 159, 161
Nudity, 212

O

Obama, Barack, 147, 148
Objectification, 1, 226
Oksala, Johanna, 47, 52n21, 53n26
Oliver, Kelly, 148, 218n38, 238n39
Ontology, 8, 60, 84, 87–90, 92–95
Optimization, 37–50
Organism, 88, 92–94, 141n39

P

Pakistan, 185–187
Palermo Protocol, 170, 172, 173, 176
 See also Human rights; Law
Pandey, Gyanendra, 186
Partition, 184–186, 195
 See also India; Pakistan
Patriarchy, 212, 232
Perception, 25, 40–42, 51n10, 70, 71, 133, 134, 205, 206, 214
Performance art, 205, 207, 214
Performativity, 87, 89, 90, 95
Phenomenology, 2, 3, 7, 8, 11, 39–43, 104, 111–114
Piero della Francesca, 211
Plato, 6, 19–21, 24
Pleasure, 20, 22, 31, 45, 48, 114, 150, 213
Poïēsis, 209–211
Pornography, 189
Posthuman, 236n9
Post-linguistic turn, 7, 83–95
Postmodernism, 3
Poststructuralism, 86
Post-traumatic stress disorder (PTSD), 168, 187
Poverty, 171, 173, 174, 176, 192
Power, 1, 3, 4, 7, 12, 21, 29, 30, 39, 42, 43, 45–48, 58, 59, 67, 73, 87, 90, 116, 151, 156, 158, 159, 170, 183, 184, 210
Pragmatism, 2, 3, 7, 8, 84–89, 93–95
Precariousness, 9, 60, 61, 74, 76n20, 149, 150, 152, 153, 161
Precarity, 9, 61, 149–154, 157, 159, 160
Pregnancy, 2, 5, 11, 117, 203–216, 221–235
Privilege, 25, 29, 103, 104, 106, 116, 118n1, 136, 172, 233
Production metaphor, 223–226, 231
Prosser, Jay, 108, 110, 120n22, 120n23, 120n26, 121n28, 121n32
Public sphere, 10, 74, 183–186, 195, 197
Purity, 188, 189, 194, 197

Q
Queer theory, 2, 8, 107, 111–114, 117

R
Race, 18, 20, 21, 25, 42, 48, 103, 110, 115, 116, 118n4, 169, 196
Racism, 24, 29
Rape, 30, 148, 153, 156, 158, 184–186, 189–198
  See also Sexual violence
Raymond, Janice, 105–107, 119n9, 119n10, 120n18
Recognition, 9, 10, 30, 44, 48, 49, 61, 62, 74, 92, 109, 115, 117, 126, 129, 150–152, 154, 158–160, 167, 186, 190–192, 194, 197, 198
Religion, religious identity, 197
Representationalism, 90
Reproduction, 10, 11, 117, 128, 129, 136, 151, 198, 207, 221, 224, 231, 232, 235
Reproductive labour, 225
Reproductive rights, 1, 5, 9, 167–177
Resistance, 10, 26, 50, 89, 158–161
Responsiveness, moral, 158
Rorty, Richard, 60, 75n12, 87
Rothman, Barbara Katz, 209, 215, 218n21, 225, 232, 236n21, 240n76, 240n80, 240n81, 240n82
Roy, Arundhati, 198
Rubin, Henry, 112–114, 121n39, 121n40

S
Salamon, Gayle, 110, 111, 113, 114, 121n34, 121n35, 121n36, 121n37, 121n41, 121n42, 121n43
Sartre, Jean-Paul, 23, 32n18
Sati, 194

Satz, Debra, 232, 240n77
Science, 125, 126, 128, 129, 137, 188, 194, 207
Sedgwick, Eve Kosofsky, 86, 96n17
Sex/gender dichotomy, 8, 105, 106
Sex industry, 2, 9, 10, 167–177, 178n2
Sex trafficking, 2, 4, 5, 9, 10, 167–177
  See also Trafficking
Sexual exploitation, 170, 176
Sexual violence, *see* Rape
Shame, 10, 28, 31, 47, 67, 150, 184, 185, 187, 189, 191, 195, 196, 207
Sharpe, Jenny, 194, 196
Simpkins, Reese, 116, 122n48
Social construction, 8, 105, 109–113, 118
Society for Women in Philosophy Ireland, 5
South Asia, 10, 186, 195
Steubenville, 148, 156–158
  See also Sexual violence
Stone, Sandy, 106, 120n19
Subjectivity, 1, 8, 9, 11, 12, 17, 47, 71, 113, 152, 204, 205, 208, 210, 215, 223, 225, 228–231, 233
Suffering, 58–60, 64–69, 71, 74, 149, 150, 174
Sullivan, Shannon, 92–94, 95–96n6, 96n10, 98n28, 99n63, 100n67, 100n71
Sympathy, 64, 65, 147

T
Technology, 5, 11, 50, 132, 204, 208–211, 215, 225
Tomkins, Silvan, 86, 96n17
Torch Bearers (Meira Paibi), 10, 198
Torture, 61, 66–68, 150, 185, 198
Toxins (and toxic bodies), 91
Trafficking, 10, 168–174, 176, 177
  See also Sex trafficking

Trafficking Victims Protection Act 2000, 171
  See also Human rights
Transaction, 8, 85, 89–94, 224, 226, 234
Transcorporeality, 8, 85, 91
Transfeminism, 3, 7, 8, 104, 115
Transgender, 8, 103–118
Transphobia, 119n5
Trauma, 4, 10, 68, 173, 183–191, 197
Trump, Donald, 148
Turner, Emily, 156, 162n42, 163n44, 163n49

U
Ulmer, Gregory, 209, 218n25

V
Van Eck, Cathy, 204, 206
Verne, Jules, 194
Victim-blaming, 148, 156
Victims, 5, 10, 147, 153, 156, 157, 159, 167–177, 195

Violence, 26, 58, 106, 147–161
  See also Sexual violence
Virilio, Paul, 49, 53n30
Vulnerability, 2–7, 26–30, 57–74, 153, 154, 169, 170, 188

W
Waldenfels, Bernhard, 70, 71, 77n63, 77n64, 78n66, 78n67, 78n69, 78n70
Walzer, Michael, 154, 155
Waugh, Louisa, 170, 179n10, 179n11, 179n12
Wexler, Laura, 207, 217n12
Willett, Cynthia, 31, 32n39
Wynn, Francine, 215, 219n51

Y
Young, Iris Marion, 25, 30, 42, 52n13, 97n23, 204, 205, 208, 210, 213–216, 217n14, 218n41, 219n49